GETTING AROUND

Exploring Transportation History

Exploring Community
History Series Editors

David E. Kyvig
Myron A. Marty

Getting Around
Exploring Transportation History

H. Roger Grant

Krieger Publishing Company
Malabar, Florida
2003

Original Edition 2003

Printed and Published by
KRIEGER PUBLISHING COMPANY
KRIEGER DRIVE
MALABAR, FLORIDA 32950

Copyright © 2003 by H. Roger Grant

Library of Congress Cataloging-in-Publication Data

Grant, H. Roger, 1943–
    Getting around : exploring transportation history / H. Roger Grant.
        p. cm.— (Exploring community history series)
    Includes index
    ISBN 1-57524-153-6 (alk. paper).—ISBN 1-57524-225-7 (pbk. : alk. paper)
    1. Transportation—History.   I. Title.   II. Series.

    TA1015 .G73 2003
    388'.09—dc21   2002066879

For Martha and Julia

CONTENTS

EDITORS' INTRODUCTION

Getting around from place to place is one of the fundamental tasks of human existence. People need to move themselves and their commodities about, whether they accomplish the deed on foot; are propelled by animals, wind, or muscle; or are conveyed via waterways, roads, rails, or the air by some modern technology. The challenge of transporting persons and goods remains as well a distinctive feature of community life. Indeed, ease of internal movement and communication helps define the boundaries of a community and serves as a means of distinguishing between it and the outside world. The nature of travel and trade beyond its borders also determines a community's identity as well as its isolation from or integration with the wider world at any time in its history. The experience of travel has changed dramatically as transportation technology has evolved. Earlier modes of getting around, not to mention their effect on restraining or encouraging movement, have too often been forgotten. Therefore, gaining an understanding of its transportation network ought to be regarded as essential to any effort to explore the past of a locale.

As different systems of transportation evolved, they overlapped and intertwined to give every individual community a particular identity. Variations of landscape, population, economy, and circumstances, combined with distinctive patterns of change over time, give each community a unique transportation past. In order to understand the evolution and present nature of a community, therefore, comprehending the history of its means of getting around becomes vital. This book provides guidance to those who recognize the value of such knowledge about a locality, who desire to acquire or enhance it, and who wish to do so effectively and thoroughly.

Most communities instinctively know that their own particular history is important to them. Recalling nothing of that past puts them in the same position as people suffering from amnesia, unable to remember their origins, their response to needs or challenges, their means of achieving success or dealing with setbacks, their sources of support or opposition, and their goals. History serves the community much as memory serves an individual. In imperfect, sometimes distorted, but most often helpful fashion both memory and history help identify familiar elements in new situations and provide a guide to appropriate behavior. History also offers a standard of comparison across stretches of time and circumstance that exceeds the span of an individual life. In this sense, history is far more than a remembrance of things past. History represents a means of coming to terms with the present, developing an awareness of previous influences, the continuities and distinctiveness in current conditions, and the range of future possibilities. Just as memory helps the individual avoid having to repeat the same discoveries, behaviors, and mistakes, historical knowledge helps a community, as well as any group or individual within it, avoid starting at the beginning each time an issue needs to be addressed.

A community's transportation history represents a vital ingredient of its overall history. Understanding its transportation history helps in comprehending the community's advantages and limitations of location, features of layout, obstacles and opportunities for growth, and patterns of disruption, development, and decay. In turn, residents' experiences and needs can be comprehended. Such knowledge can lead to better informed decisions on a variety of governmental and business issues as well as greater personal satisfaction derived from the enhanced awareness of a place.

Even if there is obvious value to community understanding of its past, the means of acquiring such self-knowledge are usually less evident, especially when the subject of interest, such as transportation, is previously unexamined. Knowledge of the past is commonly gained from books, teachers, museums, films, or other presentations. What is one to do if the subject has never been explored, if there is no book on the topic in the library, if there is no expert to whom to turn? What is to be done in the even more likely circumstance that answers obtained from such sources are insufficient or unsatisfying?

A number of years ago, we began to appreciate that many people would like to explore the past of their own families and communities. Only a lack of confidence and knowledge about how to conduct research stood in their way. We realize from working with students, local historical and genealogical society members, and independent adults that any literate person motivated to explore some question regarding the past of his or her immediate surroundings could master most historical research methods, pursue most research possibilities, critically evaluate most potential explanations, and achieve a considerable measure of understanding. We felt it important to empower people to function as historians themselves or evaluate what others historians might say and write about a personally important past.

We began our effort to identify questions of historical significance and interest as well as explain how to investigate them in *Your Family History: A Handbook for Research and Writing* (Arlington Heights, IL: Harlan Davidson, 1978). Four years later we continued the undertaking with a larger book, one more broadly focused on communities. *Nearby History: Exploring the Past around You* (Nashville, TN: American Association for State and Local History, 1982) was, nevertheless, merely an overview of a broad and complex subject. The second edition of *Nearby History* (Walnut Creek, CA: AltaMira Press, 2000) updated reading suggestions, provided information about use of the Internet for local history research, and reflected nearly two decades of our own further thought, but remained a general treatment of the subject.

The warm reception that greeted *Your Family History* and *Nearby History* encouraged us to carry our notion further by providing specific advice on exploring particular topics. Enlisting historians who were experts on schools, homes, public places, places of worship, and businesses, we edited a five-volume nearby history series, originally published by the American Association for State and Local History and currently available from AltaMira Press of Walnut Creek, California (web site: www.AltaMiraPress.com). We have been pleased to be able to expand the scope of these efforts through a series of books devoted to exploring community history produced by the Krieger Publishing Company, the first three of which were Ann Durkin Keating's *Invisible Networks: Exploring the History of Local Utilities and Public Works*, R. Douglas Hurt's *American Farms: Exploring Their History*, and Michael W. Homel's *Unlocking City Hall: Exploring the History of Local Government and Politics*.

The book in your hands is an important addition to the *Exploring Community History* series. *Getting Around: Exploring Transportation History* describes ways to pursue an inquiry into the history of transportation in a United States or Canadian community. The book is filled with ideas about topics and issues well worth examining, shrewd suggestions about how to go about such an investigation, and useful examples of successful previous inquiries that may provide models and inspiration.

We asked H. Roger Grant, professor of history at Clemson University, to write this guide to exploring the history of transportation not merely because he is our valued long-time friend but, more importantly, because he is one of the most broadly experienced and well-respected transportation historians practicing today. For over three decades he has crisscrossed North America, visiting archives, museums, and a variety of other sites in the course of his prodigious and still ongoing research career. His many publications on the history of individual railroads, railroading in general, depots, transportation workers, and travelers have been widely read and admired by both scholars and a much broader audience. He has poured his vast experience as well as his deep understanding of the varied concerns of those interested in the history of transportation into this research guide. We present *Getting Around* with full confidence that it will be a useful tool for anyone—interested citizen, beginning or advanced student, or experienced investigator—seeking a deeper understanding of this vital aspect of community history.

> David E. Kyvig, Editor
> Myron A. Marty, Consulting Editor

INTRODUCTION

Getting around has always been one of the basic challenges of every-day life. The capacity to negotiate what many American considered to be the "tyranny of distance" has changed over time but has always remained an important aspect of binding a community together and distinguishing it from the outside world. How people transport themselves and commodities helps define the nature of life in any particular time and locale.

Every place has a diverse transportation story, replete with failures and triumphs. Individuals who explore the transportation heritage of their community will quickly discover that various forms of transport have had a vital impact on ordinary life. The fate of every frontier settlement depended on transportation. Access to deep water may have sparked initial development, and canals or steam railways then surely accelerated the process. If a rail line missed an inland village, the place likely withered and died, explaining why there are examples of determined townspeople having their houses and business structures moved to a track-side location. Novelist E. L. Doctorow captured in *Ragtime* the life or death importance of railroads to Americans when he wrote, "Tracks! Tracks! It seemed to the visionaries of that day that the future lay at the end of parallel rails." With the advent of electric interurbans and then automobiles, buses and trucks, which traveled over an expanding network of all-weather roads, communities that had endured poor transportation received a second, even third chance for a better day.

The interconnectedness of a community and its transportation systems always needs to be recognized. No historical topic should ever be viewed in isolation, and the saga of transportation in America is hardly an exception. Linkages take a variety of forms. The pattern of streets and locations of factories and stores may reflect the route of a past or present transportation artery. The old commercial core of Akron, Ohio, straddled the north-south axis of the Ohio & Erie Canal, a waterway

1

that gave birth to and nurtured the future "City at the Summit" (a reference to Akron's location as the high point on the 308-mile canal). The impact of the canal on the arrangement of downtown streets can still be seen and some businesses or their remains stand at bankside. De Smet, South Dakota, immortalized by children's writer Laura Ingalls Wilder as the "Little Town on the Prairie," has its north-south main street running perpendicular to the east-west tracks of the former Chicago & North Western Railway (today's Dakota, Minnesota & Eastern Railroad). This street orientation makes De Smet one of hundreds of "T-towns" that dot the landscape, especially on the Great Plains. Specifically, the railroad formed the top of the letter "T" and the principal street created the stem. In De Smet the south side of the tracks became commercial and residential areas while the creamery, grain elevators and coal and lumber yards appeared on the north side. The oft-used phrase "wrong side of the tracks" has a clear transportation connection. Grimy, noisy businesses, houses of the poor and perhaps a "hobo jungle" filled land adjacent to the right-of-way that separated them from "respectable" sections.

Even a town name may have a transportation connection. In the places spawned by canals it is not surprising to find a Canal Winchester, Ohio; Lockport, Illinois; or Port Byron, New York. And the impact of the railroad is everywhere. In eastern Washington, for example, the village of Oakesdale honors Thomas F. Oakes, an official of the Northern Pacific Railroad; the towns of Endicott and Prescott are named for William Endicott, Jr. and C. H. Prescott, directors of a railroad holding company; and the Starbuck settlement venerates General W. H. Starbuck of the Oregon Railway & Navigation Company, remembered for providing his namesake community with its first church bell.

Ties between a railroad official and a community in Washington state are but one illustration of transportation history containing a pronounced human component. It is not to suggest that churches, schools or other dimensions of nearby history lack this element, but transportation always has involved people, and lots of people, physically and emotionally. Not only did sailing ships, steamboats, canal packets, day coaches and Pullmans, interurban cars, motor buses and other transportation vehicles carry countless individuals to and from communities, but the social fabric of thousands of places was shaped, even indelibly stamped by the presence of one or more forms of transportation. Why have some localities where time-honored "village virtues" may have been less than dominant become famous for being "wide open?" Take Buffalo, New York, for example. The well-known song "Buffalo Gals Won't You Come Out Tonight" captures a wildness that historically has

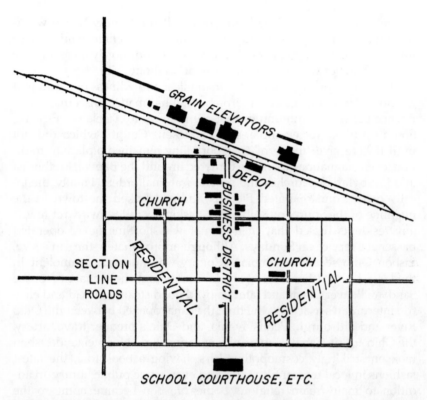

The concept of the "T-town" is demonstrated in this sketch of a typical railroad-created community.

been part of Buffalo's past, a legacy resulting from a large, transient population initially brought into the community by boats on Lake Erie and the Erie Canal, then by nearly a score of railroads and still later by several electric interurbans.

The presence in a community of a railroad shop, which also usually included an operating division headquarters, meant a nucleus of young, often single, male workers. This element of the permanent population contributed to a coarseness and diversity that nearby places probably lacked. Railroad towns, whether Alamosa, Colorado; Avery, Idaho; Creston, Iowa; El Reno, Oklahoma; Hamlet, North Carolina; Hornell, New York; Meridian, Mississippi; or San Bernardino, California, featured a multitude of boarding houses and usually places for "adult entertainment." These populations, too, might be ethnically different from the surrounding areas. By way of illustration, in the late

nineteenth century the Erie Railroad recruited a heavily Italian workforce for its passenger car shop in Susquehanna, Pennsylvania. These
immigrants came with their cultural baggage and shortly thereafter the
largest churches were ones of the Roman Catholic faith.

Transportation has done more than inject a rowdiness or a different
religious flavor into a local environment; it has made a discernable difference between communities that are more or less isolated. Pickens,
South Carolina, for example, seat of Pickens County, which did not
until 1898 receive "modern" transport, long remained a place of tradition, even stagnation. Town life centered around the Baptist, Methodist
and Presbyterian churches and several fraternal orders. Finally, the locally owned and operated Pickens Railroad linked the town to the
mainline of the Southern Railway at Easley, six miles away. Yet few, if
any residents fussed that their hometown shortline never operated
passenger service on Sundays. Although approximately the same size,
Lisbon, Ohio, seat of Columbiana County, was much less somnolent. In
the 1840s Lisbon (then called New Lisbon) became headquarters for the
Sandy & Beaver Canal and later enjoyed good steam railroad and electric interurban service. By the time the canal opened between the Ohio
River and Pittsburgh, Pennsylvania, and Ohio's premier travel artery,
the Ohio & Erie Canal, community isolation ended forever, and Lisbon
took on strikingly cosmopolitan airs, having a bookstore, the latest
fashions in local mercantile stores and even a free public library. In addition to mainstream religious bodies, Lisbon became home to the
Church of God or "Winebrennarians," and by mid-century this sect's
house of worship had developed into a public place where "lectures,
sermons, harangues on all subjects were launched . . . and it was the
seat of so-called 'advanced thought.'" At the close of the nineteenth
century, a small utopian group, the Spirit Fruit Society, felt comfortable
in Lisbon and took advantage of its transportation connections, usually
the Erie Railroad, to reach Chicago, the center for the commune's out-
reach effort.

Even today, long after the demise of most intercity railroad passenger service, it may be possible to explain why residents of a particular
community have certain outlooks and proclivities. An aspect of popular
culture is a case in point. Indeed, newer forms of travel, best represented by automobiles and paved highways and better communica-
tions, specifically radio and television, have helped to perpetuate previously established interests that the Railway Age, most of all, fostered.
For more than a century many residents of Albia, Iowa, have shown al-
legiance to the Chicago Cubs or Chicago White Sox, teams playing more

than 300 miles away. Why is this so? Historically the town benefitted from a superb rail connection with the Windy City, via the main stem of the Chicago, Burlington & Quincy Railroad. The "Q's" crack mail and passenger trains brought baseball fans in Albia and other stations along this line in Illinois and Iowa the daily Chicago newspapers, including the *Inter-Ocean*, *Tribune* and *Sun*. Residents could read about the ups and downs of their favorite major league team. Yet, Lovilia, a community nine miles northwest of Albia, had fans loyal to the St. Louis Browns and St. Louis Cardinals rather than the Chicago clubs. The probable explanation involved the direct railroad link the village had to the Gateway City, 282 miles away via the Wabash Railroad. The afternoon St. Louis dailies arrived early the next day at the Lovilia depot for local delivery. And in both places faithful fans could take the train to the ballpark city of their favorite club, something that both the "Q" and Wabash encouraged with special, low-cost "excursion" fares. Knowledge of the transportation past can help residents find their roots, even their identities in a rapidly changing society.

It should be realized that a community's transportation heritage also had influences that a researcher might not expect to find. There is even a tie to local humor. A railroad, for example, might be somewhat woebegone and residents for generations might refer to it in some lighthearted fashion. The Minneapolis & St. Louis (M&StL) Railroad, with one possible exception, never operated fast, luxurious passenger trains; instead, it dispatched mostly poky, Spartan locals. No wonder denizens of communities along the M&StL's lines in Minnesota, Illinois, Iowa, and South Dakota called it "Midnight & Still Later," "Misery & Short Life," "Missing & Still Lost," and "Maimed & Still Limping." Area residents had fun, too, with town names and used a railroad context for such humor. The text of a comic postcard, published early in the twentieth century as part of an "Ohio Whisperettes" series, went as follows:

I want to go to Morrow, Ohio. I asked a man the quickest way to get to the depot. He said, RUN. When I reached the depot, there was a train on the side-track—I asked the agent, "Does this train go to Morrow?" He said, "No, it goes to-day." I told him I wanted to go to Morrow. He said, "Come down tomorrow and go." I told him I wanted to go to Morrow today. Just as the train was pulling out, I said, IS THIS MY TRAIN?" He said, "No, the R.R. Co. wants to use it." I went way back and sat down on a truck, telling the agent he was too fresh. He said, so was the paint on the truck.

What might be learned about a community's transportation past may be surprising and unexpected. There is always that thrill of discovery!

Researchers are likely to glean "tidbits" that are remarkably significant, and in the process become bonafide experts on what legitimately is "important stuff." After all, scholars conceivably know more about trans-Atlantic travel than they do about short trips in and between American communities. If this information can be disseminated (see Conclusion), much has been achieved.

The approach used in *Getting Around* covers in roughly chronological order the topics of natural waterways, roads, canals, railroads, electric interurbans, urban transit, and aviation from the earliest trails to modern airports. Since transport forms share similarities, repetition becomes a challenge in crafting the narrative; hopefully, this has not happened to an unreasonable degree. The most detailed chapter, "Railroads," provides insights that are applicable to *all* transport forms, even natural waterways and aviation. Moreover, the length of the discussion on railroads reflects the long-time significance of the rails in the daily affairs of the nation. *Getting Around* repeatedly suggests primary and secondary sources and how they might be employed in learning more about the nearby transportation heritage. Sidebars and illustrations, too, should make it easier to sense the nature and value of resource materials for all transport forms. A final chapter, "Using Local Transportation History," suggests what might be done with the findings. When used with care, imagination and energy and perhaps in connection with other books in the Nearby History and Exploring Community series, this volume will assist the reader to appreciate a locale's means of getting around in the past.

Before anyone considers the core textual material, it is wise to think about transportation in the context of the community. What information is likely to be sought and how will it be used? The following specific queries will place the project in solid historical perspective:

How did the general topography or lay-of-the-land influence patterns of travel?

How did the earlier humans move to or through the area?

What were the initial forms of commercial transport? Sailing ship, river craft, stagecoach, canal boat or steam train?

What motivated and discouraged travel?

How were the economy, culture and society altered in both positive and negative ways by changes in transportation?

Did the community traditionally have good travel connections with the outside world?

Did major community growth coincide with arrival of a particular form of transport?

Did the appearance of the steamboat, canal barge or iron horse cause instability in the social structure?

Did transportation employees create social distinctions in the community, for example in housing, religion, values, marriages and political beliefs?

How were individuals and communities shaped by the experience of travel (or staying put while others traveled)?

What were the popular destinations of local residents?

How did travelers reach their final local destination from the station, airport or other point of entry?

What are the remaining structures (toll houses, depots, trolley barns, air hangers and the like) that make up the historic fabric of local transport?

Do sections of the community show the legacy of commercial transport? For instance, what is the appearance of the active or abandoned railroad corridor? Were amusement parks, cemeteries and suburbs created by electric railway companies? What development has occurred around old and new airports?

When and how were public roads improved? Was there a progression from dirt or corduroy to Macadam to brick, oil, asphalt and concrete?

Did any one city, which enjoyed direct transport ties, dominate or have a strong impact on local cultural, economic and social activities?

Who worked for the transportation companies?

The researcher may have other questions in mind. By writing out these queries, the process of collecting, organizing and sharing information will be easier and more effective.

As with all research and writing projects, there are individuals and institutions that have contributed to the final published product. I am especially indebted to David Kyvig, my former colleague at The University of Akron, who more than a decade ago encouraged me to explore the nearby history dimensions of transportation. He and Myron "Mike" Marty, co-editors of this imaginative and well-received series, have steadfastly supported my endeavors. Others, too, have assisted, including Susan Berg, Director, Research Library, The Mariners' Museum, Newport News, Virginia; Bette Gorden, Curator, Herman T. Pott National Inland Waterways Library, St. Louis, Missouri; Lynn D. Farrar, Lafayette, California; George N. Johnson, Jr., Lexington, Virginia; John V. Miller, Jr., Archivist at The University of Akron in Ohio; Barbara Handy Pahl, National Trust for Historic Preservation, Denver,

Colorado, and David A. Pfeiffer, Archivist, National Archives and Records Administration, College Park, Maryland. The resourceful staff at the Robert M. Cooper Library at Clemson University aided my efforts, locating a variety of books and other published materials. As with my other book projects, my wife, Martha Farrington Grant, has provided superb editorial advice.

H. Roger Grant
Clemson University

Chapter 1

NATURAL WATERWAYS

Transport on rivers, oceans and lakes has played a vital role in the historic movement of goods and people. Over time the means have evolved to include the river steamboat, coastal packet and lake schooner. Blessed with long, navigable rivers, the Atlantic and Pacific oceans and the Gulf of Mexico and the Great Lakes, Americans found it convenient to exploit these natural waterways. Much of the early settlement process of the trans-Appalachian West, for example, relied on the mighty Ohio and Mississippi drainage systems.

Unquestionably, the commercial history of the Ohio-Mississippi network reflects the overall evolution of river travel. Down these winding streams paddled Native Americans, explorers and early trappers and traders in their canoes and pirogues. Then drifted countless flatboats, loaded with men, women and children, assorted animals, household furniture, farm implements, whiskey, grindstones and other merchandise. These primitive and cheap transport vessels, commonly hewn from the pine and hardwood forests of western Pennsylvania, resembled a "mixture of log cabin, fort, floating barnyard and country grocery." Next came the popular keelboats with their rounded bows and sterns that usually carried from twenty to forty tons of cargo. Unlike flatboats, which only could move with the current, keelboats could travel upstream with the aid of a steersman and usually from six to ten men involved in hard and fatiguing poling. But it would be the steamboat that revolutionized river commerce. In 1816, nine years after Robert Fulton's famed *Clermont* made its maiden voyage on New York's Hudson River, the *Enterprise* became the first steamboat to ascend the Mississippi and Ohio rivers, reaching Brownsville, Pennsylvania, on the Monongahela River, fifty-four days out of New Orleans. By the 1850s steamboats served as the great beasts of burden; scores regularly plied hundreds of miles of riverways. They hauled manufactured goods, including iron, bricks, barrel staves; agricultural products;

"HARTFORD LINE"

DAILY SERVICE

New Steel Twin-Screw Steamers

"Middletown" Leaves New York Monday, Wednesday and Friday

Captain R. H. HILLS

Leaves New York Tuesday, Thursday and Saturday

"Hartford"

Captain CHAS R. BACON

Leave Pier 20, East River, New York, foot of Peck Slip, at 5.00 P. M., and foot of State Street, Hartford, at 4.00 P. M., Daily except Sunday

Stopping at Intermediate Landings on the Connecticut River

Fares Between New York and River Landings in Either Direction

One Way..$1.75
Round Trip, Good for Season..... ....3.50
Bedstead Rooms, Nos. 10 or 58, One Way................2.00
Outside Staterooms, One Way (Except Nos. 10 and 58).....1.50
Inside Staterooms, One Way............................1.00

Meals: Supper 75c.   Breakfast 50c.
or a la Carte.

4

SUMMER SCHEDULE
DAILY EXCEPT SUNDAY

Miles			Miles	
5.00 P. M.	0	lve........NEW YORK........arr.	160	6.00 A. M.
12.00 N'ht	102	arr....SAYBROOK POINT 1...lve.	58	9.30 P. M.
12.30 "	104	" ....LYME 2.......... "	56	b...... "
1.00 A. M.	108	" ....ESSEX.......... "	52	8.45 "
a1.15 "	109	" ....HAMBURGH....... "	51	a8.30 "
1.45 "	114	" ......DEEP RIVER...... "	46	8.15 "
2.00 "	116	" ....HADLYME....... "	44	8.00 "
2.30 "	119	" ....EAST HADDAM.... "	41	7.45 "
3.00 "	127	" ...ROCK LANDING... "	33	7.15 "
3.30 "	132	" ...MIDDLE HADDAM... "	28	6.45 "
4.15 "	138	" .....MIDDLETOWN 3..... "	22	6.00 "
5.45 "	149	" ..SOUTH GLASTONBURY.. "	11	5.00 "
6.15 "	154	" ......GLASTONBURY...... "	6	4.30 "
7.00 A. M.	160	arr.........HARTFORD........lve.	0	4.00 "

a Stops for freight and passengers Wednesday and Saturdays only.
b Stops only on trips from New York.
CONNECTIONS.—1 With Valley Branch Hartford Div., N. Y., N. H. & H. R. R.   2 With New London Division, N. Y., N. H. & H. R. R.   3 With Air Line Division, N. Y., N. H. & H. R. R., and New Britain and Berlin Branches.   4 With Hartford and Highland Divisions, N. Y., N. H. & H. R. R.; Central New England Rv.; and Trolley lines for Unionville, Farmington, Windsor, Springfield, Holyoke, Manchester, New Britain, and other points.

5

1.1   An invaluable source of information about local water transport is found in the timetable/folder issued by various carriers. The Summer 1916 schedule for the Hartford & New York Transportation Company lists stops between New York City and Hartford, Connecticut. As with most timetables, additional data is provided, including a description of the vessels used in this intercoastal river service.

the U.S. mail and passengers. In the 1840s more than two million passengers annually traveled the Ohio River alone. Yet service was slow; most boats stopped virtually anywhere to pick up "hogs and humans." The coming of the railroad, immune to high and low water levels, snags and winter ice, dramatically reduced, and in the early twentieth century virtually eliminated the steamboat passenger business. Some freight, however, mainly grain, lumber, rock and other bulk commodities, continued to move on these streams.

During World War I a new day dawned for the Ohio-Mississippi network. Increased freight traffic headed for East Coast ports overwhelmed the country's railroads, precipitating a revival in river transport. During the 1920s business grew even more when the federal government "canalized" sections of these streams. Water levels could be controlled through a series of locks and dams, and these rivers largely stopped being foaming torrents in the spring and sluggish ribbons in the summer. Barge lines quickly captured considerable bulk cargoes from the railroads, just as the latter had done during and after the Civil War. Dependable diesel engines rather than dangerous high-pressure steam boilers propelled squatty towboats that pushed along the busy channels barges loaded with oil, chemicals, coal, sand, gravel and grain. This process of improvement and modernization continues into the twenty-first century.

Coastal waterways likewise have long been vital to American transport. This has been especially true in New England and the Mid-Atlantic region. From almost the start of Euro-American settlement, a system of water transport, both for freight and passengers, thrived. Prior to the advent of steamships, the most comfortable way to travel from Boston to either New York, Philadelphia or Baltimore, for example, was to take a stagecoach to Newport or Providence, Rhode Island, and from there board a sailing packet. These boats were fast by contemporary standards and usually offered comfortable accommodations. When in the 1810s and 1820s steamboats appeared, speeds increased, and these coal-burning state-of-the-art vessels understandably attracted passengers and ever-increasing quantities of commercial goods. Even after railroads evolved, steamers traveling on Long Island Sound and especially between eastern ports and destinations along the Gulf of Mexico remained popular. Indeed, vessels operating between Gulf ports were often magnificent, at times equaling those in service on the North Atlantic. As late as 1927, for instance, the Southern Pacific Steamship Company, the "Morgan Line," launched the elegant *S.S. Dixie*. This oil-burning ship, which handled both freight and passengers, offered travelers a "luxury" trip "for health or pleasure" at "reasonable prices." Surprisingly, steamship lines themselves, because of cost considerations, did not eliminate sailing vessels until after World War I. For decades, six-masted schooners economically transported coal from Newport News, Virginia, to Boston, and three-masted ones carried cotton from Galveston, Texas, and New Orleans to East Coast ports. Although by the 1930s passenger travel disappeared, bulk

HUDSON RIVER DAY LINE

STEAMERS

WASHINGTON IRVING   ROBERT FULTON
HENDRICK HUDSON   AND ALBANY

1915   DAILY, EXCEPT SUNDAY   1915

NORTH BOUND	A.M.	A.M.	P.M.
New York			
Desbrosses St.	8 40	9 40	1 45
West 42d St.	9 00	10 00	2 00
West 129th St.	9 20	10 20	2 20
Yonkers	9 45	10 50	*2 45
Bear Mountain		12 30	*4 30
Highland Falls			4 45
West Point	11 50	1 00	5 00
Cornwall		1 25	5 25
Newburgh	12 25	1 45	5 45
New Hamburgh			6 15
Milton			6 30
Poughkeepsie	1 15	2 35	6 45
Kingston Point	2 10		
Kingston			7 45
Catskill	3 25		
Hudson	3 40		
Albany	6 10		

(May 14 to Nov. 1 — June 19 to Sept. 18 — June 1 to Sept. 18 — *Yonkers and Bear Mt. Stop from July 7 to Sept. 4)

SOUTH BOUND	A.M.	A.M.	P.M.
Albany		8 30	
Hudson		10 40	
Catskill		11 00	
Kingston	7 00		
Kingston Point		12 25	
Poughkeepsie	8 00	1 20	4 10
Milton	8 15		
New Hamburgh	8 30		
Newburgh	9 00	2 15	5 05
Cornwall	9 15		5 20
West Point	9 35	2 50	5 50
Highland Falls	9 40		
Bear Mountain			6 00
Yonkers		4 30	7 35
New York			
West 129th St.	11 55	5 10	8 10
West 42d St.	12 15	5 30	8 40
Desbrosses St.	12 45	6 00	

(June 2 to Sept. 18 — May 15 to Nov. 2 — June 19 to Sept. 18 — This Steamer will run one-half hour later on Saturdays)

☞ Over for Rates and Important Notes.

1.2   Although merely a card-type timetable, this one distributed by the Hudson River Day Line Company for the "sailing season" of 1915 indicates landings between New York City and Albany, New York.

goods, including petroleum products from the oil fields of Louisiana and Texas, continued their movement on waterways. Early in the twentieth century this artery improved significantly when the federal government financed construction of the Houston Ship Channel and the Gulf Intracoastal Waterway. Along the Pacific Coast, where nature

1.3 The Mallory Steamship Company promoted heavily its sailings between New York City and Galveston, Texas. Its 36-page public timetable for January-February 1909 provided such diverse information as drawings of its steamships *Alamo, Brazos, Colorado, Concho, Denver, Lampasas, Rio Grande* and *Sabine* and a listing of principal lights and lighthouses on the Atlantic and Gulf coasts.

13

placed coastal shipping on a competitive footing with interior railroads due to their heavy grades and curving lines, freight and passenger vessels flourished until the hard times of the 1930s. As with coastal traffic in general, eventually passengers moved to other transport forms, especially to automobiles, and freight went to pipelines and trucks. Still some business remained.

Commercial navigation on the American Great Lakes began early and became well-developed by the mid-nineteenth century. Initially, scores of sailing schooners, brigs and barks carried intercity cargoes, but steam eventually reigned supreme. In 1818 the first steamboat on the upper lakes, the 330-ton *Walk-in-the-Water*, made its historic voyage. Although the increase in steam tonnage on the Great Lakes was not as rapid as on the Ohio-Mississippi river system, by 1840, 225 sailing vessels and sixty-one steamboats operated on the five lakes. Internal improvements financed heavily by the federal government, such as lighthouses and deeper harbors, made these waterways more useful to shipping interests and hence to the general public. Canals also altered lake transport. The opening in 1829 of the Welland Canal, which linked Lake Ontario and Lake Erie, increased the value of the waterways, and construction in the 1850s of the Sault Canal around the Falls of the St. Marys River at the foot of Lake Superior had an even more pronounced effect on traffic. Most of all, the region's iron and later steel industries boomed. During the shipping season basic components of these metals—iron ore and limestone—could be cheaply and easily transported from the shores of Lake Superior to ports on Lake Michigan and Lake Erie. By the turn of the twentieth century great "freshwater whales"—long bulk carriers—became the principal type of freight vessel. Later, with completion of the artificial channels, locks and other betterments on the lakes and St. Lawrence River, the famed St. Lawrence Seaway opened in 1959 to ocean-going ships, and the mariner's map of North America changed dramatically.

Although throughout the twentieth century heavy cargoes dominated the Great Lakes trade, some passenger traffic remained until the 1940s. During the first quarter of the nineteenth century carriers instituted regularly scheduled service, and as late as the first quarter of the last century special passenger carriers enjoyed good business. The Detroit & Cleveland Navigation Company and the Cleveland & Buffalo Transit Company, for example, boomed the merits of pleasure and overnight business trips by water: "Spacious staterooms and parlors combined with the quietness with which the boats are operated insures refreshing sleep." But by World War II the automobile and airplane—the same transportation forms that decimated electric interurbans and

1.4   This picture postcard of lake boat *Eastern States*, operated by the Detroit & Buffalo Steamship Company, gives the researcher a sense of the appeal for this form of business and leisure water travel. At times the volume of traffic might be enormous, especially with special outings.

greatly reduced intercity rail passenger travel—also virtually choked off lake passenger service.

   Since riverways themselves are a vital part of transport history, a good point of departure for any study involving them would be an examination of individual bodies of water. Fortunately, high-quality literature is readily available. Examples include *The Cuyahoga* by William Donohue Ellis (New York: Holt, Rinehart and Winston, 1967); *River to the West: Three Centuries of the Ohio* by Walter Havinghurst (New York: Putnam, 1970); and *The Wisconsin, River of a Thousand Isles* by August Derleth (Madison: University of Wisconsin Press, 1985). Likewise of value are a series of books sponsored in recent years by the United States Army Corps of Engineers. Raymond H. Merritt, for one, produced *Creativity, Conflict and Controversy: A History of the St. Paul District U.S. Army Corps of Engineers* (Washington, DC: USGPO, 1979), in which he discusses the physical characteristics and general history of the Upper Mississippi, Minnesota and Red Rivers and the impact the Corps has had on these waterways and their drainage systems. This genre of work might readily answer the question of whether commer-

cial traffic ever appeared on a particular river. Did steamboats, for example, once ply the James or "Big Jim" River in South Dakota or the
Niobrara River in Nebraska? Then, too, an extensive list of monographic literature focuses on commercial development of rivers, lakes
and other bodies of water. The pre-steam era has received solid coverage. The classic work, *The Keelboat Age on Western Waters* by Leland D.
Baldwin (Pittsburgh, PA: University of Pittsburgh Press, 1941), tells
how keelboats revolutionized commerce in the trans-Appalachian
West. The steamboat era is explored in such specialized studies as *A
History of Steamboating on the Upper Missouri River* by William E. Lass
(Lincoln: University of Nebraska Press, 1962); *Steamboats on the Colorado
River, 1852–1916* by Richard E. Lingenfelter (Tucson: University of Ari-
zona Press, 1978); *Steamboats on the Western Rivers: An Economic and
Technological History* by Louis C. Hunter (Cambridge, MA: Harvard
University Press, 1949); *Steamboating on the Upper Mississippi* by
William J. Petersen (Iowa City, IA: State Historical Society of Iowa
Press, 1968); and *Stern-wheelers Up Columbia: A Century of Steamboating
in the Oregon County* by Randall V. Mills (Palo Alto, CA: Pacific Book,
1947). These books commonly contain maps, notes and references that
provide directions and clues for more specialized insights into the history of a local river site.

Tracing the past of specific river firms, their equipment and their ties
with particular locations and individuals, however, can be a challenge.
Although the secondary literature adequately covers the histories of
waterways, fewer works have appeared on specific topics. Yet appropriate strategies exist when a researcher wishes then to learn more
about the steamboat past in a particular community. If the subject involves commercial boat line operations that were once part of Ohio
River life in East Liverpool, Ohio, forty-four miles downstream from
Pittsburgh, the appropriate process might be as follows:

Identification of firms. Local newspapers and city directories (if available) are likely to be useful. Occasionally town or county histories provide such information. Only newspapers, though, regularly carried accounts of commercial river traffic, noting by name the daily arrival and
departure of boats, particularly those that accommodated passengers.
Identification of the vessel's owner may also be mentioned. Most
prominent river-town newspapers employed a staff specialist personally acquainted with the boat owners, captains and pilots. But in the
early twentieth century as river traffic waned, coverage usually declined. In 1902, the East Liverpool daily newspaper revealed that a lone
company, the Pittsburgh & Cincinnati Packet Line, headquartered in
Pittsburgh, continued to serve this pottery-manufacturing center, and

that its three steamboats, *Keystone State, Queen City* and *Virginia*, were the only ones that on a regular basis called at the public docks. "The Pittsburgh & Cincinnati Packet Line is the only line operating steamers [for freight and passengers] westward from Pittsburgh and naturally offers advantages that can not be secured by any other mode of travel out of Pittsburgh." Subsequently, the press made no further mention of the packet firm.

Vessels: While the number of extant steamboats is few, photographic images and also paintings and drawings abound. Some of the oldest daguerreotypes, dating from the 1840s show such river vessels. If a photograph or some other image is found, careful examination, perhaps by a magnifying glass, may reveal the boat's name. Frequently companies displayed highly visible signboards. Once the name is known, much more can usually be learned about the vessel. Two excellent sources of information are *Merchant Steam Vessels of the United States, 1790–1868* edited by C. Bradford Mitchell (Staten Island, NY: The Steamship Historical Society, 1975), and *Way's Packet Directory, 1848–1983: Passenger Steamboats of the Mississippi River System Since the Advent of Photography in Mid-Continent America* compiled by Frederick Way, Jr. (Athens: Ohio University Press, 1983). The former work, which is sometimes known as the "Lytle-Holdcamper List," includes hundreds of vessels in alphabetical order. Each entry contains seven columns with information about design (sidewheel, sternwheel or screw), name, tonnage, year of construction, place of construction, first home port and disposition. The book also provides a "Loss List" that names unfortunate vessels and notes their tonnage, year of construction, nature of loss ("lost," "destroyed," "wrecked" or "sunk"), date of loss, place of loss and numbers of lives lost, if any. The latter guide provides much the same type of material but it appears in paragraph format. The entry for the *Capitol City* reads as follows: "Stw p wh b. [sternwheel packet, wood hull, built] Harmar, Oh., at the Know yard, 1888. 132.2×25.7×4 Engines, 12's-41/2ft. Two boilers, each 36" by 22 ft., Ran in Gallipolis-Charleston trade, Kanawa River. Capt. Howard Donnely, with Wirt Donnely, clerk. Rebuilt 1893 and became COLUMBIA." There is then an appropriate entry for the *Columbia*.

Also available is a study that lists the more unusual showboats or floating theater vessels. This is *Showboats: The History of an American Institution* by Philip Graham (Austin: University of Texas Press, 1951), and its appendix chronicles the principal boats. A sample entry provides this data: "CHAPMAN'S FLOATING THEATER. Built in 1831 at Pittsburgh by William Chapman, Sr. Seated 200. Named changed in 1836 to the STEAMBOAT THEATER. Lower Mississippi, and Ohio Sys-

"The Lorena" on Muskingum River, Malta, Ohio

1.5   As with all forms of transport, the picture postcard offers clues to past river transport. This ca. 1910 view of *The Lorena* reveals the type of steamboat used at the turn of the twentieth century on small inland steams, in this case the "canalized" Muskingum River of Ohio.

tem. After Chapman's death in 1840, operated by his wife under the name CHAPMAN'S FLOATING PALACE. Sold to Sol Smith in 1847, and in the same year collided with a steamboat and sunk."

Supporting structures: Although physical remains of old steamboats, towboats and barges are relatively rare, structures associated with the halcyon days of river boating are less unusual. During the steamboat era river towns inevitably sported a river-front hotel, usually situated near the public wharf. Its location may be determined through newspaper accounts, fire, plat and other maps. This building type may have found adaptive use after patronage dwindled and closure followed. Water-front warehouses, often constructed of brick or stone for fire protection, may also remain, perhaps either abandoned or recycled. Remnants of the historic wharf itself may be extant; after-all, bricks and cobblestones are enduring materials. The once ubiquitous floating warehouse ("wharfboat") and the nearby steam-powered ferry and its landing float, however, have surely disappeared. Yet, the scoured-out site of some former ferry landings might be visible, especially when water levels are low.

Details of operations. Once a list of companies that served East Liverpool has been compiled, local newspapers remain an excellent source of information about corporate activities. The likely place to locate additional material is *The Waterways Journal* and *The River*, a predecessor, published since 1887 in St. Louis, Missouri. Like parallel periodicals that cover steam railroads, electric interurbans, bus companies and airlines, *The Waterways Journal*, a long-time weekly publication, reviewed company operations, including those of the Pittsburgh & Cincinnati Packet Line. Unfortunately *The Waterways Journal* has never been fully indexed, only the 1891–1910 period has been cataloged.

If even more information is needed, a primary center for research is the Herman T. Pott National Inland Waterways Library, a unit of the St. Louis Mercantile Library, located on the campus of the University of Missouri-St. Louis (8001 Natural Bridge Road, St. Louis, MO 63121-4499). This virtually unique collection, which consists of more than 450 linear feet of archival materials, includes manuscripts, posters, photographs, paintings, steamboat plans, barge and towboat blueprints and related paper ephemera. Three separate photographic groups found in the Pott Library are of enormous value: Ruth Ferris Collection containing rare views of steamboats and other vessels, river communities, and boatmen, dating from the mid-1880s through the 1970s; *The Waterways Journal* Collection featuring a variety of river subjects; the Captain Thomas E. Kenny Photo Collection and the Ray Covington Photo Collections consisting mostly of vessels on the Ohio River beginning in the 1930s. The Pott Library, moreover, holds the corporate papers of the Federal Barge Lines, launched during World War I by the federal government, when William G. McAdoo, Director General of the Railroads, commandeered all privately owned floating equipment on the Mississippi and Warrior Rivers to relieve wartime rail freight congestion. Congress subsequently created the Inland Waterways Corporation to operate the Federal Barge Lines and later this operation was privatized. A superb guide book, *An Inventory of the Federal Barge Lines Collections*, by Ann Morris is available from the Pott Library. Finally, this research facility possesses more than 10,000 volumes of other primary and secondary works. (See www.umsl.edu/pott)

Personal history. Since barge companies continue to serve East Liverpool, Ohio, it is possible to interview current crew members and those who assist with local operations. Employees, too, might suggest others, namely retirees, who can recall life on the Ohio River with specific knowledge about the community and that immediate stretch of the waterway. Because no barge lines are based in East Liverpool, former river men likely live elsewhere, perhaps in the Cincinnati, Pittsburgh or St. Louis areas. A potential source of contacts might be through a heritage-

1.6   Another illustration of the timetable/folder is the one issued for the 1893 season by the Chicago-based Goodrich Transportation Company. An artist's sketch of the *S.S. Virginia* depicts the firm's all-steel, twin screw boat that served its routes on Lake Michigan.

type organization, Sons and Daughters of Pioneer Rivermen, which publishes a quarterly magazine, *S&D Reflector* (123 Seneca Drive, Marietta, OH 45750).

Little has been done by historical societies and others to tap memories of individuals associated with inland waterways. The primary collection of such reminiscences is part of the holdings of the Herman T. Pott National Inland Waterways Library. In 1987 this library launched an on-going oral history project to record and transcribe experiences of individuals who have been closely involved with river transport. As the transcripts reveal, operating men are good sources of information of past and present river operations. They can offer "color," sharing the rich folklore of their occupation. Unquestionably, there has long existed a special "subculture" in river towns, where restaurants, saloons, brothels, hotels, boarding and rooming houses catered to these men in motion. Furthermore, operating workers typically can recall the physical features of these streams; for example, locations of long-abandoned factories, mills, mines, docks and ferry crossings or how over time the river has altered its course. The business dimensions of a company that provided local service are gleaned from executives and other white-collar employees. Unlike crew members, they can discuss such matters as revenues, shippers, regulation and over-all business strategies. As with all types of interviews, it must be remembered that at times the human memory may be unreliable; passage of time can blur even the sharpest of recollections.

If the nearby history project involves a coastal port, whether on the Atlantic or Pacific Oceans or the Gulf of Mexico, procedures employed for examination of river traffic and activities can likewise be effective. Basic works are a logical beginning point and include: *The Maritime History of Massachusetts, 1783–1860* by Samuel Eliot Morison (Boston: Houghton Mifflin, 1961); *Ports of Call* by Robert Carse (New York: Scribner, 1967); *The Rise of New York Port, 1815–1860* by Robert Greenhalgh Albion (New York: Scribner's Sons, 1939); and *The Sea and the States: A Maritime History of the American Merchant Marine* by Samuel Wood Bryant (New York, NY: T. Y. Crowell, 1947). Other titles can be found in *Naval & Maritime History: An Annotated Bibliography* by Robert Greenhalgh Albion (Mystic, CT: The Marine Historical Association, 4th ed., 1972).

Newspapers offer much. Just as for decades river commerce dominated life in hundreds of communities, the same can be said for seaports, on the Atlantic often extending back to the colonial period. Newspapers from the eighteenth through twentieth centuries contain a wealth of information about shipping, labor, structures and other topics. Along the West Coast in the first part of the twentieth century, a host of steamship companies, including Pacific Alaska Navigation, Pacific Coast Steamship, Pacific Lighterage, Pacific Steamship and Portland-California Steamship, served various coastal ports. Daily newspapers, *The Astorian* (Astoria, OR), *Humdoldt Standard* (Eureka, CA), *Los Angeles Times, Portland Oregonian, San Diego Union, San Francisco Chronicle, San Francisco Examiner, Santa Barbara News, Seattle Post-Intelligencer* and *Tacoma Ledger*, attempted to cover the waterfront of its particular locale, and most of them accomplished such tasks with voluminous results.

Just as newspapers shed light on coastal history, so, too, are trade publications valuable tools. Again, in the case of the Pacific past, any researcher may consult back issues of the *Pacific Marine Review*, for decades the official organ of the Pacific American Steamship Association and the Shipowners Association of the Pacific Coast. Over the last century there have been other trade publications of note for this region, including *Railway and Marine News, Pacific Shipper* and *Shipping Register*. Most of these trade journals and other Pacific coastal materials can be found in the maritime collection of the Honnold Library at the Claremont Colleges in Claremont, California (91711-6160).

Learning more about seaports and ocean-related commerce is aided by the resources of the comparatively large number of maritime museums. A good point of departure for identifying the appropriate ones is *The Naval Institute Guide to Maritime Museums of North America* edited by Robert H. Smith (Annapolis, MD: Naval Institute Press, 1990), and his companion volume, *A Supplement to the Naval Institute Guide to Maritime Museums of North America* (Del Mar, CA: "C" Books, 1993). Some museums possess extensive local history research collections, including manuscripts, newspaper clippings, photographs, charts and reminiscences. The largest and most comprehensive maritime holdings, especially three-dimensional objects, are housed at Mystic Seaport (P.O. Box 6000, Mystic, CT 06355). Calling itself "The Museum of America and the Sea," Mystic Seaport owns such widely diverse historic resources as the *Brilliant*, a training schooner, and the archive of the Electric Launch Company ("Elco"), which from 1892 to 1949 designed and built pleasure boats, yacht tenders, lifeboats and military craft, including PT boats used extensively during World War II.

Two other major centers for the study of the ocean past are the Mariners' Museum Research Library and the Steamship Historical Society of America. The former, located at 100 Museum Drive, Newport News, VA 23606-3759, is one of the largest and most comprehensive maritime research centers in the country, with extensive holdings on maritime history, marine technology and design, navigation, commerce and trade and shipbuilding. Archived items include ships' logs, account books, journals and the foremost run of vessel registers in North America. As with related facilities, this library owns a massive iconographic collection. The latter organization, which dates from 1935, also maintains one of the largest libraries in North America devoted exclusively to steamship and steamboat history. Its collections include books, periodicals, special reports, pamphlets, drawings and photographs. These holdings are housed at the University of Baltimore Library, 1420 Maryland Avenue, Baltimore, MD 21201.

It is an organization like the Steamboat Historical Society of America that not only offers a research center for anyone who is anxious to learn more about the nearby history associated with deep water, but provides valuable insights through its publications. In this case it is *Steamboat Bill*, an illustrated quarterly continuously published since 1940. A long-time feature is an opportunity to make contact with experts. As with all forms of transport history both professionals and amateurs who have much to offer. The popular "Deck Cargo" section in *Steamboat Bill* provides a regular forum for anyone to ask for assistance.

Learning about individuals linked to the seafaring life involves approaches employed in locating and identifying "common people" in other transport fields. Local and national historical repositories with their newspapers and other materials are potentially productive sources of information. State and federal censuses are likely beneficial. If, for example, those documents are consulted for New Bedford, Massachusetts, it becomes readily apparent that this long-time center of the whaling industry had hundreds of households involved in fishing and water transport. Excellent guidelines and related commentary about tracing these largely forgotten Americans are found in Chapter 5 of *Nearby History: Exploring the Past Around You* by David E. Kyvig and Myron A. Marty (Walnut Creek, CA: AltaMira Press, 2000, second edition).

While Baltimore, Claremont, Mystic and Newport News may be Meccas for coastal history materials, four places are premier centers for the study of transport associated with the American Great Lakes. Specifically, they include the Historical Collections of the Great Lakes housed in the Center for Archival Collections at Bowling Green State University, Bowling Green, OH 43403; Great Lakes Historical Society and Inland Seas Maritime Museum, P.O. Box 435, Vermilion, OH 44089-0435; Dossin Great Lakes Museum, Belle Isle, Detroit, MI 48207; and the Marine Museum of the Great Lakes at Queens University, 55 Ontario Street, Kingston, ON K7L 2Y2, Canada. Generally these depositories have complementary holdings, possessing photographs, critical in documentation for most nearby Great Lakes projects. Other materials relate to shipbuilding, commercial shipping, labor and the history of Great Lakes ports. These groups also produce well researched publications. Arguably the most useful for nearby history projects is *Inland Seas, A Quarterly Journal of the Great Lakes*, an organ of the Great Lakes Historical Society.

Yet before making a visit to one of the four research centers or to other libraries or societies with holdings on the American Great Lakes, an understanding of these bodies of waters themselves is recommended. Two works oriented toward a popular audience are *The Great Lakes* by Harlan Hatcher (New York: Oxford University Press, 1944), and *The Long Ship Passing: The Story of the Great Lakes* by Walter Havighurst (New York: Macmillan, 1943). A valuable, yet obscure study is the *History of the Navigation of the Great Lakes* by Ralph G. Plumb (Washington, DC: USGPO, 1911). And a check of *Great Lakes Maritime History: Bibliography and Sources of Information*, edited by Charles and Jeri Feltner (Dearborn, MI: Seajoy Publications, 1982) is also wise.

A fortunate dimension to Great Lakes research endeavors is the greater abundance of published histories of carriers. A recent example is Alexander C. Meakin's account of the Wilson Marine Transit Company, *Master of the Inland Seas: The Story of Captain Thomas Wilson and the Fleet that Bore His Name* (Vermilion, OH: Great Lakes Historical Society, 1988). Even in the case of this detailed study, most of the corporate records of the Wilson company have either been destroyed or lost. The author used documents and photographs held by various museums and libraries, including the research facilities at Bowling Green State University and interviews with executives, sailors and other company employees. Meakin's endeavor demonstrates that it is possible to piece together a company's past.

In a related fashion there exists an extensive body of works on Great Lakes vessels. Wind-powered schooners, the long-time workhorses, for example, have become the collecting focus of several museums, including the Chicago Maritime Society (North Pier Building, 435 East Illinois Street, Chicago, IL 60611), and the subject of such books as *Great Lakes Sailing Ships* by Henry N. Barkhausen (Milwaukee, WI: Kalmbach, 1947); *Schooner Passage: Sailing Ships and the Lake Michigan Frontier* by Theodore L. Karamanski (Detroit, MI: Wayne State University Press, 2000) and *Ships of the Great Lakes: Three Hundred Years of Navigation* by James P. Barry (Berkeley, CA: Howell-North Books, 1973). The Karamanski work provides insights into the lives of seamen and their associates and how they might be identified from the historical record. Not to be overlooked is this regularly updated Internet resource for Great

Lakes vessels: <www.bgsu.edu/colleges/library/hcgl/vessel.html> maintained by The Historical Collections on the Great Lakes.

A somewhat overlooked aspect of natural waterways history involves ferryboats. Such operations have been or have long continued to be part of river, deep water and lake crossings. In 1811 steam-powered ferryboat service began in New York Harbor and it has remained continuous, except diesel engines have since replaced steam boilers. And there were informal ferries across major streams almost as soon as there were settlers. With construction of bridges, whether railroad or wagon, such service usually disappeared. The range of vessels involved in these "over and back" operations has been enormous, running the gamut from steel-hulled boats, with bulky low-pressure coal-fired boilers, that accommodated hundreds of passengers and scores of railroad freight cars to primitive raft-like boats, propelled by animals pulling rope cables, that handled only a few wagons and riders.

As might be surmised, there exists a literature about the more important ferryboat operations, including those in the greater New York City and San Francisco areas. For the former there is the encyclopedic *Over & Back: The History of Ferryboats in New York Harbor* by Brian J. Cudahy (New York: Fordham University Press, 1990), and for the latter *San Francisco Bay Ferryboats* by George H. Harlan (Berkeley, CA: Howell-North, 1987). Yet for modest ferryboat operations on the major and minor streams there are few published titles, although bits and pieces appear in county and community histories and occasionally are mentioned in local reminiscences.

By employing research strategies used for other aspects of the waterway story, it is possible to learn more about local ferryboats and their operations. It is easier to gain information about the major harbor and lake ferries. For one thing, there exists the venerable U.S. government publication, *Merchant Vessels of the United States*, which was issued more or less annually between 1867 and 1981 by various federal agencies, including the Department of Commerce and the U.S. Coast Guard. It offers the definitive roster of U.S. flag merchant ships, including large ferryboats. Again, it will be materials found in historical societies, old maps and especially newspapers that will enable the researcher to reconstruct the past. Since some ferryboat operations were publicly owned, usually by county governments and highway departments, there are public records, housed locally or in a state archive. Railroads, too, operated ferryboats, some a combination of passenger, road vehicle and freight car and others for only railroad rolling stock. If the Hoboken Ferry Company is to be studied, this long-time affiliate of the Delaware, Lackawanna & Western (DL&W) Railroad, it would be fruitful to examine records, including minutes of the Board of Directors, which are part of the DL&W collection at the Byrd Library of Syracuse University in Syracuse, New York 13210. Also, conversations with "old timers" in the community should not be overlooked.

Just as railroad accidents (see Chapter 4) are part of nearby history endeavors, so, too, are shipwrecks. Learning about a particular disaster may involve careful reading of contemporary newspapers or checking shipwreck records found at a major marine research center. Contacting individuals who are fascinated by such wrecks is yet another resource. For example, the Great Lakes Shipwreck Research Group (www.bail-lod.com), an avid keeper of such data, is a promising possibility.

Some marine disasters have occurred near lighthouses, the signature structure for both coastal and Great Lakes transport. Although in recent decades dramatic changes in navigational aids have made obsolete many of these structures built a century or more ago, scores remain. If studying a lighthouse, whether in use, abandoned or even destroyed, examination of government documents is essential. Federal funds usually financed construction, maintenance and staffing. The "mother load" of such materials is Record Group 26 at the National Archives. There a researcher will find extensive manuscript materials, including correspondence, ledgers and journals. Some of these historic documents have been consolidated into folders that deal with specific light stations, but most are arranged chronologically for lighthouse districts or for the entire lighthouse establishment. Especially useful are the clippings files on individuals lighthouses—part printed and part manuscript material—and published annual lighthouse lists.

Federal records not only make it possible to trace the history of a lighthouse or related structure, but they can be a gold mine for other publicly built and maintained facilities. The voluminous papers of the U.S. Army Corps of Engineers, located in the National Archives, are one such resource. Thus, if the question involves the construction of a "pool" on the Ohio River or a dam on the Missouri River for navigation purposes, Corps materials can supply answers, just as they might for military and other special roads, part of the subject that will be explored next.

Chapter 2

ROADS

From time immemorial trails and traces have served as avenues for commercial and pleasure travel, connecting settlements, navigable streams and other destinations. When the earliest Euro-Americans moved beyond waterways, they often walked or rode horseback along paths made by wild animals or Native Americans. But as populations increased, the need grew for more and better roadways that would permit travel by cart or wagon. Therefore, in large sections of the expanding Republic, citizens "blazed" new roads by removing trees and stumps and even plowing furrows between villages. In laying out these pioneer roads, builders frequently selected ridges or highlands to avoid swamps, marshes and disruptive floods that struck in the spring and fall. As in the cardiovascular system of a living being, a network of roads branched out from main arteries. Although often such "capillaries" were barely discernible ruts, they allowed the transport of essential goods into the remotest areas.

Learning about the first roadways is not always easy, yet some materials are available. Historic maps are an excellent source. Understandably early cartographers wished to show routes of importance, whether the Upper Road between Fredericksburg, Virginia, Charlotte, North Carolina, and Greenville, South Carolina, or the Wilderness Road through the Cumberland Gap of Kentucky and Tennessee. A good place to search for such documents would be state, county and local historical societies. The Library of Congress and the National Archives, with their extensive cartographic collections, are also logical resource places. This is especially true for the extensive network of U.S. military roads that existed prior to the triumph of the Railway Age. Usually these Army-built and maintained arteries connected scattered forts and other military-related locations and likewise served as public thoroughfares. Some early maps have been published in an atlas format or used to illustrate articles and books.

If such primary sources cannot be located or if they are inadequate, first-hand travelers' accounts and immigrant guides might pinpoint such routes, albeit in a narrative format. Those interested in learning the precise location of the Mormon Trail in Union County, Iowa, for example, might consider the following suggestions. In the late 1840s and early 1850s this trail became the artery for the followers of Brigham Young of the Church of Jesus Christ of Latter-day Saints who removed themselves from Nauvoo, Illinois, to the Basin of the Great Salt Lake in Utah. There are a number of options, specifically diaries and guidebooks, some of which include rough maps. Collectively they make it possible to approximate most of this lengthy passage from the shores of the Mississippi River to the emerging Mormon Zion. Surely one of the most helpful printed documents is a detailed manual, *The Latter-Day Saints Emigrants' Guide*, which William Clayton prepared in 1847. Five thousand copies of this chatty publication, which describes the route and camp grounds through the Hawkeye state, were initially printed; originals and reprints can be found in a variety of libraries and historical societies.

In recent years historic trails, especially the most popular emigrant ones, have attracted increased interest. The premier example is the Oregon-California Trails Association (OCTA). Founded in 1982, the group emerged when some historians and trail enthusiasts gathered to see what they could do to preserve existing portions of the Oregon Trail. Quickly the OCTA developed into an organization dedicated to not only the Oregon and California trails but to all the major emigrant routes. It has actively supported the National Historic Trails status of the California, Mormon, Oregon, Pony Express and Santa Fe routes. The OCTA maintains a national headquarters at 524 South Osage Street in Independence, Missouri, with its mailing address at P.O. Box 1019, Independence, MO 64051-0519. It publishes research works, including its *Emigrant Trails Historic Studies Series*, and operates the Merrill J. Mattes Research Library. This expanding facility contains more than 2,200 trail diaries, letters and first-person recollections, making it the largest public research library in the nation that focuses on pioneer overland routes.

While trails, even the longest and most used, were often ephemeral, at times altering course because of weather, geological changes or discoveries of "short-cuts," early turnpikes sported greater permanency. Between the construction of the Philadelphia-Lancaster Turnpike in the early 1790s and the ebbing of the building boom prompted by the Panic of 1837, promoters projected hundreds of for-profit turnpike schemes, especially in New England, the Middle Atlantic states and the Old Northwest. During this period approximately 12,000 miles of toll roads opened. They commonly featured graded rights-of-way, hard surfaces usually paved with a gravel or stone mix, culverts and bridges and other betterments. Since tolls were collected (at least initially), tollgates appeared. For example, along the sixty-two mile Philadelphia-Lancaster Turnpike, the company erected nine small tollgate structures, located three to ten miles apart. Nationwide a few scattered tollgates have survived but sections of the original roadways, especially small stone bridges are more likely to be found. Auxiliary support structures, particularly taverns and hotels, are even more plentiful.

As with any transportation business turnpike companies kept records. Firms maintained accounts of tolls, improvements, property taxes and employee pay and often noted the types and volume of goods that passed. Larger companies issued regularly published reports as well. Some paper materials survive, usually found in the holdings of local and state historical societies. Since these toll roads commonly failed to generate enough revenues to meet the cost of repairs, most died on their own, frequently after short periods of operation. Usually there were no successor carriers, unlike some canals firms that were later absorbed by competing railroad companies. Nevertheless, public authorities assumed control of former toll roads, and their records, if extant, can shed light on this particular phase of operations. If the turnpike company passed through the wringer of bankruptcy, legal records, usually generated by the court-appointed receiver, may provide insight into daily operations and related aspects of corporate life. Property tax assessments and payments may also yield useful perspectives.

To learn about individual stagecoach companies and their employees, several approaches may be undertaken. Through much of the nineteenth century community newspapers frequently published small display advertisements about stagecoach services, usually including identification of the official corporate name. Names of the owner or proprietor and even the lead driver will perhaps be noted, too, and for the small concerns that predominated this might account for a substantial portion of the full-time employees. Large stagecoach companies existed, especially in the trans-Mississippi West. It is more likely that a historical society, typically a state one, will possess business papers and other items for such firms. Even if an employee worked for a major company, finding information about this person may not be easy. Federal manuscript census records for communities that served as headquarters or major stops may reveal wanted details. Notably, as railroads replaced stagecoaches, drivers commonly took jobs as conductors, while those who had mechanical or blacksmithing skills might become locomotive firemen or engineers or take assignments in newly

JAMESON'S STAGE LINE

BETWEEN

WEST OSSIPEE & CENTRE HARBOR

IN EFFECT

JUNE 27 to OCT. 1, 1892,

CONNECTING

AT CENTRE HARBOR WITH STEAMER "LADY OF THE LAKE."

WEST OSSIPEE TO BOSTON.

		A.M.
Leave West Ossipee...Jameson's Stage		7.00
" Whittier......... " "		7.30
" South Tamworth, " "		8.15
" North Sandwich " "		9.00
" Centre Sandwich " "		10.00
" Sandwich...... " "		10.30
" Moultunboro .. " "		11.10
Arrive Centre Harbor " "		12.10½
Leave Centre Harbor............Steamer		12.15
Arrive Weirs...................... "		1.20
Leave Weirs................C. & M. R. R.		1.25
Arrive Concord............. " "		2.28
" Manchester.......... " "		3.01
" Nashua Junction..... " "		3.30
" Lowell...........B. & L. Depot		3.57
" Boston............. " "		4.45
		P.M.

BOSTON TO WEST OSSIPEE.

		A.M.
Leave Boston...........B. & L. Depot		9.30
" Lowell .... " "		10.13
" Nashua Junction C. & M. R. R.		10.38
" Manchester...... " "		11.06
" Concord.......... " "		11.38
Arrive Weirs .... " "		12.34
Leave Weirs ....Steamer		12.34
Arrive Centre Harbor,.......... "		1.25
Leave Centre Harbor, Jameson's Stage		1.45
Arrive Moultonboro " "		3.00
" Sandwich " "		4.00
" Centre Sandwich " "		4.30
" North Sandwich " "		5.15
" South Tamworth " "		6.15
" Whittier " "		7.00
" West Ossipee " "		7.30
		P.M.

F. H. WEED, Manager, Sandwich, N. H.

2.1   Only occasionally will a printed timetable of a stage line be discovered. More likely such information will be found in local newspapers and guide books.

opened railroad shops. Such linkages may be revealed in federal and state census data.

Although passenger trains largely obliterated stagecoaches and hence the pressing need for good intercity roadways, technological advancements at the turn of the twentieth century changed the transport picture. With the dawning of the motor age and the growing use of the automobile and truck and then the "jitney" intercity motor bus, the nation experienced a renewed interest in building and maintaining better roads. At this time most public arteries were created as local projects, commonly financed through modest road taxes. For much of the nineteenth century farmers customarily "worked off" their annual road obligations by using picks and shovels and primitive scrapers. At times, especially in the South, convicts assisted in road construction and maintenance, just as slaves had done before the Civil War. Court house and state documents record both road taxes and employment of prisoners on public roads.

2.2   Early photographs of roads usually reveal their nearly universal poor condition. The researcher may get a sense of the materials (if any) used in road construction and overall dimensions of such primitive arteries.

With community pressure for better all-weather roads (and more of them, too), politicians began to respond. In 1895, for example, the California legislature created a Bureau of Highways to define the state's interest and responsibility in road building and construction. Then in 1909 lawmakers authorized a bond issue of $18 million for a network of paved state highways. What took place in California occurred elsewhere, albeit at times two or three decades later. State agencies involved in highway betterments generated reams of documents, with some eventually finding their way into public archives. Those in the Golden State are housed in the California Department of Transportation Library and Archives in Sacramento 94273-0001.

While state governments marshaled resources for better roads, private groups also responded. Automobile, truck, tire and other manufacturers joined local boosters who sought to make a particular road accessible, reliable and popular with motorists, whether the Lincoln Highway Association (LHA) that promoted a "coast-to-coast rock highway" between New York City and San Francisco (the future route of U.S. Highway 30) or the Black & Yellow Trail Association (largely today's U.S. Highway 14), a Chicago to Black Hills and Yellowstone Park route or the Arrowhead Trail (eventually a portion of Interstate 15) between Salt Lake City and Los Angeles. Indeed, prior to World War I numerous highway and trail associations emerged. Specifically, these interest groups printed maps, marked roadways, advertised them and sought funding for improvements. By the mid-1920s the country had approximately 250 marked "trails"; they knew no geographic bounds.

Learning about the privately sponsored named trails is generally more difficult than finding information about public ones, including those sponsored by state governments. Nevertheless, records of some trail groups have survived, most of all those belonging to the Lincoln Highway Association. The Transportation History Collection located in the Special Collections Library of the University of Michigan in Ann Arbor 48109-1205 holds its papers, offering correspondence, bulletins to directors, guides, maps and photographs. A related source is the enthusiast group, appropriately named the Lincoln Highway Association, located at 111 South Elm Street, P.O. Box 308, in Franklin Grove, Illinois 61031, that publishes a quarterly journal, *The Lincoln Highway Forum*. And personal papers of individuals intimately associated with such organizations can offer further information. For example, the voluminous papers of Frank A. Seiberling, co-founder of Goodyear Tire & Rubber Company, who along with Henry Joy, president of the Packard Motor Car Company, and Carl Graham Fischer, head of Prest-O-Lite, an automotive headlight firm, became a guiding force behind the LHA, are located in the Ohio Historical Society in Columbus 43211. The Seiberling papers reveal that the Lincoln Highway was marked four times: the first by red, white and blue bands painted on poles, rocks or other convenient objects, later with an insignia that consisted of red, white and blue rectangles with the words "Lincoln Highway" in blue above and below the letter "L" painted on telephone poles and metal signs, then with more permanent enameled steel signs and finally with 3,000 concrete roadside posts with the insignia and letter. Specifically, for locating routes of named highways these sources might profitably be consulted: reprint of *Auto Road Atlas of the United States*, initially published by Rand McNally in 1926; reprint of the 1916 Lincoln Highway Association guide (P.O. Box 255185, Sacramento, CA 95865); WPA guides to the various states, some of which have been reprinted; United States Geological Survey 1:250,000-scale maps; and an unpublished typescript, "Named Highways of the United States," (December 8, 1959), housed in the library

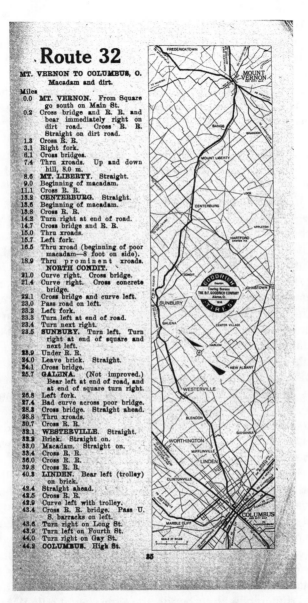

Route 32

MT. VERNON TO COLUMBUS, O.
Macadam and dirt.

Miles
- 0.0 **MT. VERNON.** From Square go south on Main St.
- 0.2 Cross bridge and R. R. and bear immediately right on dirt road. Cross R. R. Straight on dirt road.
- 1.3 Cross R. R.
- 3.1 Right fork.
- 6.1 Cross bridges.
- 7.4 Thru xroads. Up and down hill, 8.0 m.
- 8.6 **MT. LIBERTY.** Straight.
- 9.0 Beginning of macadam.
- 11.1 Cross R. R.
- 13.2 **CENTERBURG.** Straight.
- 13.6 Beginning of macadam.
- 13.8 Cross R. R.
- 14.2 Turn right at end of road.
- 14.7 Cross bridge and R. R.
- 15.0 Thru xroads.
- 15.7 Left fork.
- 16.5 Thru xroad (beginning of poor macadam—8 foot on side).
- 18.9 Thru prominent xroads. **NORTH CONDIT.**
- 21.0 Curve right. Cross bridge.
- 21.4 Curve right. Cross concrete bridge.
- 22.1 Cross bridge and curve left.
- 23.0 Pass road on left.
- 23.2 Left fork.
- 23.3 Turn left at end of road.
- 23.4 Turn next right.
- 23.5 **SUNBURY.** Turn left. Turn right at end of square and next left.
- 23.9 Under R. R.
- 24.0 Leave brick. Straight.
- 24.1 Cross bridge.
- 25.7 **GALENA.** (Not improved.) Bear left at end of road, and at end of square turn right.
- 26.8 Left fork.
- 27.4 Bad curve across poor bridge.
- 28.2 Cross bridge. Straight ahead.
- 28.8 Thru xroads.
- 30.7 Cross R. R.
- 32.1 **WESTERVILLE.** Straight.
- 32.2 Brick. Straight on.
- 33.0 Macadam. Straight on.
- 33.4 Cross R. R.
- 36.0 Cross R. R.
- 39.8 Cross R. R.
- 40.3 **LINDEN.** Bear left (trolley) on brick.
- 42.4 Straight ahead.
- 42.5 Cross R. R.
- 42.9 Curve left with trolley.
- 43.4 Cross R. R. bridge. Pass U. S. barracks on left.
- 43.6 Turn right on Long St.
- 43.9 Turn left on Fourth St.
- 44.0 Turn right on Gay St.
- 44.2 **COLUMBUS.** High St.

25

2.3   A valuable source of locating principal intercity roadways can be found in pioneer road guides. Before World War I the B.F. Goodrich Company, a leading tire manufacturer based in Akron, Ohio, issued guidebooks for most of the nation. In this one for Ohio, "Route 32" is marked, accompanied by careful directions on how to travel the "Macadam and dirt" road between Mount Vernon and Columbus. (Archival Service, The University of Akron) of the American Automobile Association in Falls Church, Virginia 22047. Various historical societies and private collectors, too, have maps, advertising materials, photographs and even the markers themselves from both private- and public-sponsored roadways.

Just as trail narratives and emigrant guides offer insights into the nature of the earliest roads, subsequent versions of this genre are published accounts of regional, interregional and transcontinental auto trips. Between 1900 and 1920 magazines such as *Overland Monthly*, *Scribner's* and *Sunset* contained articles on touring in automobiles, especially in the West. Books and pamphlets also appeared. The best guide to the latter literature is *Autos Across America: A Bibliography of Transcontinental Automobile Travel: 1903–1940* by Carey S. Bliss (Austin, TX: Jenkins & Reese Companies, 1983). In addition to sixty-six annotated entries, Bliss includes other works that cover more limited auto journeys.

With named roads becoming part of the numbered federal highway system in the mid-1920s motorists soon thereafter could take such routes as U.S. 1 along the East Coast between Maine and Florida; U.S. 2 between Maine and Washington State and the legendary Route 66 between Chicago and Los Angeles. But not until after World War II would an integrated national network of roads be developed that could accommodate large volumes of traffic at high speeds. Admittedly, there were hints of the super highway in New York City's Bronx River Parkway, which opened in 1922, and by 1940 in the nation's first bonafide freeways, the Merritt Parkway in Connecticut and the Pennsylvania Turnpike, whose first segment was then under construction.

In the decade following World War II, much enthusiasm developed for better roadways. During this period state-sponsored tollways were the most striking achievements. In 1947 Maine opened such a modern road, the forty-seven mile Maine Turnpike between Portland and Portsmouth. Other states followed, including New Jersey, New York, Pennsylvania, Ohio and Indiana. By the early 1950s, based on a combination of routes already finished, under construction or planned, motorists expected shortly to be able to drive between New England and Chicago without encountering a single stoplight. Generally, states used their borrowing capacities to finance roads, limiting projects to routes where planners anticipated substantial traffic. Only West Virginia experienced difficulty with its bonds; the eighty-eight mile West Virginia Turnpike, which was a two-lane road that opened in November 1954, failed to achieve the usage envisioned by its proponents. Eventually, by the 1970s, however, this strategic road, which subsequently linked other highways between the Midwest and the Southeast and expanded to four lanes, became financially viable.

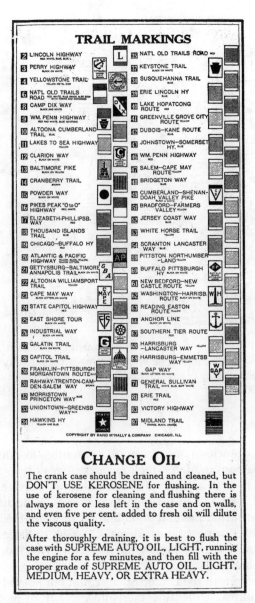

2.4 Some early road maps gave motorists a guide to "trail markings." It would not be until the mid-1920s that the federal government numbered major interstate roadways. Some states, including New Jersey, continued for a few years to use names also. If a road symbol is known, it is then possible to learn its official moniker.

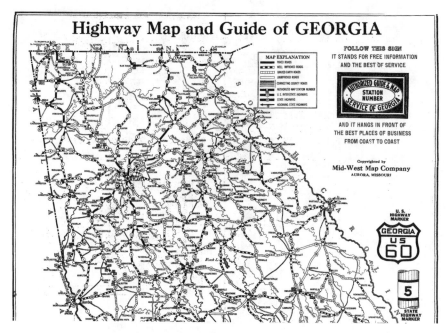

2.5   Pre-World War II highway maps offer much information. This one from
the 1930s shows the developing network of all-weather intercity roads in Georgia. Since the 1950s many of the early paved roads have either been partially or
wholly relocated.

Since state agencies, namely turnpike commissions, developed and
operated these thoroughfares, their records are readily available, either
in state archives or in an individual turnpike authority archive. For instance, records of the Ohio Turnpike Commission, including annual reports, engineering studies and photographs, reside in the headquarters
building at 682 Prospect Street, Berea, Ohio 44017. Indeed, historical
materials on this 241-mile trans-Ohio speedway, which opened on October 1, 1955, are abundant.

But vast sections of the United States could not possibly justify construction of tollways. Pressure therefore grew from motorists and a
host of interest groups, including automobile and truck makers, concrete suppliers, motor carriers, tire manufacturers and labor unions,
the so-called "road gang," for high-speed public "free ways." In 1956
the 85th Congress, stirred to action by Representatives George Fallon
and Hale Boggs, Senator Albert Gore, Sr., and President Dwight D.

Eisenhower endorsed the National Defense Highway Act, the most ambitious public works program undertaken in American history and arguably one of the most important. This landmark piece of legislation committed the federal government to pay from a Highway Trust Fund, the recipient of federal automotive and gasoline taxes, ninety percent of the cost of constructing approximately 41,000 miles of toll-free express interstate highways, a task that was to be completed in 1976. It took a decade longer, however, before this ambitious construction blitz, with its pay-as-you-go financing, was largely finished.

Materials pertaining to the federal roads system are extensive. A good place to begin is with the Bureau of Public Roads at the National Archives. Included in this massive collection (Record Group 30) are the records of the Office of Road Inquiry and the Office of Public Road Inquiries, 1892–1907; Records of the Office of Public Roads and the Office of Public Roads and Rural Engineering, 1893–1913; Field Office Records; cartographic materials and black and white still pictures. Although the bulk of these records are housed at the National Archives in Washington, D.C. and College Park, Maryland, some materials reside in regional centers. Charts and maps are located in Atlanta, Boston, Chicago, Denver, Fort Worth, Kansas City and Philadelphia. In 1970 the federal government abolished the Bureau of Roads, the successor agency, and the Federal Highway Administration (FHA) began to generate and collect its records, which have either been deposited with the National Archives or retained at the FHA headquarters at 9701 Philadelphia Court, Lanham, MD 20706.

Throughout most of the twentieth century a common sight on public roads, whether on graveled roads or paved interstates, has been the intercity bus, which made its debut not long after the dawn of the century. Initially most companies were "mom and pop" affairs that used one or more "touring" automobiles, often Bricks or Overlands, to transport passengers over short distances. Representative of such an enterprise was the Bass Rocks Motor Line. In 1909 the firm connected the closely spaced Massachusetts communities of East Gloucester, Hawthorne and Thornwold with the Bass Rock railroad station of the Boston & Maine Railroad, where patrons made direct connections to and from Boston. Learning more about such a small, ephemeral bus company is challenging. Local newspapers offer the best prospects, yet they may provide only modest coverage. Details of daily service may also be gleaned from such papers, most likely a brief advertisement or schedule. Perhaps some collector of bus memorabilia or an area historical society owns a public timetable, if one was ever issued. The chances of finding the business records of a firm like the Bass Rocks

Motor Line are slim. They might possibly exist in family-held papers or some other obscure location.

If one of the early bus companies eventually fell into the corporate hands of a larger, more durable firm, possibilities increase for much more information, including annual reports, equipment rosters and employee records. Indeed, a few of these pioneer "stages" evolved into substantial operations. A good example would be Pickwick Stages of California. At the end of the first decade of the twentieth century an "auto stage" began transporting sightseers from San Diego to nearby Oceanside. Soon service expanded to El Centro and Los Angeles. Then in 1913 this company, Pickwick Stages, linked up with another firm that tied Los Angeles with Venice. More expansion followed and company buses soon served Santa Barbara and communities in the San Fernando Valley. About a decade later Pickwick Stages became a principal component of Pacific Greyhound. Learning about Pickwick is admittedly easier than gathering data on the Bass Rock Motor Line. The merger of Pickwick with Pacific Greyhound, the latter a subsequent affiliate of the national Greyhound corporation, has meant some retention of records, mostly located in the Greyhound Corporation Collection at the American Heritage Center at University of Wyoming Library in Laramie 82071. A valuable historical sketch, "History of Pacific Greyhound Line," by Carl H. Cohres, which provides the business genealogy of this important bus carrier, is part of these holdings.

In the 1920s executives of some steam railroads began to show interest in buses. They believed that such commercial vehicles could be successfully substituted for money-losing branch-line and local passenger trains. A decade later scores of large and small railroads, including the Atchison, Topeka & Santa Fe; Boston & Maine; Chicago & North Western; Gulf, Mobile & Ohio; Missouri Pacific; Missouri Southern; New York Central and Union Pacific, had formed bus subsidiaries and had taken to the highways. Locally related materials might be found in the general corporate records of these carriers. The extensive papers of Interstate Transit Lines and Union Pacific Stages, for example, are housed at the Union Pacific Museum in Omaha, Nebraska 58179.

Few serious studies of the American bus industry exist. Yet, reading the several leading volumes helps to place a nearby bus topic in proper perspective. The best overview is *Making Connections: The Long-distance Bus Industry in the USA* by Margaret Walsh (Aldershot, England: Ashgate, 2000). Walsh also has contributed a variety of scholarly articles to state and regional historical journals, as she notes in her bibliography. A more focused study is *Intercity Bus Lines of the Southwest* by Jack Rhodes (College Station: Texas A&M University Press, 1988). And there are two popular histories of the foremost company, Greyhound: *Hounds of the Road: A History of the Greyhound Bus Company* by Carlton Jackson (Bowling Green, OH: Bowling Green University Popular Press, 1984), and *The Greyhound Story: From Hibbing to Everywhere* by Oscar Schisgall (Chicago: J. G. Ferguson, 1985).

As with other transport forms, *durability* and *growth* increase the number of artifacts, whether "flat" or three dimensional. Therefore, it is easier to find public timetables, for example, and chances are better for locating a structure or even a bus.

A parallel between the commercial bus industry and contemporary air, land and water carriers is the presence of trade journals. The premier one is *Bus Transportation*, which made it debut in 1922 as a section of the *Electric Railway Journal* and did not crease publication until December 1956. This monthly covers firms like Pickwick Stages and Pacific Greyhound and contains sections that advertise bus manufacturers and other suppliers, helpful for identification of artifacts.

Similarly, the motor bus industry developed its counterpart of the *Official Railway Guide, Russell's Official National Motor Coach Guide*. Dating from 1927 *Russell's* was published monthly by the Cedar Rapids, Iowa-based Russell's Guides, Inc. (a company begun in 1889 to produce regional timetable booklets for steam railroads). *Russell's* was the "bible" of bus operations in North America, including Cuba and Mexico, and continues to serve the industry, even though since the 1960s scheduled bus operations have waned considerably. Not only do issues of *Russell's* offer timetables of most companies but, like the *Official Railway Guide, Russell's* index reveals what carriers served a particular community. If a researcher wishes to know, for example what companies, if any, served Cresson, Pennsylvania, at the end of World War II, which incidentally was the peak of intercity bus ridership, the guide lists two: Blue & White Lines, Inc. and Pennsylvania Greyhound Lines. Then by examining the schedule pages for these two firms, one can see how these common carriers accommodated Cresson travelers.

The ubiquitous bus public timetable, which may be found in an archive or obtainable through an on-line auction service, particularly e-Bay, commonly provides useful information other than the frequency of intercity service. (See Chapter 5.) The listing of bus stations is a common feature contained in these folders. As during the stagecoach era, existing businesses regularly took on the additional function of depot. Likely the bus company paid a monthly rental fee for waiting-room and package-storage space, and an employee of the local firm received a modest commission on ticket sales. Take the case of the February 15, 1936, public timetable issued by the Lincoln Trails System. This inter-

2.6   Learning about bus equipment is aided by photographs. In the late 1920s and early 1930s several bus companies operated "sleeper" service. For a few years Pickwick Stages of California used this unusual "Nite Coach."

state carrier linked Chicago, Illinois; Columbus, Ohio; Wheeling, West Virginia, and Pittsburgh, Pennsylvania. Although the company either operated or shared bus facilities at its principal terminals, in smaller communities it relied on other commercial enterprises for its stations, illustrated in this fashion:

> Warsaw, Ind., Gill Grill, 105 East Center Street
> Plymouth, Ind., Scotty's Cafe, 222 No. Michigan Street
> Columbia City, Ind., Clugston Hotel, 134 So. Chauncy St.
> Kenton, Ohio, Colonial Restaurant, 113 W. Frankfort Street
> Zanesville, Ohio, Howell's Drug Store, 6th & Main Streets

Activities of bus companies understandably fell under the supervision of public authorities, initially states and then the federal government. By 1920 eleven states had imposed some control on bus operators, with Pennsylvania being the first. During the next five years twenty-six more followed, making three-quarters of the states, including the most heavily populated. Regulations varied widely, but most states insisted that bus firms, as public utilities, should be subject to

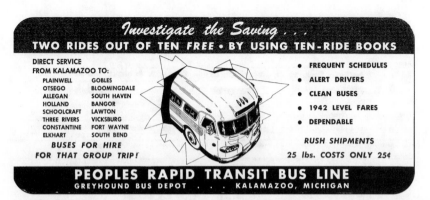

2.7   Even an advertising blotter provides a glimpse into the social history of bus operations. The Kalamazoo, Michigan-based Peoples Rapid Transit Bus Line suggests how area residents might take advantage of bus transport.

laws that protected passengers from poor service, high charges, unsafe vehicles and inexperienced drivers. Although the National Association of Motor Bus Operators, the industry's trade association, favored self-supervision, during the Great Depression the industry entered a new regulatory phase. In 1935 the federal government passed the Motor Carrier Act, which granted the Interstate Commerce Commission major controls. Bus companies, for example, had to publish and to adhere to rates and fares and give notice of any changes. The ICC could suspend these charges and prescribe maximum, minimum and actual rates. This supervision lasted largely until partial deregulation occurred in 1982.

State and federal intervention generated reams of documents. Logically these are housed in various state and federal archives. Usually the key to retrieval of wanted information is knowledge of the carrier's name. If a study involves bus service to Cresson, Pennsylvania, then the researcher should check entries for the Blue & White Lines and Pennsylvania Greyhound at the Pennsylvania State Archives and History Commission in Harrisburg and the National Archives in Washington, D.C.

The best repository of paper materials pertaining to the American bus industry, including books, trade journals, timetables, guides, equipment service manuals, news clippings and photographs is the John P. Hoschek Memorial Bus Transportation Library, which is located in suburban Trenton, New Jersey (1613 Reed Road, Hopewell Township). This research facility is sponsored by the Motor Bus Society (P.O. Box 251,

Form No. 57-2000-3-25-25   California Company

THE FAGEOL COMPANY

COACH ORDER BLANK   KENT, OHIO   DATE **August 8, 1925**

Representative's Order No. _____   Our Order No. **C-878**   Factory S. O. No. _____

Ordered for **Tri-State Transit Co., Division Caddo Transfer & Warehouse Co.**

Address	**628 Market Street**	**Shreveport**		**Louisiana**
Ship to	Street and number	City	County	State
	Same		Via **Best Route**	

Is the purchaser an individual, a corporation, or partnership   **Corporation**

Bank to which any document should be sent   **Exchange National Bank, Shreveport, La.**
                                                    (Name)   (Address)

The undersigned hereby orders, subject to the terms and conditions and at the prices herein, the following:

Quantity			Unit Price	Amount
	FAGEOL SAFETY COACHES			
One	Model **22 pass., Intercity** No. Cylinders **Four**		**6,559 00**	
	Tires **Firestone** Size Front **34 x 4** Rear Size **32 x 7 single**			
	Gear Ratio **5-4/5 : 1** Horn **Dosch** Partition **Yes**			
	Additional Specifications **Rims curst or made to accomodate 32 x 7 tire.**			
	Partition on fourth seat — No Charge			
	EXTRAS Prices on extras are subject to manufacturers excise tax of 5 per cent.			
	Dosch Horn		**24 00**	**24 00**
	Full length baggage rail		**65 00**	**65 00**
Four	**Taxi seats in baggage compartment**		**10 50**	**42 00**
	ALLOWANCES			
Prices **at Kent, Ohio**			Total	**6,690 50**

TERMS: Deposit with order **$737.50 Commission**   Acknowledged by _____

On Delivery **One-Fourth**   Balance **eighteen months**

_____notes, amount each, $ _____ at _____ % interest per annum.

DELIVERY to be made at the shipping point on or before **Immediately** _____ or as soon thereafter as possible.

If the above is not ready for delivery within 30 days after the date specified, the right is reserved to cancel this order, and the deposit shall be returned to the purchaser on written demand.

If the balance of purchase price is not paid, or satisfactory settlement made within ten days after notification that the above is ready for delivery, you may at your option cancel this order, and retain all payments as liquidated damages.

The goods herein ordered are guaranteed under the terms of the National Automobile Chamber of Commerce Warranty.

It is understood that this order shall not be binding until accepted in writing by The Fageol Company, notwithstanding that deposit by the purchaser may have been made.

I/we, the purchaser, agree to the following provisions which shall constitute a part of this contract if purchase of the above Coach equipment is made on your time payment plan:

1. That this order be supplemented by a written contract between the purchaser and The Fageol Company covering all details of the purchase and sale in accordance with this order and subject to standard provisions of Seller's Conditional Sales Contract or Chattel Mortgage.

2. That I/we will place through The Fageol Company with the insurance connections of its financial associates $100.00 deductible collision insurance, and fire and theft insurance in the amount of $ _____, on the equipment ordered herein, (UNLESS SPECIFIED OTHERWISE IN THE FOREGOING BLANK, THE EQUIPMENT ORDERED HEREIN WILL BE COVERED WITH FIRE AND THEFT INSURANCE FOR 85% OF THE TOTAL VALUE THEREOF.)

3. THAT I/WE FURNISH WITH THIS ORDER, (a) PURCHASER'S SIGNED AND WITNESSED FINANCIAL STATEMENT, (b) ROUTE ANALYSIS, (c) PURCHASER'S STATEMENT OF OPERATION, (d) INSURANCE QUESTIONNAIRE.

Sales Representative _____   Signed **Caddo Transfer & Warehouse Co., Inc.,**
                                            (EXACT LEGAL OR CORPORATE NAME OF PURCHASER)
Accepted _____ 192**5**   by _____

THE FAGEOL COMPANY _____   Title **President**

by _____   Date **Aug. 19, 1925**

STATE COLOR SPECIFICATIONS ON REVERSE SIDE

2.8   It may be possible to locate documents relating to bus equipment, largely in specialized transportation collections. This order form for the Tri-State Transit Company of Shreveport, Louisiana, which dates from 1925, is for purchase of a 22-passenger motor coach from The Fageol Company, a pioneer manufacturer of commercial buses.

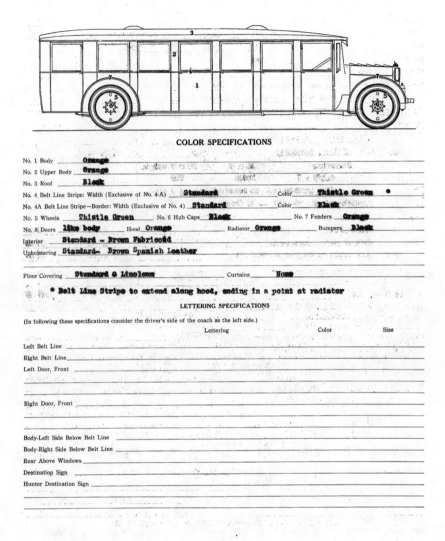

COLOR SPECIFICATIONS

No. 1 Body ___ **Orange** ___
No. 2 Upper Body ___ **Orange** ___
No. 3 Roof ___ **Black** ___
No. 4 Belt Line Stripe: Width (Exclusive of No. 4-A) ___ **Standard** ___ Color ___ **Thistle Green** ___ •
No. 4A Belt Line Stripe—Border: Width (Exclusive of No. 4) ___ **Standard** ___ Color ___ **Black** ___
No. 5 Wheels ___ **Thistle Green** ___ No. 6 Hub Caps ___ **Black** ___ No. 7 Fenders ___ **Orange** ___
No. 8 Doors ___ **like body** ___ Hood ___ **Orange** ___ Radiator ___ **Orange** ___ Bumpers ___ **Black** ___
Interior ___ **Standard – Brown Fabricoid** ___
Upholstering ___ **Standard– Brown Spanish Leather** ___

Floor Covering ___ **Standard @ Linoleum** ___ Curtains ___ **None** ___

 • **Belt Line Stripe to extend along hood, ending in a point at radiator**

LETTERING SPECIFICATIONS

(In following these specifications consider the driver's side of the coach as the left side.)

	Lettering	Color	Size
Left Belt Line			
Right Belt Line			
Left Door, Front			
Right Door, Front			
Body-Left Side Below Belt Line			
Body-Right Side Below Belt Line			
Rear Above Windows			
Destination Sign			
Hunter Destination Sign			

Paramus, NJ 07653). Founded in 1948 as the National Motor Bus Association, its ongoing purpose is the collection and dissemination of information about the history and development of bus transport. The organization also produces two quarterly publications, *Motor Coach Age* (1950–present) and *Motor Coach Today* (1994–present). Each is indexed and these finding aids are available at the Hoschek library or through the Motor Bus Society.

As with railroads especially, a valuable array of fan-oriented publications exists, albeit in considerably less volume. Useful titles for learning more about individual companies and localized areas include: *Green Pennant Special* (1983–), monthly newsletter of the Omnibus Society of America, Dolton, Illinois; *Western Transit*, originally the *Booster* until 1968, monthly newsletter of the Western Transit Association, Garden Grove, California; *The Nevada Bus Man* (1987–), monthly newsletter of the Nevada Bus Fans Association, Yerington, Nevada, and the *Paddle* (1991), bimonthly newsletter of the Pacific Bus Museum, San Anselmo, California.

By working through bus historical and enthusiast groups it should be possible to learn about bus company employees. As with some railroads and a few electric interurbans, employee clubs, with former workers, continue to function. Remaining firms and labor unions, most notably the Amalgamated Transit Union, may possess employee records. Even though a bus company, whether Arrow [Nebraska], Jefferson [Minnesota] or Martz [Pennsylvania], may have either ended or dramatically curtailed intercity bus service, it might remain active in the lucrative charter bus business; as an ongoing corporate concern, personnel records may be available.

About the time buses appeared on American roads, trucks also made their debut. Initially they replaced animal-drawn wagons for deliveries in urban areas, but by 1920 hundreds of commercial intercity trucking companies served a growing number of customers. Just as World War I spurred aviation, it had a similar impact on motor carriers. The conflict necessitated the use of trucks as cargo haulers, both in Europe and at home, resulting in rapid improvements in technology and operating performance. These advances ranged from pneumatic tires to tractor and semitrailer units. In the 1920s truck usage exploded due to a decline in vehicle prices and an increase in consumer credit coupled with substantially cheaper fuel and tires. The maturing industry also benefited from the triumph of the "good roads" crusade; better highways permitted greater speeds, allowed for more dependable deliveries and caused less wear-and-tear on equipment.

The industry continued to expand. The Great Depression of the 1930s actually hastened growth. "Mom and pop" companies sprang up, often the efforts of unemployed factory workers and downtrodden farmers. In 1932 nearly sixty-five percent of the trucks on the road belonged to one-person firms; 2.2 million truckers owned and operated only a single vehicle. These aggressive entrepreneurs siphoned off less-than-carload (LCL) traffic from steam railroads and electric interurbans, helping to cripple the latter.

With growth came regulation. By 1930 all of the forty-eight states had made attempts at regulation, demanding at least basic safety equipment and licensing of truck drivers. The federal government entered the picture with the Motor Carrier Act of 1935, placing interstate carriers under the jurisdiction of the Interstate Commerce Commission.

Federal involvement paralleled industry consolidation, a phenomenon that accelerated after World War II. Although small companies, whether common, contract or private, continued in abundance, giant common carriers, including Consolidated Freightways, Roadway and Yellow Freight, emerged. Organized labor, namely the International Brotherhood of Teamsters, also became a force for consolidation by demanding "master" contracts. This powerful union preferred to deal with the handful of giants rather than a bewildering assortment of smaller firms.

Eventually, as did other regulated forms of commerce, federal regulation of motor carriers gave way to deregulation. In 1982 Congress significantly reduced the power of the ICC over the trucking industry. This legislation caused a reshuffling of companies with several major ones unable to survive the onslaught of intense competition. Yet some historically dominant firms, including Roadway, retained their corporate status, keeping their "rigs" on the nation's highways.

As with bus companies, it is easier to discover details about the larger rather than the smaller trucking firms. Still, individual motor carriers have not been studied extensively. Two of the few works on a single company are *Perfecting a Piece of the World: Arthur Imperatore and the Blue-Collar Aristocrats of A-P-A* by David Rounds (Reading, MA: Addison-Wesley, 1993), and *The Roadway Story* by Philip L. Cantelon and Kenneth D. Durr (Rockville, MD: Montrose Press, 1996). The former is a popular account of A-P-A, which traces the rise and impressive growth of a major Eastern-based common carrier. The latter is a semischolarly account of one of the most successful nationwide trucking concerns. The authors of *The Roadway Story*, who found a limited amount of documentary materials at the company's corporate headquarters in Akron, Ohio, creatively interviewed current and former employees, creating a body of thirty-three oral history transcripts that have since become part of the Roadway archive. Even the bigger picture of the trucking industry is difficult to find in book form, although *A Glance Back: A History of the American Trucking Industry* by Gary M. LaBella (Washington, D.C.: American Trucking Association, 1977) helps.

How then does a researcher explore nearby trucking companies? To identify what companies served a community, checking city directories and telephone books might be a good first step. Some transportation collections possess back copies of the monthly, although no longer published *Official Motor Freight Guide*. Organized by state, this reference work lists a company's home office, traffic agents, equipment, type and extent of service. The March 1940 entry in the *Guide* for Miller Motor Express of Charlotte, North Carolina, provides details about its overall structure and operations, indicating that the firm owned sixty-seven tractors, sixty-three trailers and twenty-two straight (single-unit) trucks. The listing also includes a map of the company's service routes. Additional information about Miller Motor Express likely can be found in the records of state and federal regulatory bodies (See Chapter 4.) Trade publications, too, offer insights into companies and their activities. *Transport Topics*, a longtime weekly publication of the American Trucking Association, is an unusually comprehensive and reliable trade journal.

While it is rare to spot a person taking "action shots" of trucks traveling along interstate highways, there does exist an enthusiasts' organization. This is the 22,000-member American Truck Historical Society (www.aths.org), based in Birmingham, Alabama (P.O. Box 531168, 35253). As the group explains: "ATHS is made up of people who love old trucks and the history of trucking. . . . ATHS collects and preserves the dynamic history of antique trucks and the industry." Admittedly, though, members are likely to be much more interested in vintage equipment than in corporate histories, business logistics or employees.

A local researcher may find in the community a knowledgeable member of the American Truck Historical Society. If not, the Society can be contacted directly. It maintains a reference library and archive with its greatest strengths being catalogs from truck manufacturers and more than 100,000 photographs of historic trucks. Significantly, the American Trucking Association recognizes the ATHS as the "official archivist of the trucking industry."

Paralleling other fan-based transport historical societies the ATHS produces a semi-scholarly journal. Six times a year since 1985 its *Wheels of Time* provides a valuable, if not the sole source of secondary material. Although the focus is on trucks and their makers, whether Mack, Reo or White, there are articles on individual carriers and the communities that they once served or continue to serve. *Wheels of Times* is indexed by subject and that finding aid can be found on the ATHS web site.

Learning about truck drivers is challenging. Manuscript census records for 1910, 1920 and 1930 may help, but more likely information can probably be gleaned from city directories. The International Brotherhood of Teamsters and its locals have membership records, although they are not easily accessible. An alternative method would be to contact retirees. Through them and their acquaintances information about the trucking industry may be obtained. Few oral histories of individuals associated with motor carriers exist. However, the *New York Times* Oral History Program includes the Woods Highway Truck Library, a collection of more than twenty interviews with men and women (truck drivers, truck stop operators, executives and law enforcement officers) involved in the trucking industry during the 1920s and 1930s. The interviewer, Harry Woods, was a former trucker who sought to preserve the history of the industry.

Roads and the commercial vehicles that used them represent a dimension of transportation history that can often be traced through various governmental sources. After all, roads were nearly always public entities and the commercial transport vehicles that traveled them in time came under the gaze of regulators. Materials are available, albeit not as numerous or as conveniently assembled as with other transport modes. Secondary sources lack the same richness as well, although ones of value exist.

This situation necessitates that the researcher show imagination. The best strategy would be to conduct oral histories. Although most pioneers in intercity bus and trucking have died, some remain. And with motor carriers, a number of small firms date from the post-World War II era; their founders, associates and friends may still be able and willing to provide information and insights. Furthermore, if the community has an active locally based bus or truck company, it would be wise to make contacts, making certain that important records are saved. Getting the hometown historical society involved would be a good idea. With less governmental regulation, due in part to partial federal deregulation in the early 1980s of both industries, the scope of paperwork has diminished and older records are often no longer needed.

ॐ ॐ ॐ ॐ ॐ

At the end of World War II Russell A. Byrd, a veteran bus driver and independent bus operator, wrote his autobiography, *Russ's Bus: The Adventures of an American Bus Driver* (Los Angeles: Wetzel Publishing Company, 1945). In what is a unique personal narrative he reveals much about the nature of the intercity-bus business during its formative years, providing a vivid picture of travel, equipment and infrastructure. The following passages relate Byrd's adventures in the autumn of 1927 as a rookie driver for the Yelloway Bus Company, one of America's first interregional carriers. His destination was Denver, Colorado, several days of arduous driving from his home base, Los Angeles, California.

At the depot [Los Angeles], I picked up twenty-five passengers and headed for Denver. The depot agent helped me with my loading so that I experienced no ordeal at that point. . . . . .

After a few miles, or rather hours, my shifting improved. I discovered that the clutch was provided with a brake and that I had been pushing too far down on the clutch pedal. This knowledge increased my confidence, and I began to feel as though I had grained control over the bus as the miles sped by.

No one had told me about the old Cajon Pass just outside of San Bernardino. When we finally left behind us the narrow, twisting turns on the road which passed the Summit at 4,301 feet in the San Bernardino Mountains, I had a healthy respect for my new work. . . . . .

As we approached Needles, where we were to stop for the night, I relaxed my tension at the wheel. The lights of Needles were only a few miles below and we were going down grade. The road was covered with loose gravel; and the highway, which was crooked, had some very sharp turns. As I approached one turn too fast, I reached quickly for the brake pedal. As we went into the turn, I pressed the pedal completely to the floor board. The coach seemed to gain speed instead of slowing down. My heart was literally in my throat as the bus turned up on the left wheels as I turned sharper and sharper to the right, trying to keep from leaving the road. All I knew about the road was what I could see by the headlights. Just as the bus was going over on its side, the road straightened and the coach fell roughly back on all six wheels. I had used all of the roadway getting around the turn and was lucky in that no one was going in the opposite direction, as well as being fortunate enough to make the curve without upsetting my passengers. When I looked down to determine what had happened to the brake pedal to keep it from slowing the coach, I saw to my horror that I had missed the brake pedal and had jammed down the clutch pedal which had released the coach on the hill and let it coast. . . . . .

Trouble is always in the offing. That day, however, I had no fear of it. In the very midst of adventure, I was absorbed with the good of it. When we reached the long, narrow bridge spanning the Colorado river, . . . we ran into a problem. The parallel planks on the bridge were spaced for small cars, and would not fit our coach. The rafters on each side were bare, but were closely spaced. When I pulled on the bridge and found that I couldn't keep more than one set of wheels on the smooth planks, I was reluctant to bump from rafter to rafter with

the other wheels. Since there was no other way, I decided to try. . . . . .
Very slowly and with a thump of my heart at each thump of the coach,
I crept the remaining distance across the bridge. No matter what the
future held, the days ahead would be a relief to the duty of crossing
that bridge.

I was getting plenty of practice shifting the transmission now. We
stopped only long enough to get water for the radiator in Oatman [Ari-
zona]. Then, as we started over Oatman Pass immediately out of town,
I realized why the pass commanded so much attention from the old
timers. I didn't even get the coach in high gear as we started over. Third
gear was useful for only a few hundred yards. Second gear was okay
for a few miles; then we were in low gear, grinding away. A glance at
the passengers convinced me that they had more confidence in me than
I had in myself. . . . . The turns became sharper and were so narrow that
I took up the entire roadway getting around them. The motor began to
moan from its labors until I could count the last weak efforts of the
cylinder explosions as the coach coughed to a standstill.

"Well, folks, I guess you'll just have to walk over the hill," I remarked softly to the passengers. "The old hack won't make it with a
load."

No one made any objections.

"I'm used to walking over the hill. I travel this route quite often," remarked one of the men sitting near the front of the bus.

This made me feel better. I had made the right decision.

Occasionally, I would stop and help some car out of the ditch. It
seemed as if more cars were in the ditch than were on the road. I
couldn't pass them up. It took only a few minutes to get them out of
the ditch, and I always depend upon plenty of help from my own
gang as well as from those in the cars. We did good turns many a time,
that night. The help which the old time bus driver gave the tourist in
those days was responsible for the high respect he commanded. It
seemed that everyone accepted the bus driver as an authority on how
to get through.

The road was muddy after the snow was gone. Continued slipping
of the bus from side to side and the spinning of the wheels for miles
upon miles was a drain on my energy, and when we finally reached the
payment twelve miles south of Albuquerque, I was truly fatigued. A
whoop of joy rang out from within the coach. I announced breakfast
approaching from the northeast in fifteen minutes, and pandemonium
broke loose.

The seventeen miles of pavement out of town [Albuquerque] were
soon left behind, and after than, the road was only a supposition. We

were now going through the Pueblo Indian Reservation, of which the roads must surely have been made by the Indians.

The unique scenery of the reservation took our minds off the condition of the road; and regardless how bad the roads were, the strange, scenic beauty all about us made up for the rough drive.

ༀ ༀ ༀ ༀ ༀ

Chapter 3

CANALS

In parts of the United States the canal served as the principal *transition* between animal-powered vehicles and steam-propelled railway cars. America's network of canals developed rapidly and impressively. Mileage soared from approximately 100 in 1817 to 1,200 miles in 1830, about 3,300 miles in 1840, and 3,700 miles in 1850. Although New York, Pennsylvania and Ohio claimed more than two-thirds of this mileage, by mid-century twenty states had these artificial waterways.

In the early nineteenth century citizens in the North and East especially became excited about the possibilities of "ditches," transport arteries that presumably would solve the conundrum of how best to reach distant markets cheaply, reliably and safely without nearby navigable rivers and lakes. Contemporary newspapers and published travelers' accounts repeatedly told of successful canals in Europe, particularly those that served the English Midlands, and smaller ones that had appeared in scattered locations in the American East. The nearly thirty-mile Middlesex Canal, for example, which after 1803 linked Boston and Lowell, Massachusetts, effectively opened up the lower Merrimac River valley to commerce. The harbinger of what became the "canal era," however, was not the Middlesex Canal but rather the Erie Canal in New York.

Completion in autumn of 1825 by the State of New York of the 363-mile Erie Canal, which connected the Hudson River and Lake Erie, marked one of the greatest civil engineering achievements of the nineteenth century. Most of all, the massive complex of locks at Lockport, where the canal ascended the Niagara escarpment, rightly received international acclaim. This construction triumph was to canals what finishing the Central Pacific-Union Pacific forty-five years later would be to railroads. Although the latter forged a monumental iron road from coast-to-coast, the former strategically tied the Atlantic Ocean with the trans-Appalachian West.

The Erie Canal with its practical dimensions of four-foot depth, forty

51

foot width at the water line and twenty-six feet at the base proved to be enormously profitable. Even before the waterway was completed, the opened sections had generated a $1 million in tolls, about one-seventh of the canal's over-all cost. Even though critics initially viewed the undertaking as "Clinton's Folly," a reference to the role played by the canal's foremost advocate, Governor De Witt Clinton, by the mid-1820s no knowledgeable observer challenged the conclusion that this transportation marvel readily diffused "wealth, activity and vigor throughout vast parts of the Empire State." With toll revenues flowing into public coffers, state officials found it easy to meet bond obligations and to attract additional investment capital.

The profitability of the Erie Canal coupled to considerable political pressures from areas removed from it prompted New York lawmakers to authorize construction of a series of "lateral" or "feeder" canals. These ditches included the Cayuga and Seneca Canal that linked Montezuma to Geneva; the Oswego Canal that connected Syracuse to Oswego and the Chenango Canal that tied Utica to Binghamton. By the end of the canal-building era no state possessed a better network of public waterways than the Empire State.

As with canal construction in New York, states assumed the leading role in ditch digging. Prior to the Panic of 1837 and the ensuing depression, these governments were nicely positioned to turn dreams into realities: most enjoyed high credit ratings and modest public debt. Also, politicians knew that investments of public funds in canals were popular and potentially well spent. Gains from the canals themselves coupled to both short- and long-term economic development seemed to be appropriate blueprints for future prosperity.

States that led in construction of canals, most notably Illinois, Indiana, New York, Pennsylvania and Ohio, contributed millions of dollars to these internal improvements. Fortunately for anyone exploring the canal era, public entities generated and commonly retained large quantities of records, making it possible to learn much about an individual canal or a canal network.

Take the case of New York. The New York State Archives and Records Administration, a public agency located in Albany, (www.sara. nysed.gov) possesses a vast quantity of canal-related documents, ones that specifically cover the Erie Canal (later the rebuilt New York State Barge Canal) and the network of feeder canals. Included in the collection are files from the State Engineer and Surveyor covering such matters as canal construction, administration, contracts, maintenance and operation. If a lock complex is the subject of an inquiry, these archival materials would describe pertinent details.

Since most of the lateral canals in New York have long been abandoned and large segments of the original Erie Canal have been relocated, problems might arise in the task of locating the *historic* routes. Luckily the State Archives and Records Administration has about 400 maps of "Abandoned Canal Lands." These materials resulted from a 1916 law that required the State Engineer and Surveyor and the Superintendent of Public Works to document appraisals and sales of "those lands declared unnecessary for Barge Canal purposes." Prior to 1916 the state constitution had prohibited the selling of long stretches of abandoned canal rights-of-way.

Coinciding with extensive commitments made by some state governments to canal building, the private sector, too, financed projects. Some of these canals were relatively successful, lasting for decades. Others, however, failed quickly and probably should never have been built.

Anyone interested in the physical remains of a private canal will discover that if the waterway falls into the "successful" category, research may be somewhat easier. The explanation involves several factors. As with the usually enduring state canals, the longer a private one operated the greater the volume of records generated. There is also the possibility that a successor firm, probably a railroad, assumed control, thus likely maintaining the canal or portions of it and also retaining documentary materials. For these durable ditches initial operational problems were presumably solved, including water-supply sources, seepages and settling of banks. Other betterments typically followed, commonly greater channel depths and larger locks. The more that were rebuilt and improved, the more that are likely to have survived. If abandonment occurred in the late nineteenth and early twentieth centuries, the ravages of time have probably been less severe than those canals that closed during the Civil War era. Similarly, if service lasted into the age of photography, better and more extensive visual evidence eliminates total reliance on artists' paintings, drawings and sketches. For those waterways that functioned or remained in largely undisturbed ruins during the picture postcard craze (ca. 1905–1915), images abound, including "real-photo" ones (actual photographs printed on postcard paper stock).

Representative of durable privately owned waterways was the 108-mile Delaware & Hudson (D&H) Canal. Organized in 1823 by Philadelphia merchants who sought to develop coal fields in northeastern Pennsylvania, construction began two years later and completion followed in 1828. As intended, this canal tapped what turned out to be the exceedingly rich and profitable deposits of anthracite or "stone coal,"

Looking down the Canal, Akron, O.

Brother,
Will be home Sunday night,
Sisters.

3.1   The ubiquitous picture postcard of the early twentieth century can provide excellent clues about a canal corridor. This ca. 1908 view of the Ohio &
Erie Canal in Akron, Ohio, shows both the canal and an auxiliary source of
water. Although the massive Easter flood of 1913 destroyed much of the canal
that remained in service, the steel railroad bridge remains, helping the researcher to pinpoint long obliterated canal sites.

making practical delivery to New York City and ports in New England
and the mid-Atlantic region.

The D&H Canal became a strategic interstate waterway. It started at
Honesdale, Pennsylvania, a coal-mining center, and followed the Lack-
awaxen River to where that stream joined the Delaware River. The
canal paralleled the Delaware to Port Jervis, New York, and turned
eastward, following the Neversink and Roundout creeks to reach the
wide and deep waters of the Hudson River near Kingston. Once in operation coal traffic gradually increased, peaking in the early 1870s at
approximately 3 million tons annually. Canal boats, whether carrying
coal, cement or other bulk commodities, continued to ply the waters
until 1898, when railroads achieved such economies that costly canal
maintenance or improvements were no longer justified. It would be the
Delaware & Hudson Railroad, an independent carrier that survived as
a corporate entity until 1993, that assumed ownership. (The railroad

Auqueduct, Scioto River, Circleville, Ohio.

3.2   The picture postcard offers a sense of what once made up a commercial canal. Near Circleville, Ohio, the Ohio & Erie Canal used a long, wooden aqueduct to cross the Scioto River. The canal sleuth may be able to find remains, most likely quarried-stone pilings.

had, in fact, itself evolved from the canal corporation, being originally named the Delaware & Hudson Canal's Railroad Company.)

While the Delaware & Hudson Canal starred among privately owned ditches, a decidedly less financially successful operation was the Sandy & Beaver Canal in Ohio. Its backers, who hailed from along the projected route and also from Philadelphia, wanted a water connection between the developing Ohio & Erie Canal system and the Ohio River, specifically using a seventy-three mile route between Bolivar, Ohio, and Glasgow, Pennsylvania. Although officially launched in 1828, it was not until 1834 that construction began. By the time the Panic of 1837 struck the region about thirty miles of canal bed and eleven locks had been finished, mostly along Little Beaver Creek on the "Eastern Division," one of the company's projected operational units. In 1840 the intermittent work that had continued stopped. By mid-decade prosperity returned and the moribund company reorganized and pushed ahead, completing in 1847 the section between New Lisbon (Lisbon), Ohio, and the Ohio River. But the need to bore two tunnels on the "Middle Division," particularly a 3,000 foot "Big Tunnel"

3.3   Merely seeing a historic image of a canal in operation helps the researcher visualize the past. As this picture postcard of the Ohio & Erie Canal near Bolivar, Ohio, reveals, animals and their drivers walked along a relatively wide earthen towpath.

east of Sandy Creek in Columbiana County, delayed until 1848 a connection with the "Western Division" and opening to Bolivar on the
Ohio & Erie Canal. In 1852, only four years after the $1.3 million canal
handled its first through traffic, owners agreed to abandon service and
liquidate their assets. Severe and recurring water shortages, tunnel-
maintenance woes, competition from the parallel Pennsylvania-Ohio
Canal to the north, emerging railroads in the vicinity and mounting
debts prompted this draconian action. Soon along portions of the waterway the screeching steam whistle of the iron horse replaced the bel-
lowing horn of a canal boat.

Research opportunities on the once prosperous Delaware & Hudson
Canal are markedly different from those for the woebegone Sandy &
Beaver Canal. Unquestionably, the former is still remembered, partly because of the ongoing activities of the Delaware & Hudson Transportation Heritage Council. Its stated mission is "to heighten awareness,
recognition and appreciation of the archeological and other historical
remnants of the Delaware & Hudson Canal. . . ." Through the group's
vigorous activities the physical remains of the canal have been largely
preserved. Moreover, records, including photographs, have been gathered and archived, principally at the Minisink Valley Historical Society,
located in the Fort Decker-St. John's Canal Hotel in Port Jervis, New
York, and the Delaware & Hudson Canal Historical Society and Museum in High Falls, New York. A collateral organization, the Bridge Line
Historical Society (P.O. Box 7242 Capitol Station, Albany, NY 12224), a
railroad enthusiasts' group dedicated to preserving the corporate memory of the Delaware & Hudson Railroad, provides research opportunities into the railroad phase of the Delaware & Hudson Canal.

What can be learned about the ill-fated Sandy & Beaver Canal? Since
most of the company's records have disappeared, the researcher initially should check what is by default the "standard" history, *The Sandy
and Beaver Canal*. Written in the early 1950s by two amateur historians,
R. Max Gard and William H. Vodrey, Jr., and locally printed (East Liverpool, OH: East Liverpool Historical Society, 1952), this book attempts
to tell the story of the canal. Even though the narrative is badly organized, poorly written and lacking in interpretations, Gard and Vodrey
collected most surviving documents, which usually involve construction and financial matters, and assembled photographs, including
some that they took. (The authors were unable to find any contemporary images of the canal.) In the course of their study, Gard and Vodrey
walked the length of the canal (where possible) and painstakingly
chronicled what they discovered nearly a century after abandonment.
Here is an example of their findings:

Mile 12—Dam No. 8. Lock No. 33. Williamsport. This is the only dam and lock in Madison Township [of Columbiana County]. The dam has stone abutments on both banks and timber in the creek. Lock on left bank. Below are ruined stone foundations of old Crawford Grist Mill. The Canal leaves Madison Township and enters St. Clair Township. Lock No. 34 is below Williamsport on left bank. Below here the Middle Fork of the [Little Beaver] creek has broken into the Canal and the long bank between the West and Middle Forks is the old bank between the Canal and the Creek. Soon the West Fork also breaks through into the Canal and the old bed of creek to the south is dry.

Augmenting the mile-by-mile account of the physical remains of the Sandy & Beaver Canal are two exceptional maps that the printer placed in an end pocket of the book. Co-author Vodrey drew two 18x28 inch maps of the entire canal corridor. Platted from U.S. topographic maps, these supplements reveal locations of the canal bed, dams, locks and tunnels and appropriate political subdivisions, including township roads and state and federal highways. Even though these drawings are fifty years old, the area remains much the same as when Vodrey did his cartographic work. No interstates, few road relocations and little urban growth have affected the territory.

Fortunately, a basic *scholarly* work exists for *every* major and nearly every small canal. The latter, however, may have appeared only in history magazines or professional journals. Regional studies, too, can be helpful. One such outstanding work is *Canals and Railroads of the Mid-Atlantic States, 1800–1860* by Christopher T. Baer (Wilmington, DE: Hagley Museum and Library, 1981). This particular volume offers an authoritative tabulation of the history and ultimate disposition of every canal built prior to 1860 in the region and six large map inserts that show the extent of canals from 1800 to 1860 at fifteen-year intervals. The "big picture" of this transportation phenomenon in America is superbly provided in the comprehensive *Canals for a Nation: The Canal Era in the United States, 1790–1860* by Ronald E. Shaw (Lexington: University Press of Kentucky 1990).

This copious and diverse body of published literature, including the Shaw tome, offers insights into the economic dimension of a canal's operations. Not only can the overall economic health be learned, but the traffic mix is frequently discussed. What did the canal boats haul and why? Often, too, the type of equipment, including freight boats and passenger packets, is revealed.

When examining primary and at times secondary sources, the canal researcher may need a grasp of the technical and "slang" language

Canals 59

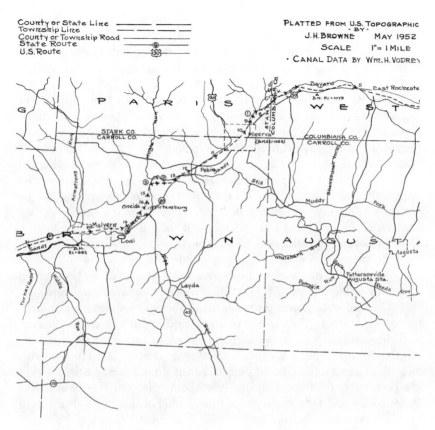

3.4 Maps are indispensable for canal research. They might be the readily available U.S. topographic maps or special ones, at times based on these government drawings. This is a portion of a detailed map of the Sandy and Beaver Canal, based on data supplied in 1952 by a local canal enthusiast.

used. Admittedly, such terms as "cuddy" (the sleeping room on a canal boat), "foo-foo" (an immigrant canal worker), "snubbing" (anchors used to control boats in the locking-through process) and "tumble bugs" (sluices that carried excess water around rather than through lock chambers) are hardly part of most people's vocabulary. Fortunately, "dictionaries" of sorts exist, including a section found in *Here and Now—Ohio's Canals* by Linn Loomis (Sugarcreek, OH: Schlabach Printers, 2000).

After completing appropriate background reading, a canal researcher can take additional steps, whether the canal was a durable public waterway (many of the most important fall into that category) or private ditch or one of the less successful ventures like the Sandy & Beaver. If the subject to be studied is an aqueduct, lock or other "work of art" (as canal engineers commonly called them), the following approach is wise.

1. Examine carefully the physical artifact itself. Perhaps the builder left carved markings or a cornerstone revealing his identity and date of construction. Occasionally locks received officially designated numbers that were inscribed in the stone blocks.

2. Check land records in the county courthouse to learn who owned of the site at the time of construction. A history of the canal, even a brief one, will provide dates of construction and operation. Since the landowner's name frequently became assigned or informally associated with the lock, this information will help to identify the lock in source materials, particularly newspapers.

3. Read *local* newspapers for the periods of construction and operations. Since most of these publications appeared weekly and contained only four to eight pages, it is possible to review extant issues rapidly.

4. Consult with area and state historical societies about the availability of local canal records and to obtain introduction to area historians.

5. Investigate guides to collections in historical societies that may point to manuscripts that contain canal-related materials. For example, a German utopian group, the Separatists at Zoar, Ohio, participated in the construction of the Ohio & Erie Canal through the Tuscarawas River valley and later these communitarians became large shippers of agricultural products to points on the canal, lateral canals and the Erie Canal. The Society's papers are housed in the Ohio Historical Society in Columbus.

6. Check with canal historical and enthusiast groups. A point of beginning is the American Canal Society (P.O. Box 842, Shepherdstown, WV 25443). This organization, launched in 1972, promotes the historic American canal through programs of research, preservation and restoration. The Society's illustrated quarterly, *American Canals,* offers canal news, history, activities and a variety of practical information. Its ongoing projects include a national inventory of American canals; a series of regional canal guides and other publications and committees focusing on canal boat design and construction, canal parks, canal engineering and maintenance and navigable canal boating and restoration. Moreover, local and state organizations exist; for example, the Canal Society of Ohio (550 Copley Road, Akron, OH 44320). This group has knowledgeable and dedicated members and other useful resources.

Canal organizations and their members can often provide investigators with answers to many of their questions. The experiences of Larry E. Tise, former Director of the American Association for State and Local History, are revealing. "The extent to which American history has become the possession and pursuit of American people came through most vividly to me some years ago when I chanced upon the remains of a canal that had been built along the Yadkin River in North Carolina. A beautiful stone wall more than a thousand feet long simply existed in the middle of nowhere, miles from any road and wholly unknown to local residents." As he further relates, "Suspecting that it was part of an early failed canal operation, I went to the local library and found virtually nothing about canals. The same was true at two major university libraries. Finally, I turned up a little book on Pennsylvania canals published by the American Canal Society and wrote to the Society for more information. I soon found myself in receipt of a monthly newsletter, forms for the recording of canals, and a spate of pamphlets on all facets of American and international canal history. I was next recruited to help survey all the early canal remains in North Carolina and was visited by two utterly knowledgeable members of the society to provide instruction and helpful guidance on the project." Concludes Tise, "Among the members of that society is more knowledge and understanding of America's largely forgotten canal history than all of the libraries and professional historians put together in the rest of the world."

Even though published accounts of a particular canal offer basic historical points, they are hardly definitive. Yet these works can help the researcher learn more about a specific aspect of an individual waterway, especially matters relating to canal finances and general economic development. By checking footnotes and other citations, exact locations of primary canal documents can be ascertained. *Indiana Canals* by Paul Fatout (West Lafayette, IN: Purdue University Press, 1972) indicates that some lock receipts for Fort Wayne, Indiana, on the Wabash & Erie Canal, are available in a local depository. These receipts reveal precisely what goods moved along the canal and the names of the vessels and their captains.

Learning details about the human component of canals can be more difficult than gleaning facts about their physical remains. Although information, including biographical sketches of politicians, promoters and investors associated with a particular waterway, may appear in state, county and city histories and comparable references, material about construction and operating workers may be tantalizingly obscure.

Since a pre-industrial workforce built, maintained and operated most canals, they left behind limited records. A contributing factor was their overall, low-level of education, explaining the paucity of diaries, letters and other firsthand accounts. A few foreign-born laborers, most often English and Welch, may have penned letters to friends and relatives back home and occasionally native-born laborers may have done the same. Even if canal workers were literate, they were hardly in an environment conducive to letter writing. Yet these unheralded individuals may have created a family oral tradition about their canal experiences. Irish immigrants in particular, who contributed greatly to the canal era, were strictly speaking not illiterate but *preliterate:* through the *oral* medium they transmitted a rich, robust culture, and that information might still be tapped through their decendents.

Still, historical records may allow some piecing together of the canal workforce. Although Irish laborers, the largest single ethnic group to build and maintain canals, may have left a modest paper trail, coverage of specific individual workers might occur in local newspapers and especially two metropolitan ones: *Boston* (Massachusetts) *Pilot* and the *Truth Teller* (New York City). In the 1830s and 1840s these newspapers published "Information Wanted Notices" that usually listed personal data about an individual's home county, last known place of employment and similar information. Since the overwhelming majority of Irish "canalwers" embraced Roman Catholicism, parish records may provide listings and more biographical information if they remained in the community. Cemetery records, too, can supply personal data. For example, a list of Irish epitaphs at St. James Cemetery in Lamont, Illinois, a settlement on the Illinois & Michigan Canal, shows twenty-seven were of the age to have been canal workers.

In addition to church records federal manuscript censuses offer an important source of information about canal workers. Take the case of the Wabash & Erie Canal. At the time enumerators conducted the census of 1840, construction on what was to become America's longest waterway was progressing through Carroll County, Indiana, with Reed Case as one of the contractors. This explains why the census for Carroll County shows Case as head of a 117-member household! There are similar entries in the canal counties of Vanderburgh and Vigo; some households contain forty or more members. Likely these "family members" consisted of canal workers and their immediate families.

With the 1850 census more specific canal information appeared. In that year federal census takers listed name, age, occupation, financial worth and place of birth of those enumerated. In 1850 the Wabash & Erie Canal was being extended through Daviess, Greene and Pike counties. Timothy Donovan, a contractor, is listed in the census for Pike County as the head of a household that contained a clerk and ninety-four canalers, blacksmiths and stonemasons. These men, who were all but three born in Ireland, probably lived in a hastily built camp and worked on the contract that Donovan held to remove rock at the Patoka summit.

Census records also reveal another lesser-known type of canal laborer, the one with a wife and family. These individuals usually lived alone or with a few other families. Although in the case of the Wabash & Erie Canal heads of these households often hailed from Ireland, their wives generally came from Indiana. In families where wives were born elsewhere, most children over the age of fifteen were born in New York or Ohio, while those under fifteen had Indiana birthplaces. This data suggests movement of laborers' families along the westward progression of canal construction, New York to Ohio to Indiana and Illinois.

As with most forms of transportation, public interest in the past remains strong and in the case of canals it focuses on these nearly always abandoned waterway routes. In recent years with support of public agencies, including the National Park Service, several "linear" canal parks have been established. Representative of this phenomenon is the Illinois & Michigan Canal Heritage Corridor, which Congress established in 1984. Centered around the defunct Illinois & Michigan Canal, this approximately 100-mile corridor includes remains of the waterway, related historic sites and active communities tied to the I&M Canal. In the process of preservation and interpretation, the Illinois Department of Natural Resources, which owns and manages most of the canal property, has gathered data about the canal and its immediate environment. This information can be tapped by those who wish to learn more about aspects of the I&M Canal story and others who seek to broaden their general understanding of canals.

These public agencies and their "friends" groups may have embarked on important archaeological work. In the case of the federally backed Ohio & Erie Canal National Heritage Corridor, which maintains portions of the towpath between Cleveland, Akron, Massillon and Zoar, one of its support organizations, the Clinton Canal Corridor Committee, has been involved in excavations at Locks 2 and 3 and a guard lock on North Main Street in this Ohio community. Such efforts in historical archaeological reveal much, including aspects of overall engineering and construction. The process of learning about what many consider to be the romantic Canal Era is ongoing.

ༀ ༀ ༀ ༀ ༀ

This account, which appeared in *The Ariel*, a periodical published in Philadelphia, Pennsylvania, was printed in 1829–1830 under the title, "Notes on a Tour through the Western Part of the State of New York."

The author provides valuable insights into the daily workings of a "packet" boat and offers interesting commentary about the canal corridor itself. The importance of the newly completed Erie Canal to communities that it directly served is readily apparent. This first-hand description is also useful in interpreting a canal artifact, whether a boat, bridge, lock, tavern or warehouse.

[May 7, 1829] We arrived at Schenectady about one o'clock. As all the passengers in our stage were bound to Utica, one of the number proposed that he be appointed to bargain for our passenger in one boat. . . . As soon as the stage stopped at the Hotel, even before the driver with all his activity to undo the door, up stepped a large muscular fellow, and bawled out at the highest pitch of polite etiquette, "Gentlemen, do you go to the West?" "We do." "The packet starts at 2 o'clock, gentlemen; you had better take your passages and secure your births; only 3 ½ cents a miles, gentlemen, and two shillings a meal, with best accommodations, and a very superior boat, gentlemen." "Hang his boat gentlemen, don't take passage in her," said a second fellow. "I'll take you for less than half the money in a devilish fine boat, and charge you but a shilling a meal." By this time there were at least a half a dozen more, all anxious for us to engage our passage with them at almost any price we pleased. But our Contractor very properly remarked, that he must see the boats himself before he would take passage in any. We therefore all sallied forth to the canal which passes at right angles through the town. We selected a very superior boat of the Clinton Line, calculated to accommodate thirty persons. This boat is calculated for carrying freight, and the cabins are furnished in good style. The Captain actually engaged to take us to Utica, a distance of 89 miles, for one cent and a quarter mile! A York shilling of each meal extra, and to make no charge for births, which are a very necessary accommodation, as the boats run day and night. . . . . . I had only time to take a casual peep at Schenectady, but it appears to be a thriving, pleasant town, and is located principally between the Mohawk and the Canal. Very few persons take the boats between this place and Albany, on account of the delay occasioned by the numerous locks. We "set sail by horse power," as the Irish man has it, about 2 o'clock p.m., the horses being attached to a rope about 30 yards long, made fast to the boat amidships, with our ideas pleasingly elevated at the thought of traveling on the Grand Clinton Canal for the first time. The afternoon was cool and pleasant and never was I more delightfully situated as a traveler than on this occasion. A majority of my companions were Western merchants, well informed respecting the localities and prospect of the country we were passing through, and ready and willing to give the required information. The Canal, this afternoon's passage, has been for the most part immediately on the south bank of the Mohawk, which flows through a narrow valley of good land, but the hills on either side have a poverty-stricken appearance.

At the close of twilight we arrived at Schoharie creek. This is the first place of danger I have yet observed. The creek is about 30 yards wide at this place, and is crossed by means of ropes stretched across the stream, which ropes are your only security; should they give away, you must inevitably go down the current and pass over a dam immediately below, of several feet perpendicular descent. In times of a freshet it is very dangerous. Two or three boats have already been forced involuntarily over it, and so far in safety. The horses are ferried over in scows, pulled by the same ropes. As darkness soon covered the face of nature, I retired to the cabin, and after sketching my observations, and enjoying a pleasant confab with my fellow travelers, retired to my berth, while our boat skimmed its peaceful way along this artificial and wonderful water communication.

8th.—I arose early, having but a disturbed rest during the night, owing to the continued blowing of trumpets and horns at the approach of every lock, and now and then a tremendous jar received in passing a boat; but there is the strictest caution and observation of rules respecting the mode of passage, &c., a precaution highly important, or, owing to the immense number of boats, great confusion and no little danger would be the consequence. The boats on the canal have a beautiful appearance at night, being each illuminated by two large reflecting lamps on either side of the bow, which has much the appearance of a street brilliantly illuminated. I endeavored to count the boats which we passed yesterday, but I soon gave it up for a troublesome job. On going on deck this morning, I found a cold air and a heavy front; we were just passing the village of Conojoharie, being the most considerable place since leaving Schenectady. I shall not attempt a description of all the numerous villages growing along our route. We are still in the valley of the Mohawk, which is narrow and fertile, but the surrounding country has nothing to boast of as to soil. The river at this place is not, I should suppose, over 50 or 70 yards wide, and is, wherever I have seen it, chequered with little islands, which give it a pleasing appearance. The locks and bridges are very numerous, and it requires great attention and care in passing them, or you may be knocked down, and rise up without your head on your shoulders, which, before you can say "look out," may be in possession of the canal fishes. The bridges being low—the highest of them not more than 10 feet above the water,

and some not even over 8 feet, while the boat is full seven, we have occasionally only one foot between the two objects, which hardly admit
a boy to pass under them. The bridges are cheap structures, being nothing more than two stone abutments, having sleepers thrown across the
canal covered with planks, and a handrail on each side. The main
width of the canal at the water line is about 40 feet, and the locks 25.
The captain informs me that six persons have lost their lives by being
crushed between the bridges, which is a greater number than have
been killed during the same time by the bursting of steam engines in
waters of the middle or eastern States.

The locks I shall not attempt to describe. They are very simple, very
strong, well built, and permanent, being uniformly about one hundred
feet long. Our boat, which is of a superior class for freight boats, is
about 80 feet long by 20; the bow and stern are 4 feet lower than the
middle section, which is divided into three apartments—the two end
ones for the accommodation of passengers, the stern to eat in, and the
bow to sleep and sit in, each about 23 feet long, and sufficiently high
for a six-footer to stand erect with his hat on. The roof is in the form of
the back of a tortoise, and affords a handsome promenade, excepting
when the everlasting bridges and locks open their mouths for your
head. The centre apartment is appropriated to merchandise. The only
difference between this and a passage or packet boat, is, that their centre cabins are also for the accommodation of passengers, and in some
instances a little more expensively finished, and travel at the rate of 4
miles an hour, while we rarely exceed 2 3 ¼, they with three horses,
and we with only two. It is evident the freight boats very much injure
the packets by the cheapness with which they run, but as they go with
freight, their passage money is clear gain, and competition is the result.
The packets pay heavier tolls, and of course levy it on their cargo of live
stock.

. . . . . It takes 4 hands to manage a boat of this size: they are the steward, the helmsman, and two drivers, who relieve each other as occasion
may require: we have relays of horses every 20 miles, and thus we are
gliding to the West. At 12 a.m. we arrived at the little falls of the Mohawk, distant 88 miles from our place of embarkation, and this being
the wildest place on the canal, I shall notice it particularly. The river
falls in less than half a mile 50 feet, by one continued rapid, which is
surrounded by five locks, one directly above the other. There being
about 20 boats waiting to pass the locks, which would occupy some
time, the captain very politely offered to accompany me to the village
situated on the opposite side of the river, which is crossed by a very
handsome aqueduct of hewn stone, to supply the canal as a feeder. The

village is of considerable size, with several very pretty buildings. There is a splendid water power at this place, ...

The passenger can supply himself with provisions and grog at all the lockhouses along the line at a very low rate. We arrived at 5 o'clock at the long level commencing at the village of Frankfort; the canal is now one entire uninterrupted sheet of water for 70 miles, without a solitary lock; we have passed enough however to suffice for a while, having ascended upwards of 40 since leaving Schenectady, a distance of 80 miles. . . . . .

We arrived at Utica just at sunset, and found our water course literally choked up with boats, and as there was considerable freight on board ours to be discharged here, we were notified that we would be detained about two hours, of which space we determined to avail ourselves by taking a peek at the town, all agreeing to continue our voyage with the obliging Captain and steward. . . . . .

We left Utica at 10 p.m. and the ear was saluted from a great distance up and down the canal by the music of bugles, horns and trumpets, some of the boatmen sounding their instruments most sweetly. After enjoying these sounds for some time, I tumbled into my birth to partake of the necessary blessing of a nap.

జు జు జు జు జు

Chapter 4

RAILROADS

"Americans take to this little contrivance, the railroad," remarked Ralph Waldo Emerson, "as if it were the cradle in which they were born." Although he made this observation in the mid-nineteenth century, it would remain true for years. Steam railroads were *the* transportation form that for generations most affected the daily lives of Americans. Few, if anyone would challenge the notion that the railroad has been an incredible instrument of change. For more than a century, the railroad resembled the Internet of the present day. It was the iron horse that shattered the isolation of much of the nation, hauling shipments of freight and express, transporting passengers, carrying the U.S. mails and making the electric telegraph part of every station that had an agent or operator. In the 1830s the "Railway Age" dawned, and by the era of the Civil War it had become firmly established. Intercity route mileage soared: 23 in 1830; 30,626 in 1860; 92,147 in 1880; 193,346 in 1910 and 254,251 in 1916, the peak year. Railroad mileage, however, did not shrink rapidly until confronted by increased modal competition, most of all from automobiles and trucks, which massive interstate highway construction accelerated after 1956. Other contributing factors were widespread corporate mergers within the railroad industry in the 1960s and 1970s and landmark regulatory reforms, especially the Staggers Act of 1980, that allowed for easier abandonment of trackage ("line rationalization"). By the beginning of the twenty-first century the national network had dropped to less than 100,000 miles.

In large sections of America railroads literally shaped the built landscape. The impact ranged from patterns of settlement to town development. By World War I the railroad corridor, as vividly described in *Metropolitan Corridor: Railroads and the American Scene* by John R. Stilgo (New Haven, CT: Yale University Press, 1983), with its distinguishing railroad and non-railroad buildings, had become fully developed. When a carrier operated a station, it maintained not only the depot, official center of company activities, but a host of supporting structures.

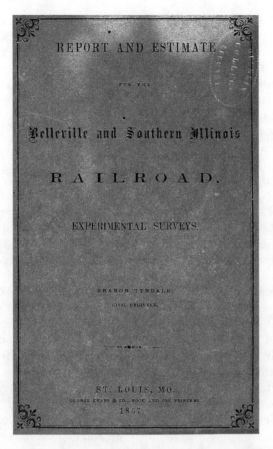

REPORT AND ESTIMATE

FOR THE

Belleville and Southern Illinois

RAILROAD.

EXPERIMENTAL SURVEYS.

SHARON TYNDALE,
CIVIL ENGINEER.

ST. LOUIS, MO.
GEORGE KNAPP & CO., BOOK AND JOB PRINTERS.
1857.

4.1 It is likely that any major depository of railroad-related materials will have an array of company-generated publications, including annual reports, timetables and the like. An example of the type of paper available is this report on various line surveys made in the late 1850s by the Belleville & Southern Illinois Railroad.

Likely one of these was a water tank for slaking the thirst of the iron horse and inevitably the one that held an irresistible attraction for most youngsters. Then there were the "railroad towns" that possessed special qualities. The facilities found there were considerably more extensive than in the typical community that had its single or perhaps multiple depots, depending, of course, upon the number of carriers. Railroad towns, commonly spaced about 100 miles apart, the distance a freight train crew in the nineteenth century could reasonably expect to travel in a work day, usually possessed a larger depot. Probably multistoried, it contained space for freight and passenger agents, perhaps an express company representative, and for operating personnel, including dispatchers who oversaw train movements, and supervisory personnel, including superintendents, road and train masters. The most distinctive railroad structure was the roundhouse or engine shed, where a bevy of workers attended to the always labor-intensive steam locomotive. And surrounding the railroad facilities were a host of commercial ones, usually hotels, eateries and saloons that catered to trainmen.

Arguably, the railroad depot (station is the technical term for the depot building *and* all additional structures, including water tanks, loading docks and privies) is the most recognizable and common three-dimensional architectual artifact of the Railway Age. For more than a century that began in the 1830s, at least 75,000 of these buildings (not including replacement ones) appeared at track side. At the beginning of the twenty-first century only 12,000 or so depots have survived. In urban centers or at junction points there might be a "union station," where two or more steam roads (and at times one or more electric interurbans) provided local service. Also in larger places, whether a county seat or state capital, railroads customarily erected a separate "freight house" or freight depot. Its floor space bulged with shipments of less-than-carload (LCL) freight. Attached docks and ramps allowed for the transfer of goods to and from dray wagons and later motorized trucks.

For generations depots served as community gateways. From the bustling eastern metropolis to the sleepy prairie village, "train time" had multiple meanings for the local citizenry. The depot was the conduit through which people, freight, mail and express moved. Travelers planned their itineraries, purchased their tickets and awaited their trains. Onlookers greeted and bid farewell to passengers or watched who was coming and going. A town's newspaper editor might assign a reporter to gather newsworthy items for a weekly "depot" or "railroad" column. And, too, residents made arrangements to send and receive freight, either at the "combination" freight and passenger depot or separate freight house. If no access existed to a canal or a navigable waterway, virtually everything arrived by rail: boxes of bread, cook stoves, window glass, a seemingly endless array of items. Local manufacturers would have the depot agent bill a carload of outbound goods or a shipment of LCL freight. Postal employees would drop off and pick up sacks of U.S. mail, and packages after enactment in 1913 of the Parcel Post Act. Agents of express companies, including Adams, American, National, Southern, United States and Wells-Fargo, handled packages until World War I when the federal government forced creation of

4.2   As with most forms of transportation, the picture postcard provides helpful information. This ca. 1910 "real photo" postcard of the Pennsylvania Railroad station in Spring Valley, Ohio, shows much, including location of the Railway Post Office mail crane. In addition to the depot sign there is one for the
local express carrier, Adams Express Company. Even if the date of the card is
not known, the Adams Express "clue" indicates that the photograph was taken
prior to 1918 when the federal government fused the major express firms into
the American Railway Express Company.

the American Railway Express Company, later the Railway Express
Agency and finally, before liquidation in the 1970s, REA Express.
    There is a good chance that anyone who wishes to learn more about
the *importance* of a local depot can discover such information in the
columns of a community newspaper. Researchers, too, may profitably
consult records of the state railroad commission (now almost universally known as the public service commission) for complaint letters,
hearing transcripts of inquests and final decisions. After all, it is hardly
remarkable that residents of villages, towns and cities continually
sought to improve the physical aspects of their depots and to maintain
or expand service.

DEPOTS

Learning more about a locale's once throbbing depot usually involves several steps. Some of the following suggestions, but likely not all, may apply to a particular place.

Location: If the depot has survived, the location is immediately apparent. Yet there is a caveat. When a railroad ended agency service, it may have ordered the depot moved away from its original site, particularly if it had been sold to an outside party. The company may have demanded that the structure be relocated several hundred feet away from the right-of-way because of liability issues, legal and safety concerns. If a replacement depot had been erected, the original one may have been torn down or relocated and the trackside site itself altered. When the depot has been demolished but the rail line remains active, the location might easily be discovered by looking for a station (town) sign post. Companies frequently erected a sign, often at the exact location of the former depot or directly across the tracks from it. If both the depot and trackage have been removed, conversations with local residents or railroad enthusiasts, can often pinpoint the site. Old town maps, including ones issued for fire-insurance purposes, also may provide the desired information.

Photographic images, including real-photo postcards, can offer clues to the placement of that missing structure. The railroad corridor had its share of buildings, many substantial, whether a brick warehouse or a concrete grain silo, and some may remain. The juxtaposition in the picture of the depot to a remaining landmark can reveal much.

Another possibility for determining location involves simple "industrial archaeology." The actual depot site usually included sidewalks and platforms, commonly constructed of brick. Parts of them may remain at or near the ground surface. Foundation rubble may be visible, as well. Pipes, broken posts, glass chards and the like may indicate the correct site. Occasionally, remains of the "depot park," which a number of carriers built adjoining their stations (usually to the left or right of the depot), might be found. It was common in these local beautification projects to have cement letters that spelled out the name of the community (AKRON, Ohio or AMES, Iowa) as part of the overall park setting. These may remain after years of neglect, buried under a few inches of topsoil.

Dating the Depot: Even though surviving depots may have been replacement ones with substantial additions or alterations, there are several ways to determine dates of construction and any modifications.

Local newspapers are appropriate initial sources for solving a dating

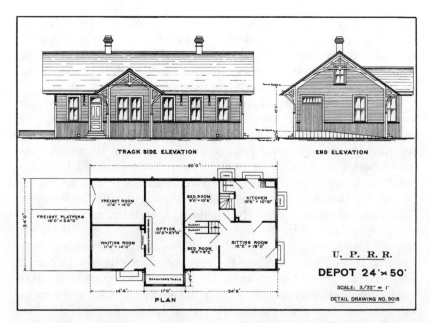

4.3 Railroad companies created a rich variety of plans for their depots. Early in the twentieth century the Union Pacific produced this "standard" 24' × 50' "combination" plan that included apartment space for the agent and his family. Several railfan organizations have reproduced depot drawings and hundreds are found in the valuation files of the Interstate Commerce Commission located in the National Archives.

problem. If the community possessed a daily newspaper, this might be a lengthy process but much less so when such a publication appeared weekly or semiweekly. When the railroad preceeded the town's establishment, a common occurrence in the trans-Mississippi West, then it is doubtful that such coverage exists at all. In most pioneer communities, it took months or possibly one or more years for the first newspaper to make its debut, long after the depot had opened. Carriers typically made depot construction a top priority; they needed places for agents/ operators to work as soon as service began. These employees usually did not devote much of their work time to the freight and passenger business, which might be virtually nonexistent, but handled train-control activities. Division dispatchers needed to know when trains arrived, departed or passed every station. Later, however, newspapers are a reliable source. "Depot news," such as a fire, storm damage or an addition or actual replacement, received front-page attention. Newspapers, too, eventually reported when the railroad ended passenger service and when it finally closed the facility. Toward the end of the twentieth century dramactic changes in business technologies, including toll-free telephone numbers and computers, made depot agents obsolete, first in small towns and then in larger places.

Railroad annual reports are a second likely source of information. From the dawn of the industry until depots disappeared, companies regularly noted their construction and major betterments. They might record destruction or major damage. For instance, the *Twenty-Sixth Annual Report of the Chicago, St. Paul, Minneapolis & Omaha Railway Company* (The Omaha Road), which covered corporate activities for 1907, reported: "Depots were erected as follows: At Augusta and Caldera, Wis., Lake Elm and Dovray, Minn., Riverside, S.D., and Bancroft, Neb., and a brick addition of 40 by 296 feet made to the freight house at Duluth, Minn." Annual reports may not be readily available, but major railroad research collections, including those at the the Newberry Library in Chicago, Mercantile Library in St. Louis and the California State Railroad Museum in Sacramento, usually have runs of major and regional carriers and their predecessors. Reference holdings maintained by a company-oriented historical society, for example, the Chicago & North Western Historical Society and the Erie Lackawanna Historical Society, commonly have old annual reports for the companies that make up their collecting focus. (See appendix for individual railroad societies.) Records of the Interstate Commerce Commission (ICC) at the National Archives (Record Group 134) contain a large variety of annual reports, dating from 1833 to 1971. (A box and folder list is available in the "Annual Reports Binder.")

Early in the twentieth century some carriers, led by the Erie Railroad, inaugurated monthly employee magazines. By mid-century they had proliferated among the larger roads. Although designed primarily for an in-house audience, companies distributed these publications to shippers, regulators, journalists, politicians and other interested parties. Inevitably, editors included feature stories about depot betterments. In the early 1950s *The Erie Magazine* ran a series of articles about new and refurbished depots located in its Greater New York City commuter zone, and was especially proud of these "all asbestos" structures. Major railroad-oriented research libraries and single-company historical societies might possess such serials.

Occasionally depots, usually the larger brick ones, may contain dated cornerstones. These inscriptions can reveal more than date of construction, perhaps names of the railroad president and directors. But such a feature, commonly found on public buildings, including

CHICAGO & NORTH-WESTERN RAILWAY

(Lines West of Missouri River)

BLACK HILLS DIVISION

No. 39 **TIME TABLE** No. 39

Effective Sunday, Sept. 24, 1911

AT 11:00 O'CLOCK P. M. MOUNTAIN STANDARD TIME

FOR THE GOVERNMENT AND INFORMATION OF EMPLOYES ONLY

F. WALTERS,
General Manager

S. M. BRADEN,
General Superintendent

TIME TABLE NO. 39.	BETWEEN CHADRON AND DEADWOOD.	TIME TABLE NO. 39.

No. 91 is superior to No. 92

From 5:15 a. m. until 6:00 a. m. all trains and engines will move very carefully around curve just west of freight depot at Deadwood expecting to find narrow gauge passenger crew making up train on main line at west switch of three-rail or coach track.

Rapid City yards will extend from the spur track switch opposite the National Smelter to the north passing track switch north of the Passenger Station and all trains will approach and move within this district under full control expecting to find main line occupied. These instructions do not modify in any respect rule 98 B.

ALL TRAINS RUNNING IN THE SAME DIRECTION MUST KEEP AT LEAST FIFTEEN MINUTES APART.

4.4 One of the most useful sources of detailed information about the railroad corridor and train operations is the "operating," "employee" or "working" timetable. This one for the Black Hills Division of the Chicago & North Western Railway, dated September 24, 1911, not only indicates freight and passenger train operations between Chadron, Nebraska, and Deadwood, South Dakota, but support facilities at various locations. There is a water tank, for example, at the Smithwick, South Dakota, station.

courthouses, libraries or schools, is rare on depots. Somewhat more frequent are carved corporate logos. Until its demolition in the early
1960s, the two-story Minneapolis & St. Louis (M&StL) Railway depot
in Oskaloosa, Iowa, long-time headquarters for the road's Eastern Division, sported under its end gables two stones emblazoned with "IC."
These logos indicate that the Iowa Central Railway, which in 1912 the
M&StL acquired, had built the structure.

A potentially rewarding resource for dating any railroad structures,
including depots, is the collection of the valuation records generated by
the Interstate Commerce Commission. These documents, which were
created mostly between 1915 and 1925, resulted from passage of the federal Valuation Act of 1913. Reformers, who spearheaded this measure,
believed that railroad securities frequently suffered from "watering,"
and that interstate rates, set by the ICC under previously passed pro-
gressive measures, reflected inflated rather than "real worth." Therefore, these consumer-oriented politicians wished to determine the *actual*
dollar investment that had been made in the railroad enterprise so that
charges to shippers could be adjusted appropriately. The law required
that *every* part of the physical plant, including depots, be examined.
Specific data about depots are found in the Bureau of Valuation Engineering Building Notes, part of the records of the ICC (Record Group
134) in the National Archives. This information, which covers all major
carriers and numerous smaller ones, is generally of high quality and
often contains detailed descriptions of structures, frequently supplemented by blueprints, drawings and photographs. The valuation officer
commonly recorded the exact or approximate date of construction and
that of any subsequent alternation. Also found in these voluminous
notes are inventories of furnishings for depots, office buildings and
other railroad facilities. A convenient way to know the all important valuation number and whether information is available for a particular
carrier, whether the Aberdeen & Rockfish or Zanesville Terminal Railroad, is to check Appendix B of *Records Relating to North American Railroads,* compiled by David Pfeiffer (Washington, DC: National Archives
and Record Administration, 2001).

Depot Styles: Apparently the earliest railroad leaders did not fret
much about depot design. They needed to construct their lines, acquire
suitable locomotives and rolling stock and recruit dependable employees. Their nearly universal goal was to start operations as rapidly as
possible in order to generate revenues. Since most companies began
with limited traffic, this was a challenge. Throughout the pre-Civil War
period, and occasionally thereafter, railroads utilized *existing* buildings, including conveniently located hotels, stores and occasionally

houses. Frequent references to such structures are included in the massive descriptive work written by Franz Anton Ritter von Gerstner, a leading European authority on railways who in 1838 and 1839 visited the United States. An 800-page English translation of his book has appeared as *Early American Railroads*, edited by Frederick G. Gamst (Stanford, CA: Stanford University Press, 1999).

As the railroad industry passed the gestation period, railroad-created depots gained favor. For the vast majority being built, companies opted for some type of "combination" floor plan, designed for places "where the amount of freight or the volume of passenger business does not warrant the construction of a separate freight house or a separate passenger depot." Usually these depots contain three track-level sections: a waiting area (or perhaps separate rooms for gender and/or racial segregation later); a central office, which featured the popular bay window, and a freight-baggage room. Some railroads, especially those that operated on the Great Plains and in the West, opted for living space because of the paucity of available rental housing for agents and their families. Usually the apartment area was located on a second floor, largely to keep the family members removed from the public space.

A common feature of the small-town depot was that it may have been constructed to a basic plan. Although the earliest buildings may have been custom-designed (as would be the case of virtually every urban terminal or "temple"), those depots erected from the 1870s to the 1920s, especially, were fashioned from *standardized* plans. "Cookie-cutter" structures were the result. The Minneapolis, St. Paul & Sault Sainte Marie Railroad (Soo Line), for one, built several hundred of its "Number 2" depots throughout the Upper Midwest and Northern Great Plains, so many, in fact, that these distinctive two-story buildings with their modest architectural detail became a three-dimensional corporate logo for the company.

The explanation for the popularity of standardized depots largely involved cost. In the East and South most communities predated the coming of the iron horse. Railroads, therefore, could predict, with some certainty, the traffic potential of every station. A manufacturing town, a county seat or an important trading center deserved a depot that reflected its standing. Frequently, however, that was not the case in large sections of the Midwest and West. Carriers through their townsite affiliates or in conjunction with real estate promoters usually planned communities every five or ten miles along their lines. The economic prospects of such new places were uncertain. Although boosters might paint glowing pictures of these "new Edens" or "future Chicagos," harsh reality dictated that a sizable number of these raw villages would at best remain whistle-stops. Town promotion was risky. Often hard pressed for funds because of construction charges and modest revenues, builders of pioneer roads did not wish to spend lavishly in a place that might fizzle. Similarly, they did not want a depot that would be too large for local needs during the foreseeable future, so they designed common plans of various sizes. Since costs of preparing these drawings were internal, railroads did not have to pay architectural fees. Companies, moreover, purchased building materials in bulk and already employed ample work crews, part of their "bridge and building" (B&B) departments, which further kept expenditures at reasonable levels. Between the Civil War and World War I standard depots typically ranged from $500 to $2,000 each, somewhat less than average-size contemporary commercial structures.

Convenience was another factor that popularized standardized depot plans. A railroad's central or divisional headquarters could prepare a set of depot drawings suitable for various community sizes, real or anticipated. The structures engineer or an assistant merely selected an appropriate plan and made any modifications, a procedure that was particularly useful when a company undertook major new-line construction. When the Atchison, Topeka & Santa Fe Railway (Santa Fe) expanded dramatically in the 1870s and 1880s, it created a series of standard drawings, ones that it updated with some regularity. In 1910 the Santa Fe files contained five standard plans for main-line depots and four for branch lines. Size and architectural attractiveness were the principal variables in these drawings.

During the Railway Age major communities saw the appearance of truly impressive structures, the largest terminals receiving monumental head houses and imposing train-sheds. Although the New York Central and Pennsylvania Railroads became internationally recognized for their *own* terminals in New York City, designed by prominent architectural firms, most cities had union stations, commonly operated by terminal companies that participating roads had created for that purpose. When the St. Louis Union Station, designed by local architect Theodore C. Link, opened in 1894, it was owned by the Terminal Railroad Association of St. Louis (TRRA). This terminal company was the property of six proprietary roads. The services of TRRA, including those for the St. Louis Union Station, were rented to several additional carriers. Since these massive terminals have often been considered to be architectural gems, not only have they been listed on the National Register of Historical Places, but usually they have been the subject of detailed studies, whether master's theses, doctoral dissertations, scholarly articles or full-fledged books.

Basic works to consult about the architecture of the depot, both large and small, include *Buildings and Structures of American Railroads: A Reference* by Walter G. Berg (New York: John Wiley & Sons, 1904); *Passenger Terminals and Trains* by John A. Droege (New York: McGraw-Hill, 1916, Kalmbach Publishing Company reprint, 1969); *The Country Railroad Station in America* by H. Roger Grant and Charles W. Bohi (Sioux Falls, SD: Center for Western Studies, rev. ed., 1988); *Living in the Depot: The Two-Story Railroad Station* by H. Roger Grant (Iowa City: University of Iowa Press, 1993); *The Railroad Station: An Architectural History* by Carroll L. V. Meeks (New Haven, CT: Yale University Press, 1956); and *Great American Railroad Stations* by Janet Greenstein Potter (New York: John Wiley & Sons, 1996). The more recent publications, particularly the Potter book, contain excellent bibliographies and other source materials.

Expanding Knowledge of the Depot: If the extant depot is no longer railroad-owned and has some adaptive use—museum, office, restaurant or the like—an oft-asked question is "Who built it?" Various local residents and railroad enthusiasts surely know. The answer also may be found by examining city or county histories and, of course, newspapers. But an excellent way to make certain that the information is correct is to consult *The Official Guide of the Railways.* From 1868 through most of the twentieth century this monthly compendium of railroad timetables for virtually every common carrier in North America featured an index of stations. Fortunately the 1,504-page January 1910 issue has been reprinted by Hilton Publications, 675 VFW Parkway, Boston, MA 02467. Each entry identifies the road or roads that served an individual community. The listing in the January 1911 *Guide* for Defiance, Ohio, tells much:

```
Defiance, O. Balt & Ohio (a)
 "            "  Ohio Electric (c)
 "            "  Wabash (b)
(a) and (b) connect at crossing; depots ½ mile apart
(c) about 1 ½ miles from (a) and (b)
```

Not only does the *Guide* reveal three separate depots in Defiance but it notes approximate locations of the two steam railroad stations, ones operated by the Baltimore & Ohio and Wabash Railroads, and the Ohio Electric Railway, the region's principal interurban.

Additional guides are commonly found in research facilities with a railroad orientation. They, too, contain keys to unlocking a depot's past. Some of these historic volumes have been reproduced, thus increasing their availability. In 1945 Kalmbach Publishing Company of Milwaukee reprinted an issue of the popular nineteenth-century

"Dinsmore's Guide," specifically the *American Railway Guide and Pocket Companion* (New York: Curran Dinsmore, 1851). But one of the most useful yet often forgotten reference works is *Bullinger's Postal and Shipping Guide for the United States and Canada*, which has been published for much of the twentieth century. This massive tome, similar in size to a contemporary *Official Guide*, organized post offices alphabetically by place, county and state and noted the railroad or railroads on which these facilities are located or the nearest railroad station that served them. Also included on these pages are names of private express companies that offered service. (Prior to the Parcel Post Act of 1913, the U.S. Post Office did not handle packages, only letters and postal cards.) In another section of *Bullinger's* is a list of railroads and their terminal points. Large carriers, for example, the Chicago, Rock Island & Pacific (Rock Island), were broken down by operating divisions, with a list of all lines, including branches. In the case of the Rock Island, the entries for its Louisiana Division are a follows:

Fordyce Line, Haskel, Ark.—Eldorado, Ark. . . . . .100.4 miles
Crossset Branch, Tinsman, Ark—Crossett, Ark. . . . . 47.3 miles
Arkansas Southern Line, Eldorado, Ark—Eunice, La. . 199.0 miles

Some depots may have had an ownership pattern that causes confusion. The carrier that built the depot might have gone through a series of reorganizations, mergers and other corporate changes. Take the case of the "AC&Y" depot in Medina, Ohio. While residents may immediately refer to this depot by the initials AC&Y (Akron, Canton & Youngstown), its background is considerably more complicated. Admittedly the Akron, Canton & Youngstown Railroad existed for nearly seventy-five years and after 1920 controlled the facility. The builder, however, was the Pittsburgh, Akron & Western Railroad (PA&W) and the Medina structure dates from the early 1890s. But in 1895 the PA&W dissolved into the Northern Ohio Railroad, a company that the Lake Erie & Western, an affiliate of the New York Central Railroad, in turn controlled. Then in 1920 the AC&Y, which had originated eight years earlier as a small switching road in Akron, leased the Northern Ohio and during World War II finally absorbed it. In 1964 the Norfolk & Western Railway leased the AC&Y and eighteen years it bought the company outright. Later the N&W became a core unit of Norfolk Southern Corporation. In 1990 Norfolk Southern spun off the old AC&Y to a new "regional" railroad, the Wheeling & Lake Erie Railway, whose freight trains continue to pass the historic Medina depot.

The best way to learn the corporate genealogy of a depot like the one in Medina, Ohio, is to consult one or more standard references. These include *Poor's Manual of Railroads, Moody's Railroads* and the *Official Railway Guide*. An answer may be gleaned more easily by checking a compendium of company names and dates, *Railroad Names: A Directory of Common Carrier Railroads Operating in the United States, 1826–1989*, compiled and published by William D. Edson (10820 Grainsborough Road, Potomac, MD 20854). Somewhat less useful is *Railroads of North America: A Complete Listing of All Railroads, 1827–1986*, compiled and published by Joseph Gross (28 Parkhurst Drive, Spencerport, NY 14559). A few specialized regional or localized studies are available, including *Names First-Rails Later: New England's 700-plus Railroads and What Happened to Them* (Stamford, CT: Arden Valley Group, 1989), compiled by L. Peter Cornwall and Carol A. Smith, and *Florida's Railroads* (P.O. Box 1878, Apoka, FL 32704), compiled by Gordon MacLeod and R. Ken Murdock.

Perhaps a particular depot (or one of a similar architectual type) has been the subject of a research article. State, regional and topical publications, whether *South Dakota History, The Old Northwest* or *Pioneer America*, occasionally contain pieces about depots. Yet an even better place to check are issues of the regularly published *Bulletin of the Railroad Station Historical Society*, available from the Railroad Station Historical Society, Inc., 430 Ivy Avenue, Crete, NE 68333.

Not to be overlooked in the course of a depot research project are materials that have been created by the National Trust for Historic Preservation and located at its Mountains/Plains Office at 910 16th Street, Suite 1100, in Denver, CO 80202. The National Trust's database covers about 500 depots and the focus is on adaptive use ideas, sources of funding for such undertakings and the like. This information may allow an abandoned or underutilized depot to have a long, useful live beyond its railroad days.

COMPANIES

As previously mentioned, *Poor's Manual of Railroads* and *Moody's Railroads* are appropriate places for learning more about a specific railroad, especially if it operated as a "common carrier," a general-purpose freight and passenger carrier subject to the obligations of "carriage for all on equal terms." There were some railroads, however, that lacked this legal status. These were "tap" roads, private ones that likely hauled for their owners a single commodity, whether minerals, lumber or an agricultural product. Some were short-lived, operating for only a few years. Ones that functioned before the era of state and federal regulation may have histories that are tantalizingly obscure. Local newspapers and rail enthusiasts probably are the best sources for information. Later tap roads, including such remote ones as the Acme, Red River & Northern Railway (Texas); Augusta Railroad (Arkansas), Little River Railroad (Tennessee) and the Mississippi & Alabama Railroad (Alabama), may have left a paper trail among records of state railroad commissions.

Although usually common carriers, "narrow gauges" were a distinct yet relatively obscure railroad genre that may have left considerable physical remains—depots, stone bridges and earthen rights-of-way. Shortly after the Civil War a cadre of railroad promoters considered standard gauge lines (4' 8 ½") to be impractical for certain transportation needs. Instead, they argued that slimmer pikes (usually 3 feet in width) held several crucial advantages, namely that they were easier to build, maintain and operate. A sizable number of their dreams became reality: between 1871 and 1882 a nationwide building boom produced by scores of roads resulted in approximately 12,000 miles of narrow-gauge lines. By using several companies in the mid-1880s it was possible to journey *continuously* 1,581 miles on narrow-gauge lines between Ironton, Ohio, and Searly, Texas, but likely no one ever did.

Although a few narrow-gauge railroads lasted into mid-twentieth century, most did not, either widening their gauge to standard width or abandoning their operations. One of the longest and most enduring "slim" carriers, the nearly 175-mile Rio Grande Southern Railroad, which served the mountainous region of southwestern Colorado, gave up the ghost in 1952. Unquestionably, "smaller and cheaper" usually did not translate into "better" in the context of American railroading.

If a researcher has learned that an old bridge abutment belonged to "the narrow gauge," a common designation for any of the hundreds of individual narrow-gauge roads, it is easy to make the correct corporate identification. In 1990 Stanford University Press published *American Narrow Gauge Railroads*. This encyclopedic tome by George W. Hilton provides the history of this largely neglected dimension of American railroading and also offers summaries of virtually every narrow-gauge carrier. Maps and references to secondary services are included.

An example of the entries for individual narrow-gauge roads, which are arranged by states, is this one for the diminutive and obscure Milton & Sutherlin Railroad:

> Major William T. Sutherlin of Danville [Virgina] conceived of this narrow gauge to serve the local transport demands of Milton, a village in

Caswell County, North Carolina, a short distance south of the Virginia state line. He incorporated it in 1876 and in the following year began building it from a point, which he named for himself, on the Richmond & Danville 11 miles east of Danville. The railroad was completed from Sutherlin to Milton (7 miles) in February 1878. It was a modest operation of a single locomotive, one combine, and two freight cars. Sutherlin considered an extension to reach the Deep River coal mines, but never undertook it.

To complete his railroad Sutherlin negotiated an agreement by which the R&D should grant him a rebate of 25 percent on all traffic from the narrow gauge up to $20,000, to be repaid to the R&D in stock of the M&S. This odd arrangement resulted in the R&D's rapidly gaining stock control of the M&S. On May 19, 1882, the R&D arranged to lease the M&S for 999 years in return for payment of interest on the narrow gauge's debt and guaranty of the principal. Sutherlin sold his interest in the road to M.M. Watkins and other local businessmen.

The usefulness of the narrow gauge declined greatly in 1889 when the Atlantic & Danville built its main line through Milton. When the Southern Railway succeeded to the properties of the R&D in 1894, it listed the M&S among the R&D's holding, "believed to be of no value." The Southern operated the narrow gauge for the R&D's receivers in July and August of 1894, but then shut it down. L. M. Warlick of Winston, North Carolina, bought it late in 1896, but proved unable to restore it to operation. The railroad track was removed in the spring of 1898.

The larger steam (and later diesel) railroads are chronicled in a rich and abundant variety of book-length studies. Three types of works predominate: ones often by and for railroad enthusiasts; ones of a semischolarly nature, at times company sponsored, and ones that are wholly academic. Most important or ("Class 1") roads have been covered in a book format, although there are major exceptions. Enthusiasts, however, seem much more interested in shortlines and roads that have been abandoned. It is easier for these authors "to get their hands on" a smaller operation and there is a strong romantic element to some abandoned operations.

Illustrative of coverage of smaller carriers is *The Ulster and Delaware Railroad Through the Catskills* by Gerald M. Best (San Marino, CA: Golden West Books, 1972). The author, a renowned railfan and photographer, assembled an impressive collection of illustrations of this 129-mile New York shortline to complement his engaging narrative. Common with this genre, Best meticulously researched the rolling stock of the "Rip Van Winkle Road" and its predecessor and affiliated companies. A detailed locomotive roster of the Ulster & Delaware, with representative photographs, is part of an extensive appendix.

Railroad enthusiasts, too, repeatedly have long found abandoned roads, usually situated in popular tourist areas, to be irresistible. The Colorado Midland Railway is an outstanding example. In the late nineteenth century this 310-mile standard-gauge road opened between the Colorado communities of Colorado Springs and Grand Junction, but during federal control in World War I it suspended operations and soon thereafter much of it was abandoned. A fifty six-mile section between Colorado Springs and Divide, however, continued until 1949 to serve area mines, operating under the banner of the Midland Terminal Railway. Several books, or parts of books on the "Midland" have appeared. The most detailed account is *Colorado Midland* by Morris Cafky, which the Rocky Mountain Railroad Club of Denver published in 1965. A long, heavily illustrated text offers what one wag has called a "tie-by-tie and spike-by-spike history." Cafky even provides a set of five pocket maps, which include ones of the system, the Leadville Mining District, Aspen and vicinity, east and west approaches to Hagerman Pass, and a profile-rail chart of the line.

While *The Ulster and Delaware* and *Colorado Midland* represent railroad company histories that have targeted a railfan readership, another category would be corporate histories, perhaps company sponsored, that were more scholarly in their orientation. Often to celebrate centennials or other notable landmarks, firms hired professional researchers/writers to "tell the story," usually in glowing terms or at least suggesting that progress had been a hallmark of the past and undoubtedly would be so in the future.

From the prospective of the sleuth seeking information about a local railroad topic, the railfan study frequently is preferable to the semi-scholarly book, since the latter is more likely to focus on corporate policies and personalities. Still, much can be gleaned from such a work. Following World War II management of the Chicago & North Western Railway (C&NW) hired two journalists from Chicago, Robert J. Casey and W. A. S. Douglas, to produce a corporate history. This they did. *Pioneer Railroad: The Story of the Chicago and North Western System* (New York: Whittlesey House) appeared in 1948. Although the book is badly flawed in places and the authors' emphasis is on company executivies, the reader can get a good sense of the impact this Chicago-based rail giant had on its multistate service territory. An enormously useful feature is found in an extensive appendix; namely, "Construction of Lines Now Part of the Chicago and North Western Railway Company," which is organized on a year-by-year basis from 1848 ("Chicago to Harlem, Ill., 10 miles, constructed by the Galena & Chicago Union Rail Road Company") to 1948 ("Belle Fourche, SD to Aladdin, Wyo., 18.2 miles, constructed by the C&NW Ry"). A similar construction history exists for the long-time affiliate of the North Western, the Chicago, St. Paul, Minneapolis & Omaha Railroad (The Omaha Road).

Just as the semischolarly tome possesses value for the railroad researcher, so, too, does the academic one. Although there is an abundance of such books, there are some spectacular gaps, including such leading carriers as the Chicago, Rock Island & Pacific; Northern Pacific; St. Louis-San Francisco (Frisco); Southern and Wabash railroads. But carriers like the Atchison, Topeka & Santa Fe; Chicago & North Western; Chicago, Burlington & Quincy; Illinois Central; Louisville & Nashville; Southern Pacific and Union Pacific have either one or more scholarly works. As indicated, the "nuts and bolts" railfan history may be preferable, but arguably *every* type of study on a particular railroad will make a contribution.

There are other avenues that may be profitably traveled in the quest for company history. Trade journals are valuable, especially *Railway Age* (1876–present), the longest continuously published trade journal in the industry. An excellent way to tap this type of resource is to consult *Railroad Periodicals Index, 1831–1999*, compiled by Thomas T. Taber III (504 South Main Street, Muncy, PA 17756), which covers eighty Canadian and U.S. periodicals. *Poor's Manual of Railroads* and *Moody's Railroads* provide material, especially for such matters as corporate history, mileage and finance. Periodically, *Poor's* published an extensive entry for a company, often prompted by a merger or a reorganization.

Everyone who seeks to learn more about an individual railroad should investigate the presence of "single-road" historical societies. More than eighty currently flourish. These fan-based organizations usually collect historical materials, which are often deposited in an archive; publish newsletters and journals and respond to inquiries about their favorite road. They run the gamut from those that cover the largest roads to ones that deal with some of the smallest. Most groups center on "fallen flag" carriers, namely those that have entered the business boneyard. For example, there is The Milwaukee Road Historical Association that focuses on the former 10,500-mile giant Chicago, Milwaukee, St. Paul & Pacific Railroad. This group of more than 3,000 members publishes a well-crafted quarterly magazine, *The Milwaukee Railroader*, and holds annual conventions, usually in communities once served by The Milwaukee Road. Likewise, the Missouri & Arkansas Railroad Research Group studies this former 368-mile Joplin, Missouri, to Helena, Arkansas, shortline. This obscure carrier did much to open up the Ozarks to commercial agriculture, especially fruit farming, but in the late 1940s abandoned much of its trackage, although segments operated for a few more years as the Arkansas & Ozarks and the Helena & Northwestern Railroads.

If one wishes to determine what *primary* sources might be available, two guides are highly recommended. In 1988 a meticulous compiler, Thomas T. Taber III (see page 85) produced for the Railway & Locomotive Historical Society, *A Guide to Railroad Historical Resources, United States and Canada.* (In 1993 an updated edition appeared.) This four-volume work is organized by railroad company and includes shortlines, tap roads and narrow-gauge carriers. The *Guide* provides a researcher with an indication of the types of reference materials that are located at public and private libraries, historical societies and museums. Taber, however, provides an important caveat: "Very few libraries and museums have railroad knowledgeable personnel responsible for their material. You should therefore expect when visiting that help by staff will be little." A less encyclopedic, yet at times useful publication is *The Directory of North American Railroads, Associations, Societies, Archives, Libraries, Museums and Their Collections,* assembled in 1999 by Holly T. Hanson (1950 N. 6900 E. Croydon, UT 84018) that is also organized by carrier. This 130-page paperback came about, according to the compiler, because "While trying to locate information on an early Georgia railroad I discovered that there was no easy way to locate records of defunct railways." A valuable regional reference volume is the *Guide to Railroad Collections in the Intermountain West* by Ronald G. Watt (Salt Lake City, UT: Inter-Mountain Archivists, 1984).

Finally, the researcher should realize that a few carriers, including some important ones, often used nicknames rather than their legal corporate titles or even these initials. A major railroad, historically controlled by the New York Central, was the Cleveland, Cincinnati, Chicago & St. Louis. The proper name appeared in print, often in small type, on company timetables and other publications, and the road used "CCC&St.L" on its rolling stock. Nevertheless, this company was known by all as the "Big Four" Railroad. Other examples include the "Clover Leaf" (Toledo, St. Louis & Western), "Nickel Plate Road" (New York, Chicago & St. Louis) and the "Cotton Belt" (St. Louis Southwestern). Because of the confusion of names the Railroad Retirement Board distributes a pamphlet on common railroad nicknames, and *A Treasury of Railroad* Folklore, edited by B. A. Botkin and Alvin F. Harlow (New York: Crown, 1953), covers the topic in some detail.

INTERSTATE COMMERCE COMMISSION
DIVISION OF VALUATION

Page ....

.... for Carrier
.... for I. C. C

NORFOLK & WESTERN RAILWAY
Valuation Section 2Va.
Collection Section 2-1
GILMERTON,VA TO PETERSBURG,VA.
Station 422/33 to Station 4382/33
Roadway Party #8.
A. T. Dean
A.F.E.

NARRATIVE NOTES

Pages
Collection Section Schedule 1
Narrative .... 2 - 4

INTERSTATE COMMERCE COMMISSION
DIVISION OF VALUATION

Page ...4...

Date ...Jan. 1918...
Carrier ...Norfolk & Western Ry.
Valuation Section ...2Va
Coll. Sect. 2-1

a c .... I.C.C

     Sand used in concrete on this line came from Petersburg,Va. Stone came from Lone Jack,Va, about 130 miles from the west end of this section.

     The stone used in old masonry probably came from Lone Jack or from around Petersburg and Richmond,Va where there are quarries. No information could be obtained on the source of stone used in original construction. The stone used in later structures came from Ohio.

     Timber for bridges and ties can be obtained from the sur--rounding country at an average haul of from 10 to 20 miles.

     This line is ballasted with cinders, crushed stone, slag, and sand. The cinders came from Norfolk,Va, Petersburg,Va and Crewe,Va. Most of the stone came from the quarry at Pembroke,Va., about 240 miles from the west end of this section. Some stone has been used from the Lone Jack quarry. Slag came from the furnaces at Roanoke,Va Pulaski,Va and Buena Vista,Va, 176, 234, and 230 miles respectively from the end of this section. Sand ballast came from the pits at Petersburg,Va.

     Construction work can ordinarily be carried on throughout the year in this section of the country, as the weather during the winter months is not severe.

4.5   A bonanza of historic railroad material is found in the voluminous collection of records generated by the industry and the Interstate Commerce Commission to comply with the Valuation Act of 1913. In the holdings for the Norfolk & Western Railway, a file exists on the physical plant of the line between the Virginia communities of Gilmerton and Petersburg. The valuation team reported on such minutiae as the origination of sand used for concrete work.

EMPLOYEES

If a researcher wishes to learn about railroaders, there are good starting points. The published literature is plentiful with autobiographies, edited primary sources and interpretative secondary books. Helpful in the two former categories are *Brasspounder* [depot agent] by D.C. Saunders (New York: Hawthorn Books, 1978); *Brownie the Boomer: The Life of an American Railroader*, edited by H. Roger Grant (DeKalb: Northern Illinois University Press, 1991); *Goin' Railroading: A Century on the Colorado High Iron*, by Sam Speas as told to Margaret Speas Coel (Boulder, CO: Pruett, 1985); *Railroad Voices*, edited by Linda Niemann (Stanford, CA: Stanford University Press, 1998); *Southern Railroad Man: Conductor N. J. Bell's Recollections of the Civil War Era*, edited by James A. Ward (DeKalb: Northern Illinois University Press, 1993), and *Workin' on the Railroad: Reminiscences from the Age of Steam*, edited by Richard Reinhardt (New York: Weathervane Books, 1970). Recommended in the latter category are these titles: *Men of the Steel Rails: Workers on the Atchison, Topeka & Santa Fe Railroad, 1869–1900* by James H. Ducker (Lincoln: University of Nebraska Press, 1983); *Set Up Running: The Life of a Pennsylvania Railroad Engineman, 1904–1949* by John W. Orr (University Park: Penn State University Press, 2001), and *Working for the Railroad: The Organization of Work in the Nineteenth Century* by Walter Licht (Princeton, NJ: Princeton University Press, 1983).

Another useful source to learn about the nature of work on railroads is the rulebook. In the mid-nineteenth century the industry developed books of rules. Since railroads adopted a semimilitary style in the workplace, employees, upon pain of punishment or dismissal, were expected to obey a plethora of rules. Typically rule books, which remain in use today, provide three kinds of information: they list lines of authority, establish standards of personal behavior and give exact instructions for the exercise of workers' tasks. Most railroad-oriented libraries and societies have examples of rulebooks. Usually they were produced for a particular carrier, but some served the needs of several railroads and an occasional electric interurban. The Strahorn Library of the Illinois Railway Museum (www.irm.org), located at 118 East Washington Street in Marengo, Illinois, has perhaps the best collection of late nineteenth- and twentieth-century rule books.

Once the nature of railroad work is understood, there are several ways to find information about an engineer, station agent, or section hand. Some of the single-road historical societies assistant the public with queries about former railroad employees. Indeed, the Chicago & North Western Historical Society has a volunteer who handles genealogical and related questions. As with other forms of transportation, locating information about former employees can be challenging. The number of railroad employees is staggering: in 1910 the national railroad workforce stood at nearly 1.7 million and increased steadily until about 1920, and then declined, at times dramatically, until by the early 1970s the total dropped below a half million. Since railroad companies, especially the major ones, literally filled warehouses with records, they often discarded personnel files as quickly as regulatory authorities allowed. As a result of mergers since the early 1960s, carriers have disappeared and personnel, payrolls and related materials, if retained, have been scattered or destroyed. Also, a few roads pushed hard to get rid of employee records that might make them legally liable for certain health-related problems, especially asbestosis. Still several important collections of personnel records exist, including the Atchison, Topeka & Santa Fe; Missouri-Kansas-Texas; and Missouri Pacific (the former can be found at the Kansas State Historical Society, 6425 S.W. Sixth Avenue, Topeka, KS 66615 and the later two at the Union Pacific Railroad, 1416 Dodge Street, Omaha, NE 68179). Some companies kept payroll records, "personal injury registers" and similar reports. Understandably, saving worker-related materials has been a collecting objective of some single-road historical societies.

It might be in the records of a railroad company that will supply clues about employees. Papers of the General Manager, Vice-President for Labor Relations, Trainmasters and the like are potentially rich sources. A sense of corporate recruitment stategies, for example, is found in this 1906 communication about trainmen from Iowa Central Railway Trainmaster J. H. McCarthy to station agents: "It is the purpose of this company between now and fall to place a number of young men on the road as students . . . to learn the duties of brakemen and to be employed in that capacity when they have become familiar with work." Added McCarthy, "If you are acquainted with any young men at your station who desire to enter this service, I wish you would have them make application to me, but endorsed by you." Specifically, he wanted "young men between the ages of 21 and 26 years, weighing from 125# to 160#, of steady habits and fair education. . . ."

One group of preserved records that may help in learning about former railroad employees are those generated by the U.S. Railroad Retirement Board, the agency that administers a federal retirement benefit program. As does the Social Security Administration, the Railroad Retirement Board dates from the New Deal; specifically, in 1936 it began to maintain its own records. Not all railroad employees were covered; exluded are those who worked for carriers not tied to the Rail-

SURGICAL DEPARTMENT

East St. Louis—Dr. V. P. Siegel, Local Surgeon.
Granite City—Dr. R. W. Binney, Local Surgeon·
Edwardsville—Dr. E. C. Ferguson, Local Surgeon.
Worden—Dr. C. E. Dorr, Local Surgeon.
Staunton—Dr. A. H. Hunter, Local Surgeon.
Mt. Olive—Dr. Otto Hauser, Local Surgeon.
Litchfield—Dr. G. A. Sihler, Jr., Local Surgeon.
Alton—Dr. H. P. McCuistion, Local Surgeon.

When any person is injured upon or about the tracks, trains, structures or grounds of the Company, it shall be the duty of the Station Agent, Conductor, Section Foreman or any other person in the service of the Company who first learns of the injury, to wire the General Manager and obtain authority to provide surgical attendance or to direct the injured to report to the Surgeon for treatment.

The authority of the General Manager must be secured before the service of a Surgeon is invoked, EXCEPT in cases of serious injury, where life or limb is involved, making immediate attention necessary, when the nearest competent surgeon shall be called to attend the injured. If it becomes necessary to call other than one of the Company's Surgeons, be particular to notify such surgeon his services are required for first attention only or until the Company's Surgeon arrives.

In making requests of General Manager a full explanation must be made of all circumstances surrounding the accident, and if injury is result of collision with a train of another railroad or Street Car Company, full particulars as to cause of collision must be given.

The names and addresses of all witnesses to the accident must be secured and shown on regular report form 1167, which must be carefully filled out and forwarded to the General Manager by first mail.

In the case of employes of this Company being injured while in its service and requiring the attendance of the Company or other Surgeon, a discharge certificate must be procured from the attending Surgeon, and the same presented to the head of the department in which the employee is engaged, together with a release of the Company, properly signed, before he will be permitted to return to the service of the Company.

First-aid materials and litters or stretchers for use in case of personal injury to employees of this Company or other persons on or near the premises, have been placed at East St. Louis Freight House, Madison Yard Office, Edwardsville Car Shop Office and Edwardsville Dispatchers' Office.

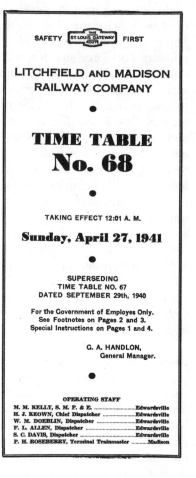

SAFETY [ST. LOUIS GATEWAY ROUTE] FIRST

LITCHFIELD AND MADISON RAILWAY COMPANY

•

TIME TABLE
No. 68

•

TAKING EFFECT 12:01 A. M.

Sunday, April 27, 1941

•

SUPERSEDING
TIME TABLE NO. 67
DATED SEPTEMBER 29th, 1940

For the Government of Employes Only.
See Footnotes on Pages 2 and 3.
Special Instructions on Pages 1 and 4.

G. A. HANDLON,
General Manager.

•

OPERATING STAFF

M. M. KELLY, S. M. P. & E. ....Edwardsville
H. J. KEOWN, Chief Dispatcher ....Edwardsville
W. M. DOEBLIN, Dispatcher ....Edwardsville
F. L. ALLEN, Dispatcher ....Edwardsville
S. C. DAVIS, Dispatcher ....Edwardsville
P. H. ROSEBERRY, Terminal Trainmaster ....Madison

4.6   The April 27, 1941, operating timetable for the Litchfield & Madison Railway Company is typical of such "for employees only" schedules in that it lists local physicians who serve the railroad's surgical department.

road Retirement Act and employees who had only brief careers or merely a casual relationship with a company. Requests for genealogical information should be sent to the Board's Office of Public Affairs, 844 North Rush Street, Chicago, IL 60611-2092.

A diligent researcher who cannot locate company- or government-generated records likely can still discover some information about past railroad employees. With their heavy coverage of railroad happenings during the industry's Golden Age, newspapers are valuable for tracing who worked for the local road. In African American communities, for example, the black press regularly covered the comings and goings of Pullman Company porters. This is understandable since these men were part of the African American elite. City directories and manuscript federal censuses for the mid-late nineteenth and early twentieth centuries should be consulted. As noted elsewhere, some states also created their own censuses. Records of railroad brotherhoods, especially their monthly periodicals, are another potential source of information. *The Brotherhood of Locomotive Firemen and Enginemen's Magazine,* published in Columbus, Ohio, for years noted membership and activities in its various "lodges" as well as reported deaths. It was common to find listings of "brothers" who received insurance payments. After all, a major factor in the popularity of these brotherhoods involved their role as "coffin clubs"; that is, they offered health and burial insurance benefits.

A researcher should realize that railroad workers joined more than the appropriate brotherhood, thousands became active members of fraternal societies, especially the Freemasons. Indeed to advance through the ranks of either the white-collar or blue-collar workforce, it was necessary on many roads for an employee to be a Protestant and also a Mason. But the Masonic order was not the only group. Take the case of employees of the Denver & Rio Grande Western (now part of the Union Pacific), who worked out of the Salida, Colorado, terminal. Scores belonged to the chapters of the Ancient Order of United Workmen (AOUW), International Order of Oddfellows and the Order of the Knights of Pythias. If these local fraternal units exist, membership files should be checked. And some records of the defunct fraternals, for example the AOUW, and locals of ongoing orders have been preserved by local and state historical societies.

In a few cases records of "veterans" associations remain, perhaps part of the archive of a single-road historical society. In the first part of the twentieth century some carriers sponsored such groups and others followed. Often the largest veterans organizations were associated with medium-sized roads, like The Omaha Road, which operated less than 2,000 route miles. From that company's earliest history a sense of kinship developed. The Omaha management endorsed institutionalization of these bonds of comradeship through creation of The Omaha Veteran Employees Association, a voluntary social organization. Older and retired workers enthusiastically joined. Most of these associations, frequently with female auxiliaries, tapered off in the 1950s and a decade later disappeared. Their publications and other printed materials commonly discuss the railroad careers of individual members.

Statement of Death and Disability Claims

FILED WITH THE GENERAL SECRETARY AND TREASURER DURING THE MONTH ENDING DECEMBER 15, 1913.

No. of Claim.	NAME OF MEMBER.	No. of Lodge.	Date of Filing.	Character of Claim.	Amount of Ben. Cert.	When Payable if Approved.	Cause of Death.	Cause of Disability.
4160	Benj. B. Brandt.....	65	Nov. 20, '13	Disab.	$1500	Jan. 15, '14	....	Consumption of lungs
4163	John J. Pasler.....	797	Nov. 20, '13	Disab.	2000	Jan. 15, '14	....	Consumption of lungs
4164	Frank E. Durfey.....	326	Nov. 20, '13	Death.	500	Jan. 15, '14	....	
4165	Henry D. Whitney...	485	Nov. 20, '13	Death.	1500	Jan. 15, '14	Typhoid fever.	
4166	Lemuel M. Huffman..	299	Nov. 24, '13	Death.	1500	Jan. 15, '14	Collision.	
4167	Edward Herman.....	300	Nov. 24, '13	Death.	1500	Jan. 15, '14	Acute rheumatism.	
4168	Joseph Retty........	321	Nov. 24, '13	Death.	1000	Jan. 15, '14	Collision.	
4169	Walter P. Kimball...	352	Nov. 24, '13	Death.	1500	Jan. 15, '14	Collision.	
4170	Thos. A. Maxwell....	528	Nov. 24, '13	Death.	500	Jan. 15, '14	Derailing of engine.	
4171	Fred Yeomans.....	645	Nov. 24, '13	Death.	1000	Jan. 15, '14	Collision.	
4172	John E. Sharp.....	604	Nov. 24, '13	Death.	1500	Jan. 15, '14	....	
4173	Geo. L. Gillig......	662	Nov. 24, '13	Death.	1500	Jan. 15, '14	Stabbed.	
4174	E. W. Hoover	107	Nov. 24, '13	Disab.	1000	Jan. 15, '14	....	Bright's disease.
4178	John Schmidgall.....	231	Nov. 24, '13	Disab.	1500	Jan. 15, '14	....	Consumption of lungs
4179	Norman E. Cram ...	327	Nov. 24, '13	Disab.	500	Jan. 15, '14	....	Blind one eye.
4181	Wilmer Gwynn	405	Nov. 24, '13	Disab.	1000	Jan. 15, '14	....	Consumption of lungs
4183	Wm. F. Swanston...	90	Nov. 26, '13	Death.	1500	Jan. 15, '14	Pneumonia.,	
4184	Wm. H. Titzell.....	179	Nov. 26, '13	Death.	500	Jan. 15, '14	Peritonitis.	
4185	Harry Condram.....	249	Nov. 26, '13	Death.	1500	Jan. 15, '14	Consumption of lungs	
4186	John A. Winters	331	Nov. 26, '13	Death.	1500	Jan. 15, '14	Bronchitis.	
4187	W. J. J. O'Connor...	387	Nov. 26, '13	Death.	1500	Jan. 15, '14	Derailing of engine.	
4188	Harry Odenthal.....	3	Dec. 2, '13	Death.	1500	Jan. 15, '14	Circomas.	
4189	Ora L. Tuttle........	191	Dec. 2, '13	Death.	1500	Jan. 15, '14	Exposure–snow storm	
4190	Clarence A. Russell..	192	Dec. 2, '13	Death.	1500	Jan. 15, '14	Typhoid fever.	
4191	John R. Cove........	229	Dec. 2, '13	Death.	1500	Jan. 15, '14	Derailing of engine.	
4192	Frank L. Hanes.....	472	Dec. 2, '13	Death.	1500	Jan. 15, '14	Tumor.	
4193	Peter Ruffer........	543	Dec. 2, '13	Death.	1500	Jan. 15, '14	Kidney disease.	
4194	Edward A. Reiff	553	Dec. 2, '13	Death.	1500	Jan. 15, '14	Consumption of lungs	
4195	Thos. E. Metz......	570	Dec. 2, '13	Death.	1500	Jan. 15, '14	Collision.	
4196	George Allen	656	Dec. 2, '13	Death.	1500	Jan. 15, '14	Pneumonia.	
4197	Geo. E. Siple, Jr....	673	Dec. 2, '13	Death.	1000	Jan. 15, '14	Typhoid fever.	
4198	Oliver G. Leiter	673	Dec. 2, '13	Death.	1500	Jan. 15, '14	Typhoid fever.	
4199	Geo. W. McClanahan	688	Dec. 2, '13	Death.	1000	Jan. 15, '14	Septicæmia.	
4200	R. R. Welch........	237	Dec. 2, '13	Disab.	1500	Jan. 15, '14	....	Blind one eye.
4201	Harry Nelson........	298	Dec. 2, '13	Disab.	1000	Jan. 15, '14	....	Blind one eye.
4202	Conrad J. Schafers.	578	Dec. 2, '13	Disab.	1500	Jan. 15, '14	....	Amputation of foot.
4204	Clark J. Lalande....	92	Dec. 5, '13	Disab.	1500	Jan. 15, '14	....	Amputation of foot.
4205	G. C. Gearheiser	107	Dec. 5, '13	Disab.	1500	Jan. 15, '14	....	Amputation of hand
4207	Geo. R. McGinnis ...	441	Dec. 5, '13	Disab.	1500	Jan. 15, '14	....	Amputation of foot.
4208	Frank D. Winters...	174	Dec. 5, '13	Death.	1500	Jan. 15, '14	Pneumonia.	
4209	Patrick Briceland....	241	Dec. 5, '13	Death.	1500	Jan. 15, '14	Heart disease.	
4210	Guy Karr	482	Dec. 5, '13	Death.	1000	Jan. 15, '14	Collision.	
4211	Lester C. Thomas...	324	Dec. 6, '13	Death.	500	Jan. 15, '14	Collision.	
4212	Jos. E. Gray	411	Dec. 6, '13	Death.	1500	Jan. 15, '14	Derailing of engine.	
4213	Jos. E. Taylor.......	536	Dec. 6, '13	Death.	1500	Jan. 15, '14	Collision.	
4214	Geo. H. Hoffman ...	718	Dec. 6, '13	Death.	1500	Jan. 15, '14	Paresis.	
4218	V. L. Winkworth....	5	Dec. 10, '13	Death.	500	Jan. 15, '14	....	Consumption of lungs
4219	Elmer Sanford......	21	Dec. 10, '13	Disab.	1500	Jan. 15, '14	....	Bright's disease.
4220	Andrew J. Cress	159	Dec. 10, '13	Disab.	1500	Jan. 15, '14	....	Consumption of lungs
4222	Jos. V. Elmore......	316	Dec. 10, '13	Disab.	1500	Jan. 15, '14	....	Paralysis.
4223	Hooper C. Van Vorst.	230	Dec. 10, '13	Death.	1500	Jan. 15, '14	Nephritis.	
4224	Walter O. Chambers.	409	Dec. 10, '13	Death.	3000	Jan. 15, '14	Heart disease.	
4225	Patrick D. Mulcahy.	424	Dec. 10, '13	Death.	1500	Jan. 15, '14	Struck by engine.	
4226	Jacob H. McDavid .	453	Dec. 10, '13	Death.	1500	Jan. 15, '14	Pneumonia.	
4227	R. M. Weatherford..	714	Dec. 10, '13	Death.	1500	Jan. 15, '14	Collision.	
4228	Geo. H. Bracken	14	Dec. 12, '13	Death.	1500	Jan. 15, '14	Collision.	
4229	Henry C. Randall....	14	Dec. 12, '13	Death.	1500	Jan. 15, '14	Heart disease.	
4230	John Kramer........	123	Dec. 12, '13	Death.	1500	Jan. 15, '14	Collision.	
4231	Donald McDonald....	181	Dec. 12, '13	Death.	1000	Jan. 15, '14	Drowned.	
4232	Arthur Knapp	799	Dec. 12, '13	Death.	1500	Jan. 15, '14	Run over by cars.	
4233	Jas. W. Hathway....	12	Dec. 12, '13	Disab.	1500	Jan. 15, '14	....	Consumption of lungs
4235	Lewis Argersinger...	334	Dec. 12, '13	Disab.	1500	Jan. 15, '14	....	Blind left eye.
4240	Wm. L. Behnke.....	711	Dec. 15, '13	Disab.	1500	Jan. 15, '14	....	Amputation of feet.
4241	Will C. Chance.....	80	Dec. 15, '13	Death.	1000	Jan. 15, '14	Run over by train.	
4242	Harry O. Bernd......	318	Dec. 15, '13	Death.	1500	Jan. 15, '14	Apoplexy.	
4243	Harry F. Koop......	378	Dec. 15, '13	Death.	1500	Jan. 15, '14	....	
4244	Wm. P. Cassidy.....	562	Dec. 15, '13	Death.	1500	Jan. 15, '14	Struck by street car.	
4245	John D. Chaplin....	789	Dec. 15, '13	Death.	1500	Jan. 15, '14	....	
4246	Howard S. Martin ...	810	Dec. 15, '13	Death.	1000	Jan. 15, '14	Falling from engine.	

4.7 A good place to attempt finding a former railroad employee is in back runs of labor union publications. In a 1914 issue of the *Locomotive Firemen and Engineman's Magazine*, official publication of the firemen's union, considerable information is listed about disabled and departed brothers.

In a similar fashion information about employees may be gleaned from company magazines. Just as these in-house publications featured stories of new or remodeled depots and other betterments, they also extensively covered employees' activities, especially those who had made a special contribution or who had retired after a long career. The Louisville & Nashville Railroad, which introduced in March 1925 *The Louisville & Nashville Employees' Magazine* (later *L.& N. Magazine*) made much of workers who earned their 15-year, 25-year, 35-year, 45-year and 50-year service buttons (female employees received pins). Editors of these magazines were fond, too, of human interest stories, whether a feature about a third or fourth generation employee or one who was "different;" for example, a woman who during World War II labored in the car or machine shops.

Railroad officials, including minor ones, can be traced. The best place to look are back issues of *The Pocket List of Railroad Officials*, which dates from the 1870s and was long compiled by the Railway Equipment and Publication Company of New York City. This quarterly publication provides information for most carriers, even shortlines. For example, the entry in the *Pocket List* for October 1916, gives the names of these officials for the forty-mile Pecos Valley Southern Railway Company (of Texas): president, assistant to the president, vice-president, vice-president and general manager, general counsel, secretary, treasurer, auditor and general freight and passenger agent, master mechanic and division engineer. Higher ranking officers of major roads can be found, complete with full biographies, in copies of *Who's Who in Railroading* (prior to the 1930 edition *The Biographical Dictionary of Railway Officials of America*) prepared by the Simmons-Boardman Publishing Corporation of New York City and more recently of Omaha, Nebraska.

Oral histories of former and current rail employees usually offer important clues about railroaders and the nature of their work. Some organizations and groups have conducted extensive oral history projects, producing both tapes and transcripts of interviews. The John W. Barriger III National Railroad Library, a division of the Mercantile Library in St. Louis, for one, has an ongoing series of interviews with top officials and financial personnel who led the industry prior to the coming of the quasi-public Consolidated Rail Corporation (Conrail) in the mid-1970s. Representative of more modest endeavors have been interviews begun in the late 1970s by the West Chicago Historical Society with individuals associated with the Chicago, Burlington & Quincy and especially the Chicago & North Western railroads in West Chicago, Illinois. A number of single-line historical societies have their own specialized projects. Of course, nearby history researchers can do

NKPersonals

News briefs reporting activities of employes of The New York, Chicago and St. Louis Railroad Company

CLYDE H. WARE, *Editorial Assistant*

GENERAL OFFICES
CLEVELAND, OHIO

Traffic Department

Charlie Weiss, Frank Tesar and Bill Becker while in Chicago attending meetings were interviewed on a radio breakfast program in a Loop restaurant. As they answered each question, they received groceries. They were so successful that, when C h a r l i e loaded his prizes in his traveling bag, he broke the zipper and it cost six dollars to be repaired . . . Tom Walsh is assistant basketball coach of the Cleveland NKP team, working under Marty Markworth . . . Ken Shea had a turkey and a chicken on his h a n d s for the Thanksgiving holiday . . . A strep throat confined Leonard Schirmer for a while but he's back in good shape . . . Al Dietsche's eighth-month-old grandson is banging around the house already in his Taylor-Tot . . . Again Mike Schobel saw the Thanksgiving day football game between Case and Western Reserve . . . Charlie Steffen was really surprised when he saw Tom Kilcullen, traffic representative in our New York office, on the Arthur Godfrey television show recently. Tom sponsored a quintet which won first prize for the evening.

Supt. Transportation and
Supt. Car Service

K. A. DAGGETT, *Correspondent*
Our offices now are located on the ninth floor of the Terminal Tower. We are beaming with pride over the lighting system . . . Everyone wishes a quick and complete recovery to D. M. Bender, superintendent of transportation, who recently underwent surgery and to Mrs. A. Klima who also was hospitalized . . . Both A. R. Morse and Ken Daggett had good luck during hunting season . . . R. S. Lewis and Ed Kubik are in their new homes . . . Thirty couples attended the Car S e r v i c e Office Party at the Hilltop Club in No-

vember . . . Travelers: L i l l i a n Blasko and Corine Burton to Chicago; S. C. Russo to Columbus and Retired Supervisor of Demurrage W. S. Cotterman to Hot Springs, Ark.

Central Machine Bureau

IRENE WALLACE, *Correspondent*
Latest dress creations will be the fashion in our office as Marion Walsh, Elsie Gallagher, Shirley Tamkin, Betty Sutter and Pat Medley are studying dressmaking . . . Marie Habrat and Elsie Gallagher joined the NKP swimming class at the "Y" and, after hearing about the swim meets some of us wish we also had joined.

Engineering Department

JEAN BROWN, *Correspondent*
Welcome to the W&LE employes in our department . . . Our deepest sympathy to Emil Vanik on the death of his mother . . . Glad to see Gus Metzdorf back to work after a recent illness . . . Congratulations to Ed Thacker, a proud grandfather . . . Mr. a n d Mrs. Robert L. R o a c h finally have moved to the city . . . Recent vacationers: Gene Matlock to Conneaut, his home town; and John Morrow to Huntingdon, Ind.

Auditor of Revenues

HERB SHATTUCK, *Correspondent*
Charles Robinson of the Interline Bureau will direct the first play given in January by the newly organized Avon Lake Little Theater. Charlie was long associated with the Lakewood Little Theater, both as an actor and a director. Born in England, he toured with stock companies in Canada and the United States, serving on the staff of the Montreal Community Theater and the Montreal Repertiore Theater . . John Petruska of the Station Accounting Bureau is on leave of absence, attending Cleveland College under the GI Bill . . . Betty Besida's infant daughter is home from St. Alexis Hospital . . . John Fabris of the Station Ac-

counting B u r e a u attending the banquet honoring the championship Westlake Softball League team on which he played center field . . . Paul Satterfield of Muncie, Ind., formerly of the Revision Bureau, was the guest of Mr. and Mrs. George Pike . . . Our sincere sympathy to the families of Helen N. Bishop of the Station Accounting Bureau and of Henry H. Bates of the Overcharge Claim Bureau who passed away recently . . .Mary C. Pallein recently was on jury duty . . . Eugene J. Andres attended the Notre Dame-North Carolina game in New York City . . . Among those attending the John Carroll-Canisius game at Buffalo were Lloyd Jones, Joe Geshke and son, Jack Tenhagen, Norma Ferrara and Arlene Wallman . . . Lee Andrews, retired accountant who now lives in Ashtabula, Ohio visited the department recently . . . Robert Green, who broke his leg while skating in Akron several months ago, has had to have it reset . . . Travelers: Evangeline Stephan visiting her sister in Maumee Valley, Ohio; Fran Berry in Buffalo, N. Y.; John Andreski in Virginia Beach, Va.; Regina Karpowicz in Youngstown, Ohio; Carolyn Mieldane to North Bay, Canada; and Hazel Stieglitz to Pittsburgh.

CLOVER LEAF DISTRICT

A. McGINNIS, *District Editor*
Frankfort, Ind.
R. D. Henry, former NKP employe and now C&O car inspector at Muskegan, Mich., recently visited the superintendent's office and the car shops . . . Retired General Yardmaster and Mrs. J. J. Downer celebrated their golden wedding anniversary on October 23. They received gifts and the best wishes from many friends . . . Our sympathy to Engineer H. M. Johnson on the death of his mother, to Engineer J. L. Reagan on the death of his mother and to Mrs. T. V. Hinton on the death of her husband . . . S. T. Crispin visited his sister at Fort Worth, Texas, returning home via the Grand Canyon and

16

4.8 Throughout much of the twentieth century major railroad companies produced employee magazines, often providing information about employees. An illustration is the January 1950 issue of *The Nickel Plate Road Magazine*, which contains its regular section, "NKPersonals."

FIRST DISTRICT CENTRAL DIVISION
ALBERT LEA TO ANGUS

Distance from St. Paul	No. of Station	STATION	COUNTY AND STATE	AGENTS	Class of Agency	CONNECTIONS
119.0	119	ALBERT LEA (See1stDist.W.Div.)				
123.0	123	Kansota.............*Prepaid	Freeborn,Minn.			
126.2	126	Twin Lakes...............	"	C. H. Carter....	FT	
132.2	132	Emmons................	Worth...Iowa	H. L. Opdahl...	FT	
138.4	138	Lake Mills...............	Winnebago "	E. R. Jeffords...	FTC	
147.1	147	Leland................	" "	L. M. Peterson..	FT	
152.9	153	Forest City.............	" "	C. S. Kruchek...	FTC	
....	154	C. R. I. & P. Transfer.......*X				C. R. I. & P.
158.8	159	Hawley.............*Prepaid	Hancock			
167.5	168	Britt................	"	A. Anderson....	FTC	C. M. St. P. & P.
173.4	173	Stilson................	"	Miss G. Martin..	FT	
178.2	178	Corwith.............C	"	S. S. Young....	FTC	
182.6	183	Hanna.............*Prepaid	Kossuth			
187.0	187	LuVerne................	"	J.M.Christensen	FTC	C. & N. W.
192.7	193	Livermore...............	Humboldt	C. O. Gustafson.	FTC	C. R. I. & P.
196.7	197	Arnold.............*Prepaid	"			
203.1	203	Humboldt...............	"	L. E. Chambard.	FTC	
206.1	206	Rogerton.............*X	"			
212.4	212	Badger................	Webster	H. J. Rudolph..	FT	
221.6	222	S FORT DODGE, Freight.....C	"	C. E. Hill......	F	Ill. Cent.
....	"	Pass. (Jt. with Ill. Cent.)..	"	W. J. Kearney..	TC	
226.3	F226	Kalo Jct.............*Prepaid	"			
229.4	F229	Otho................	"	R. H. Richey...	FT	
235.1	F235	Burnside...............	"	T. F. Mulligan..	FT	
241.3	F241	Dayton................	"	E. C. Connor....	FT	
244.4	F244	So. Dayton...........*Prepaid	"			
249.4	249	Pilot Mound................	Boone	D. C. Wiley....	FTC	
251.0	F251	Wolf.............*Prepaid	"			Ft. D. D. M. & S.
257.5	F258	Ogden................	"	O. M. Olson....	FT	C. & N. W.
265.7	F266	Berkeley................	"	G. W. Beaman..	FT	
270.3	272	ANGUS................	"	A. Berglund....	FT	

SECOND DISTRICT CENTRAL DIVISION
SPENCER TO DES MOINES

Distance from St. Paul	No. of Station	STATION	COUNTY AND STATE	AGENTS	Class of Agency	CONNECTIONS
197.2	B197	SPENCER (See Third Dist.)...				
210.0	C210	Ruthven Pass(Jt.with C.M.St.P&P.)	PaloAlto, Iowa	P. G. Bowers...	T	C. M. St. P. & P.
....	"	Freight.............	"	V. M. Steidl...	F	C. M. St. P. & P.
217.5	C218	Ayrshire.............	"	C. A. Spitler....	FT	
223.9	C224	Curlew...............	"	E. A. Arndt....	FT	
228.0	C228	Mallard.............C	"	H. B. Turner...	FTC	
233.0	C233	Plover...............	Pocahontas	J. W. Ferguson..	FTC	
239.7	C240	Rolfe...............	"	E. D. G. Weiland	FTC	C. & N. W.
245.2	....	Cement Plant.............*X	"			
247.1	C247	Gilmore City.............	"	H. Granseth....	FTC	
252.8	C253	Pioneer...............	Humboldt	G. C. Stanz....	FT	
257.9	C258	Clare...............	Webster	D. M. Dickenson	FT	
227.6	228	TARA (Jt. with Ill. Cent.).....	"	E. E. Rector....	FT	Ill. Cent.
231.7	232	Moorland................	"	M. W. Lothringer	FTC	C. G. W.
237.1	237	Callender................	"	C. K. Ferguson..	FTC	C. & N. W.
242.7	243	GOWRIE (Jt. with C. R. I. & P.)	"	P. A. Strobel....	FTC	Ft. D. D. M. & S.
246.9	247	Lena.............*Prepaid	"			C. R. I. & P.
251.2	251	Paton................	Greene	C. O. Knutson..	FTC	
255.3	255	Dana................	"	G. D. Johnson...	FTC	
260.4	260	Grand Jct., Freight.........C	"	W. J. Boyle.....	F	C. & N. W.
....	"	Grand Jct., Pass. (Jt. w C&NW)	"	W. J. Boyle.....	TC	
267.8	268	Rippey................	"	J. P. Eshouse...	FTC	
272.1	272	ANGUS (See First Dist.)........	"			
276.0	276	Perry.....................	Dallas	J. C. Rhode....	FTC	C.M. St. P. & P. / D. M. & C. I.
282.9	283	Minburn................	"	A. H. Nelson....	FTC	
289.0	289	Dallas Center...............	"	C. F. Beard....	FTC	
295.4	295	Waukee................	"	J. C. Sandmier..	FTC	C. M. St. P. & P.
302.5	303	Ashawa.............*Prepaid	Polk			
305.1	305	Valley Junction.........	"	C. E. Gearhart..	FTC	C. R. I. & P.
310.1	310	S DES MOINES, Freight.....C	"	C. A. Ziehlke...	F	With Lines Diverging
....	....	City Ticket Office.......	"	D.L.McCaughan	TC	With Lines Diverging
....	....	C. R. I. & P. Depot, Tkt....	"	W.M.Daugherty	TC	
....	....	C. R. I. & P. Depot, Bag...	"	D. C. Shafer....		

5

4.9   Occasionally railroad companies produced lists of employees. In 1931 the
Minneapolis & St. Louis Railway distributed a booklet, "No. 26," *List of Officers,
Stations, Etc* that indicated its various employees by operating divisions and
districts. A female agent is listed for Stilson, Iowa.

their own interviewing, following accepted oral history techniques. See Chapter 6, "Oral Documents," in *Nearby History: Exploring the Past Around You*, second edition, by David E. Kyvig and Myron A. Marty (Walnut Creek, CA: AltaMira Press, 2000).

Active and retired railroad employees may have much to tell about their railroad, community, themselves and other employees. Often their testimonies complement and expand the written records. In some cases an oral tradition can lead to the distant past, even to events that occurred in the nineteenth century. It is not unknown for tales of the rails to have been passed from generation to generation.

A story still related among railroaders on the Denver & Rio Grande Western (now part of Union Pacific) involves the community of Nephi, once the terminus of the forty-two-mile San Pete Valley branch in central Utah. Early in the twentieth century a troubling situation developed in Nephi, directly related to the Rio Grande. After entering the town limits, the company's tracks crossed a number of streets before they reached the depot. According to state statute the engineer had to pull the whistle cord and ring the bell at every road crossing. The steam whistle blast was the prolonged signal of two longs, a short and a long. A newly scheduled train usually arrived in town about 4:00 a.m., and the continuous whistling and bell ringing awakened everybody. As time passed there were so many babies born locally that the rapidly expanding infant population became a community concern. Residents demanded that the Rio Grande alter the timetable so that this noisy train would arrive later in the morning. Management agreed and the population explosion subsided.

ROLLING STOCK

A visible part of the railroad legacy has been equipment, whether steam locomotive, passenger coach or freight caboose. Other types of rolling stock have survived as well, being found along the railroad corridor, in a farmer's field, along a city alley or even as part of an existing structure. It might be an old Pullman sleeping car, tank car or boxcar, often an inexpensive and suitable place for storage. How then can the past of a historic piece of rolling stock be traced?

Steam locomotives and other pieces of motive power usually pose no problems. Inspired by British "train-spotters," beginning in the formative years of the twentieth century American railroad enthusiasts started to collect lists of locomotive data by company, manufacturer, engine number, builder's plate number and wheel arrangement. Rosters of virtually every railroad, large and small, have been gathered and frequently published. The Railway & Locomotive Historical Society provides a comprehensive series of steam and diesel-electric locomotive rosters and also offers copies of locomotive builders' records. (Railway & Locomotive Historical Society, P.O. Box 1674, Sacramento, CA 95812-1674) Moreover, there is a rich literature of the locomotive, including one basic work, *A Short History of American Locomotive Builders* (Washington, DC: Bass, 1982). Simple identification of pieces of diesel-electric motive power is possible by checking *Diesel Spotter's Guide Update* (Milwaukeee, WI: Kalmbach, 1984).

Passenger coaches, Pullman sleepers, diners, Railway Post Office and baggage cars and cabooses have similarly caught the fancy of railroad enthusiasts. Equipment rosters for various railroads are available, often through the single-road historical society or some national railroad group. Various railroad museums have employees and volunteers who can assist in identification and with restoration. The umbrella organization is ARM, the Association of Railroad Museums (P.O. Box 370, Tujunga, CA 91043 or www.railwaymuseums.org). This group publishes the *Railway Museum Quarterly*, which highlights major projects at member museums and features articles on preservation, conservation and restoration of equipment.

The caboose is one of the most commonly found pieces of railroad rolling stock. Not only have they been used since the mid-nineteenth century but in the 1980s and 1990s railroads disposed of them in large numbers as states repealed their "caboose laws," allowing for today's ubiquitous "end-of-train-device," which permits the engineer to keep watch on air-brake pressure, instead of relying on crewmen who rode the historic red (or other color) caboose. An appropriate source of information is the American Railway Caboose Historical Education Society, Inc. (P.O. Box 2772, St. Louis, MO 63116).

Just as there is a national organization that focuses on the caboose, a similar one exists to honor and enjoy the lowly track inspection vehicle or motor car. This type of equipment dates from the nineteenth century, although more modern ones use gasoline engines rather than muscle power. In the early 1990s hundreds of enthusiasts created the North American Railcar Operators Association (NARCOA). The group has a far flung membership that is extremely knowledgeable about motorcars, sometimes called "speeders," and their manufactures, most of all Faribault Motor Car Company, the largest maker of this motorized maintanence-of-way equipment. NARCOA maintains an informative web site: www.narcoa.org and publishes a newsletter.

Much more can be learned about rolling stock by checking old equipment registers. Just as the *Official Railway Guide* offers timetables for virtually every railroad in North America, a parallel volume for rolling stock is the *Official Railway Equipment Register*. What this reference work provides is a compendium of all equipment, including freight and passenger, that common carriers possessed. If an "ancient" livestock car were to be discovered, a careful examination, perhaps in a palimpsestic fashion, may reveal its owner and number (railroads universally placed both on their rolling stock). With this information, it is relatively easy to ascertain more about this car. Let's say that the road is the Wabash and the number is 16981. By examining old copies of the *Equipment Register* it is possible to learn that the road name and number correctly match and that the car was thirty feet in length and held a capacity of 40,000 pounds. Number 16981 was one of 468 livestock cars that the Wabash owned in the early 1890s.

With passage of the Valuation Act of 1913 the federal government demanded that railroads keep copious records on money spent for rolling stock. The specific bureaucratic form was known as the "Authority for Expenditures" or "AFE's." Clerks noted, for example, when a locomotive was purchased, its cost and other vital statistics. Similarly, when the locomotive was scrapped or sold, that information was duly recorded. This data, together with a host of other materials that related to a variety of financial matters, including track construction, signals and bridges, trestles and culverts, was reported annually on "Form 588" and sent to the Interstate Commerce Commission in Washington, D.C., records that make up the papers of the ICC, now administered by the National Archives. Some railroads' runs of AFEs have been saved by either railfan-related groups or by libraries and historical societies. For instance, the extensive AFE records for The Milwaukee Road are in the possession of the Barriger Library in St. Louis.

Although not providing specific information about an individual piece of railway rolling stock, *The Car and Locomotive Cyclopedia*, which for decades the Association of American Railroads compiled and edited, provides detailed data and specifications about various car types and their components. This huge tome, which first appeared in 1879 as the *Car Builders' Directory*, and later absorbed the *Locomotive Directory*, which initially appeared in 1906, is a bible for railway preservationists.

A variety of trade-oriented periodicals may also be profitably consulted. The principal ones are the *American Journal of Railway Appliances* (1883–1901); *National Car Builder* (1870–1895); and *Railroad Car Journal* (1890–1902). And, of course, nonspecialized trade organs, especially

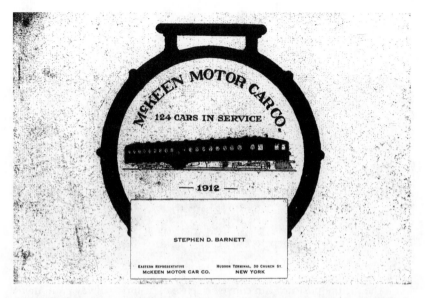

4.10 Equipment manufacturers produced a plethora of catalogs. In 1912 the McKeen Motor Car Company of Omaha, Nebraska, issued an illustrated seventy-four page brochure, describing its gasoline-electric cars and providing a listing of railroads, mostly shortlines, that operated them.

Railway Age, are of value. Originally *Railway Age* devoted limited space to rolling stock until about 1890 when the subject became covered extensively. Two encyclopedic secondary works on the overall subject should also be checked. Both are by John H. White, Jr., former curator of transportation at the Smithsonian Institution: *The American Railroad Passenger Car* (Baltimore: Johns Hopkins University Press, 1985) and *The American Railroad Freight Car: From the Wood-Car Era to the Coming of Steel* (Baltimore: Johns Hopkins University Press, 1993). And White's specialized book, *The Great Yellow Fleet: A History of American Railroad Refrigerator Cars* (San Marino, CA: Golden West Books, 1986), offers encyclopedic information on this type of rolling stock.

There are collections of car builders' records. For example, the Newberry Library, 60 West Walton Street, Chicago, IL 60610, holds records of the Pullman Company, a major producer of sleeping cars, freight equipment and other pieces of railway rolling stock, and the Barriger Library in St. Louis has the ACF Industries Archival Collection. The lat-

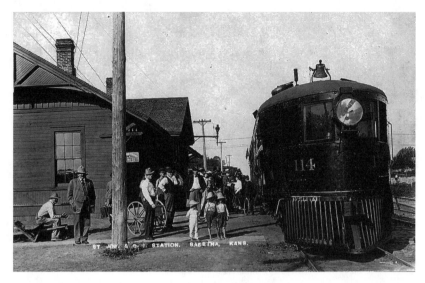

4.11   The picture postcard can convey a sense of historic railway equipment. About 1910 McKeen Motor Car No. 114 of the St. Joseph & Grand Island Railroad is captured at the Sabetha, Kansas, station. By examining the adults and children at track side, it is possible to estimate the car's size.

ter consists of records from the corporate archive of the American Car & Foundry Company as well as thousands of interior and exterior photographs of ACF-built equipment.

Restoration of a piece of rolling stock requires the services of experts. As mentioned, ARM is an organization that can serve as a clearing house for vital information on the task at hand. Since there is a railroad museum in virtually every state and Canadian province, sometimes several, one should be contacted. A tool for locating such an organization is the *Guide to Tourist Railroads and Museums, 36th ed.* (Waukesha, WI: Kalmbach, 2001). A literature also exists. On the subject of color and paint there are such titles as *Pullman Paint and Lettering Notebook: A Guide to Colors Used on Pullman Cars from 1933 to 1969*, by Arthur D. Dubin (Waukesha, WI: Kalmbach, 1997) and *Pennsylvania Railroad Car Painting and Lettering* by Charles Blardone, Jr. and Peter Tilp (The Pennsylvania Railroad Technical & Historical Society, 1988). The Dubin book even provides examples of popular color samples, including Lackawanna gray, North Western yellow, Rio Grande orange and Pullman green.

ARTIFACTS

As America's first big business, railroads for more than a century and a half have generated a staggering array of objects, everything from locomotive bells to switch locks and keys to lanterns of an amazing variety. Since companies frequently stamped their initials on these three-dimensional items, identifying the original owner is often a simple task. A brass switch key marked "NYC" undoubtedly belonged to the New York Central. But one with the markings of "NYP&O RR" is somewhat more challenging. Several reference works, however, usually provide the correct answer. *Railroad Names*, compiled by William D. Edson, lists only one possibility, the New York, Pennsylvania & Ohio, which operated between 1878 and 1895 as the intermediary company between the Erie Railway and the Erie Railroad, a carrier that periodically went bankrupt and changed its corporate name. Another source is *Railroads of North America: A Complete History of All North American Railroads, 1827 to 1986*. More difficult initials exist, however. Does "B&MR" refer to Boston & Maine or Burlington & Missouri River? Does "MC" stand for Maine Central or Michigan Central? Does "IC" mean Illinois Central or Iowa Central? This is where the "hardware" collector should be consulted for the correct identification of the marking.

Usually understanding an artifact demands more than simply knowing about its original railroad owner. If the manufacturer is desired, an examination of the piece may quickly yield the information. A kerosene-burning hand lantern nearly always had the maker's name stamped on the top, whether "Adlake" or "Adlake Reliable" (The Adams & Westlake Company), "Amspear" (Amspear Manufacturing Company), "Dietz" or "Dietz Vesta" (Dietz Company), "Dressel" (Dressel Railway Lamp Works), "Handlan" (Handlan-Buck Manufacturing Company), or "Star," (Star Head Light and Lantern Company). Some railroad reference libraries own collections of manufacturers' catalogs. By examining them it is possible to determine nearly the exact date of production, original cost and other details of manufacturing. Dating, however, can often be approximated by looking for the patent dates placed on the top of the lantern. For example, one Pennsylvania Railroad hand lantern contains the following information: "PATENTED SEPT. 21, 1897–MAY 5, 1908-2 PATS. Jan. 26, 1909–NOV. 28, 1911. 2 PATS. JULY 2, 1912–APR l, 1913." In all likelihood this Pennsylvania lantern dates from the time period shortly after 1913. Just by quickly "eye-balling" a railroad lantern, the *general* time period can be estimated: a "fixed globe" lantern likely dates from the 1840s to the immediate post-Civil War years; a large, removable globe lantern (5 ³⁄₈" to 6") belongs in the period from the 1870s to the 1920s and the somewhat smaller ones, or "short globe" style (3 ¼") are of more recent vintage. In fact, these latter lanterns were manufactured until the late 1960s. For overviews of the lantern, see *The Railroad Lantern, 1865 to 1930* by William A. Cunningham (Hiram, OH: Hiram Press, 1998), and *The Illustrated Encyclopedia of American Lighting*, Vol. 1, *The Railroad Lantern* by Richard C. Barrett (Rochester, NY: Railroad Research Publications, n.d.).

Since World War II collecting railroad artifacts has been a popular hobby. An indication of its present-day appeal is found in the hundreds of daily listings on e-Bay, the Internet auction house. Moreover, a variety of books and booklets have been published that focus on the collecting of "railroadiana," whether the overall variety of items or on something as specific as dining car china. Understandably, collector groups have emerged, the two principal ones being Key, Lock & Lantern, Inc.: An Organization for Railroadiana Collections, and Railroadiana Collectors Association, Inc. The former publishes a quarterly magazine, *Key, Lock & Lantern* (www.keylocklantern@aol.com), and the latter produces the quarterly, *The Railroadiana Express* (www:railroadcollectors.org). Many members have expertise in identifying and valuing the rich range of railroad artifacts.

IMAGES

For those individuals who seek photographic images of railroad rolling stock, structures along the railroad corridor or other railroad subjects, their quest should be successful. One scholar of American railfans concluded that virtually all enthusiasts share two things in common beyond their fascination for trains; namely, they buy books about railroading and they take and/or collect pictures of their favorite railroad subjects, whether locomotives, depots or the railway landscape. Since millions of railroad photographs exist, dating from the inception of the camera, it is difficult to pinpoint their specific locations. Yet, nearly without exception, *every* general railroad collection contains some images. Companies themselves employed photographers to record the construction of their lines, especially in the West, for purposes such as public relations. Not surprisingly the Union Pacific Railroad at its museum in Omaha, Nebraska (soon-to-be-relocated to the former Carnegie Library in Council Bluffs, Iowa), maintains an extensive collection of modern and historic images, including ones that depict construction of the transcontinental railroad in the 1860s and its rebuilding in the late 1890s and early 1900s. The single-road historical society usually has a collection, commonly placed in a library, museum or member's home. For example, the photographic holdings of the Gulf, Mobile & Ohio Historical Society are housed in the Barriger Library. These societies can also surely provide leads on how to find and identify a desired image.

Similar commentaries can be made about general railroad groups. The National Railway Historical Society, for one, maintains an extensive photographic library at its headquarters (110 North 17th Street, Philadelphia, PA 19103, www.nrhs.com). In addition to negatives, prints and slides, holdings include company-produced films, often prepared for corporate promotions, centennials and other special events, and movies taken by enthusiasts. Some railroad societies and enthusiast groups have banded together to preserve and make available to the public their largely photographic holdings. Recently, for example, several in Ohio formed the Northern Ohio Association of Railway Societies, and this body works with Special Collections at the Cleveland State University Library 44115 in collecting, cataloging and maintaining photographic materials.

Some depositories have produced descriptive photographic guides. The Smithsonian Institution in Washington, D.C., has published a representative one, a two-volume catalog of the Charles B. Chaney Photography Collection, housed in the Division of Transportation at the National Museum of American History. The Chaney holdings, which were donated in the late 1940s to the Smithsonian, contain approximately 20,000 postcard-size negatives and have particular depth on carriers in the East.

Excellent opportunities exist for locating desired images on the Internet. One good site is www.donross.railspot.com. "Railspot: Don's Rail Photos" has been developed by an enthusiast who began his photographic collecting in 1946. Like many others, this individual provides a print-making service for photographs shown on the site. These images, which have been scanned from the originals, are arranged by railroad name, a common organizational technique.

The value of the picture postcard should not be underestimated. The popularity of this nationwide phenomenon soared during the first two decades of the twentieth century and coincided with the golden age of rail transport. Tens of thousands of images of nearly every conceivable aspect of railroading appeared on these 3 ¼ x 5 ½-inch size pieces of stiff paper. These cards are seemingly ubiquitous with the largest single collection located at the Lake County Museum, Lakewood Forest Preserve, in Wauconda, IL 60084. Here is found the Curt Teich Postcard Archive. Between 1898 and 1974 the Curt Teich Company operated in Chicago as a printer of postcards, advertising pamphlets and brochures, maps, blotters and sundry other printed items.

Commercially distributed videotapes are still another source of visuals. The pages of popular railfan magazines, especially *Trains* and *Classic Trains*, contain advertisements for these popular items. Although many are of contemporary railroad scenes, historic ones are also being marketed. Most of the extant "centennial" railroad films, movies that usually date from the late 1940s and early 1950s, have been reproduced. Similarly, post-World War II promotional films, typically twenty-five to thirty minutes in length, are available. Hopewell Productions (1714 Boardman-Poland Road, Poland, OH 44514), for example, reproduced the 1952 "The Nickel Plate Story" and the 1953 "Once Upon the Wabash," in Volume 3 of its "Collector's Series." Single-line historical societies, too, collect and often sell such videos.

A tangible indicator of continuing interest in the imagery of railroads has been the creation of the Center for Railroad Photography and Art, based in Madison, Wisconsin (P.O. Box 259330, Madison, WI 53725-9330, www.railphoto-art.org). This nonprofit organization, launched in 1997, publishes a quarterly magazine, *Railroad Heritage*, which focuses on historic railroad photography, and maintains an archive at the Donnelley Library at Lake Forest College in Lake Forest, Illinois 60045.

ACCIDENTS

Accidents and wrecks, with their accompanying inquiries and deaths, have always been part of American railroading, a gruesome dimension of the nearby history story. Yet few major wrecks occurred during the first several decades of rail operations. Slow speeds and light traffic accounted for this good record. By the time of the Civil War, however, faster and more frequent train movements reduced the margin of safety considerably. Although important technological improvements—steel rails, wheels and axles, airbrakes, automatic couplers, block signals, steam heating and electric lighting—gradually made travel by rail speedier, more comfortable and theoretically safer, the number and severity of accidents actually increased. Even with the best equipment, mechanical problems occurred. Boiler explosions continued to take place as did other accidents caused by defective bridges, tracks, brakes, signals and

4.12 Although this picture postcard lacks identification (it was also never mailed), it is possible to guess at the location and date of this nasty head-on collision. The station sign shows "Tyrone," and a check of the *Official Railway Guides* indicates that the place is probably Tyrone, Iowa, a hamlet on the main line of the Chicago, Burlington & Quincy Railroad in Monroe County. Then by checking wrecks investigated by the state or national regulators the date and other data will be revealed. If these documents cannot be found, a review of any nearby local newspaper may tell the story.

the like. Nor could human error be overcome; this factor proved to be the *principal* cause of fatalities.

In a community there may be evidence or memories of a historic railway accident, even a disaster. There may be a series of commercial photographs or a picture postcard that shows a wreck scene with a few words of identification. Individuals or an organization, usually a local museum, may possess "souvenirs" picked up at the accident site: a crumpled piece of metal, chards of melted or broken window glass (perhaps stained glass from a dining or sleeping car) or in rare cases fragments of human bones from bodies of victims. Occasionally, the site itself is marked in some fashion. How then does one discover more about such tragic railway occurrences?

There are several ways to learn details of a railway accident. If ever a story grabbed headlines in contemporary newspapers, this was such an event. The public eagerly sought to read every detail. If the approximate date is known, local newspapers should be consulted. If the accident resulted in major injuries and loss of life, the regional and even the national press likely provided coverage. Another source is trade journals. Beginning about 1880 these speciality publications regularly analyzed major disasters or accidents. Court records offer another opportunity. A large number of mishaps led to jury trials, the records of which have been saved by the appropriate courts. With the advent of regulatory bodies, including the Interstate Commerce Commission (1887), these public agencies frequently provided exhaustive reports of major accidents. Starting in the immediate post-Civil War period the legislatures of certain states, notably Illinois, Massachusetts and New York, charged their state railroad commissions with the responsibility of providing full reports of each serious railroad accident. In most instances these investigations were comprehensive and more valuable than the early ones conducted by the ICC. Then beginning in 1902 the ICC published *Accident Bulletin No. 1*, which covered accidents in the last quarter of 1901, and since then it (or its recently designated successor) has produced reports on all important mishaps. The general subject of railroad wrecks is covered in *Notes on Railroad Accidents* by Charles Francis Adams, Jr. (New York: G. P. Putnam's Sons, 1879), and even more extensively in *A History of Railroad Accidents, Safety Practices* by Robert B. Shaw (Potsdam, NY: Privately Printed, 1978).

ADDITIONAL POINTERS

If locating a railway accident site is the goal, maps usually provide a valuable resource as they do with all community-history transportation research undertakings. Maps abound. Frequently railroads, even small ones, provided "system" maps in their public timetables, similar to the ones in most railroad entries in the *Official Railway Guide*. Less common are maps, including divisional ones, found in operating or "employee" timetables. (These schedules themselves may be indispensable in determining exact locations for accidents or other places or events, since accident reports and related data usually refer to milepost numbers. Distances from a terminal or division point are always listed in operating timetables.) Larger carriers commonly printed separate map folders, often accompanying promotional materials. Although such timetable and promotion items are readily available, albeit widely

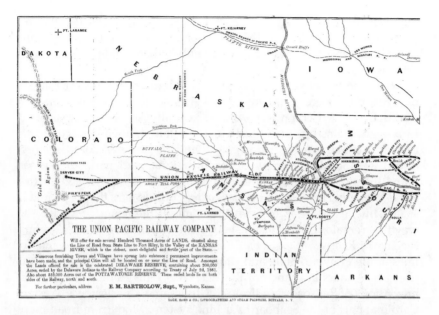

4.13   Railroad maps come in an array of types and sizes. This one from the early 1870s shows the main line of the Union Pacific, Eastern Division Railway (Kansas Pacific). It is contained in a folder, "Union Pacific Railway, Eastern Division, New Route by Steamer and Railway, to Lawrence and all Central, Southern and Western Kansas."

scattered, outstanding holdings are the Charles Rupp Railroad Time-table Collection found at the Barriger Railroad Library and the collections of the Railway & Locomotive Historical Society (strong on Eastern and nineteenth-century roads) and the California State Railroad Museum (depth on Western and twentieth-century carriers) both housed at the Museum, 111 "I" Street, Sacramento, CA 95814. In some railroad annual reports companies included detailed maps, especially during the period of new line construction. Indeed, the earliest annual reports for the Baltimore & Ohio Railroad focused on the building of this Baltimore-based road. Maps and detailed written descriptions of surveys for routes, including alternate ones, were provided, even though it might take years before the B&O actually built in these places. Topographical maps should not be overlooked and can be obtained for nearly every part of the country either from the U.S. Geological Survey or state geological survey offices. Operational, out-of-service and abandoned lines are usually marked. Moreover, county atlases feature a plat or map of each township or district (the latter the political unit prevalent in the South of the nineteenth century) and show locations of railroads as well as public roads and other transport arteries.

When the objective is to use a map to identify a particular railroad or piece of trackage, there are a number of choices. Some carriers produced their own commercial atlases, usually showing maps for all forty-eight states but may offer greater detail for their service territories. Map-making firms, principally Rand McNally & Company, produced an abundant variety of state, regional and national railroad maps. Indeed, Kalmbach Publishing Company has reproduced the first Rand McNally *Handy Railroad Maps of the United States* that appeared in 1928. Thus, if you seek to learn the name of the abandoned right-of-way that remains clearly visible between Iva and Starr, South Carolina, the *Handy Railroad Maps of the United States* reprint contains a map of lines in the Palmetto State and shows this piece of trackage as the McCormick-Anderson branch of the "C&WC." The guide's "Key to Abbreviations of Railroads" indicates the full name: Charleston & Western Carolina, part of the Seaboard Air Line system. Modern railroad maps are also available, including ones produced by the U.S. Department of Transportation.

Actual railroad locations within or near a community may require more specialized maps. Those produced by the Sanborn Map and Publishing Company of New York City help to locate specific railroad structures, as well as urban and industrial trackage, including complicated layouts common to manufacturing and mining operations. Railroads themselves produced their own versions of Sanborn maps, what they call "track charts," showing every piece of trackage by terminals or operating divisions. Railroad historical groups, museums and related bodies have gathered extensive collections of these maps, rightly sensing their overall historic value. Often they are physically bulky, with some individual maps measuring four to six feet in length. A related map type covers a particular station. In June 1919, for example, the Office of the Chief Engineer for the Wabash Railway in St. Louis, Missouri, produced the "Station Map, Lands, Tracks and Structures" for its facility at Peru, Indiana. This document reviews *every* aspect of the physical presence of the Wabash in this Hoosier State community.

There are two other kinds of specialized maps that might provide beneficial information. One is the "profile" map that railroads have long produced to show grades along a line, allowing train crews to know what to expect. If one wishes to learn more about the "big hill" outside of town, the profile chart pinpoints location and tells percentage of grade. Railroads and bond firms also created on an annual basis "traffic density" maps that reveal the volume of freight business (tonnage miles) on a particular piece of trackage. The amount of revenue service through a community can be understood, likely showing a major drop during the Great Depression of the 1930s or perhaps shortly before an abandonment. Those interested in the rails-to-trails movement, which over the past fifteen years has converted more than 10,000 miles of abandoned railroad rights-of-way into bicycle and hiking trails, may find both map types particularly useful.

Even with the best maps, field work may become necessary. As indicated, local residents might possess the knowledge to answer questions. Long-time property owners, for one, may recall the precise location of an abandoned rail line, perhaps partially obliterated by a public road, plowed field or housing development. Although not applicable to every situation, the right weather and natural conditions may reveal extant sections of a forgotten right-of-way. With a light dusting of snow on the ground and favorable lighting, grades, depressions and other artificial features become readily visible. These factors of nature resemble the precise angle of the sun illuminating words on a cornerstone, gravestone or some other hard-to-read marking.

Today's railroad environment continues to be modified, whether through line abandonments, track relocations or replacement of structures. But individuals interested in railroads and communities, including enthusiasts and preservationists, are sensitive to change. The rate of photography, for example, is arguably at an all-time high, providing data for future efforts to learn about this vital, albeit shrinking dimension of nearby history.

ॐ ॐ ॐ ॐ ॐ

ROAD-MASTERS

377. Road-masters will report to and receive their instructions from the Division Superintendent. They will have supervision of the track and right of way.

378. They must go over their division frequently and carefully examine the condition of the road-bed, ballast, ties, tracks, culverts, bridges, trestle work, tunnels, and other structures, and see that they are kept in good repair; that ditches are properly maintained, switches are kept clean and work easily, semaphores and other fixed signals are in good condition, and that track and bridge watchmen are attentive to their duties.

379. They must inspect all ties, rails, and other material intended for

BEAUTIFUL
SUBURBAN
TOWNS

Within
easy
reach
of Chicago
by means of
the fast suburban
train service
of

THE NORTH-WESTERN LINE

1904

4.14 As the nation's first big business, the railroad industry generated count-less publications. In 1904 the civic- and profit-minded Chicago & North West-ern Railway issued a descriptive folder on "Beautiful Suburban Towns" along its three principal lines radiating out of Chicago, which contains a wealth of in-formation about the interrelationship between railroad and community.

use on their division; see that ties are of the standard size and quality, and that all materials are received and are as represented and suitable for the purposes required, and must see that proper use is made of material and supplies furnished them.

380. They must see that the track foremen thoroughly understand and are faithful in the performance of their duties, and must hold them strictly accountable for the manner in which work is done on their sections; that the time of the men and rate of pay is truly made and correctly stated, and must give them such instruction and assistance in the discharge of their duties as they may request, or the nature of the case may require.

381. In case of accident, or other detention of trains, they must promptly go to the point of detention and provide facilities for movement.

The above commentary about the work duties of a roadmaster appeared in *Rules and Regulations for the Government of Employes of the Operating Department* (Chicago, IL: Chicago & North Western Railway, 1893), p. 92

ॐ ॐ ॐ ॐ ॐ

Chapter 5

ELECTRIC INTERURBANS

During the waning years of the nineteenth century a newly perfected form of intercity travel garnered widespread attention. The debut of the electric-powered interurban railway signaled a transportation advance that many believed would yield enormous benefits. At the time one optimist considered its potential to be "as great as that rendered by its steam-operated precursor." Although the roughly thirty-year craze for constructing interurbans did not affect every American community, the impact was considerable.

Prospective patrons and backers liked what they had read about interurbans or perhaps had even seen. Their enthusiasm is understandable. If a community or area lacked adequate steam railroad service, an electric or "juice" road could solve the problem. An electric line would provide farmers, villagers and others convenient access to the opportunities offered by urban centers. And merchants, bankers and other business and professional people could profitably tap a larger trading region. Other factors contributed to the immense popularity of electric intercity railroads. When in operation these carriers scheduled frequent passenger service; cars often ran hourly during most of the day. Steam roads, on the other hand, typically dispatched fewer trains daily and they might arrive and depart at inconvenient hours. Moreover, interurbans, unless operated on a "limited" fashion, stopped at farmsteads, road crossings or virtually anywhere. Electric cars were sleek and clean, producing "no cinders, no dirt, no dust, no smoke," a common annoyance for riders of soft-coal-burning steam-powered trains. Interurban cars were also potentially fast. If track conditions warranted, they could accelerate within a few minutes to fifty or more miles per hour. Furthermore, companies provided express and package service. At times these items were transported in the "baggage" compartment behind the motorman's seat or in a freight-only self-propelled "box motor," in reality an electric boxcar. Some carriers handled carload freight, usually a short string of boxcars pulled by a box motor

PUBLIC MEETING!

A Meeting will be held at AMMON'S HALL in

GEORGETOWN
THURSDAY,
JULY 21, 1910
(AT 8 O'CLOCK P. M.)

For the purpose of discussing the practicability of building an

ELECTRIC ROAD
With Terminals at
UNION AND VERSAILLES

Connecting Phillipsburg, Georgetown, and other intervening Towns. All persons interested in the proposed improvement are requested to be present.

COMMITTEE

5.1 If a piece of local paper ephemera about an interurban is discovered, information that it contains can help in learning more about this form of transport. This broadside about a proposed electric interurban between Union and Versailles, Ohio, gives an important date, one that can be checked in area newspapers. However, this project, which involved construction of approximately 30 miles of line, never developed beyond the talking stage.

or an electric locomotive. These pieces of rolling stock might be inter-
changed with steam roads, depending upon the electric road's physical plant and the willingness of the steam roads to accept such
business. The public, too, welcomed the usually cheaper charges for
passenger, express and freight services.

Starting in 1889 with a seven-mile trolley line between the Ohio
communities of Newark and Granville, electric interurbans had grown
a decade later to a nationwide total of more than 1,500 miles. By 1905
mileage stood at 7,940 and in 1916 peaked at 15,580 miles. Although
Illinois, Indiana, Michigan and Ohio were centers of interurban construction, lines could be found connecting such remote locations as
Busbee and Warren, Arizona; Monarch and Sheridan, Wyoming; and
Parsons, Kansas, and Nowata, Oklahoma. Companies could install
lines with considerable speed. Most were lightly and economically
built. In many places, for example, interurbans took advantage of existing rights-of-way, such as in streets, alongside dirt roads and over
public bridges. By 1910 interurbans had become so ubiquitous that it
was possible to use them for extensive journeys. A few adventuresome
souls even traveled between the Northeast and Chicago, Milwaukee
and St. Louis.

Ohio's impressive network, for example, "jelled" early in the twentieth century. On December 31 1905, a much-publicized "golden
spike" ceremony occurred in Findlay. On that winter day, scores of well-
wishers—traction-company executives, business leaders, politicians,
journalists and the curious—celebrated the official joining of the Western Ohio Railway with the Toledo, Bowling Green & Southern Traction Company. The former tied Findlay with Lima and made direct
connections to Dayton, Cincinnati and Indianapolis, while the latter
linked Findlay with Toledo and ties to Detroit, Cleveland and Buffalo.

During the brief "interurban era" promoters envisioned hundreds
of plans for additional service, including "missing links" between existing lines. A good illustration is Texas. Although the state never
emerged as the leading interurban center, it ultimately claimed nearly
500 miles of electric lines, the greatest mileage in any state west of the
Mississippi River except California. The Dallas-based Texas Electric
Railway, with its 226 route miles, became the largest system in the
western half of the country. Yet the story of the interurban in the Lone
Star state involves more than a chronicle of the eleven companies that
actually opened: between the 1890s and 1920s scores of additional
firms were proposed. Even though statistical evidence is sketchy, projected traction mileage in Texas ranks at or near the top of any listing
of unbuilt proposals for a single state. The total reached an astonishing

22,500 miles! For example, a proposal emerged to tie the Texas Electric network to lines that served Houston and the Gulf Coast.

With 20/20 historical hindsight, it was probably well that dreams of more interurbans remained unfulfilled. After World War I trouble arose. Increased popularity of trucks, buses and most of all private automobiles together with the prolonged depression that followed the Crash of 1929 led to the collapse, first of the weakest roads and then most of the surviving ones. Carriers that developed substantial less-than-carload (LCL) and carload interchange freight business generally weathered competition and hard times. Mileage dropped from 15,337 in 1920 to 10,422 in 1930 and plummeted to 3,197 in 1940. And by 1960 less than 200 miles remained.

Physically, not much exists of America's once-vigorous interurban industry. Several roads continue to function, nearly always as diesel-powered shortlines, and some additional trackage serves as appendages of larger nonelectric systems. Also, scattered portions of abandoned rights-of-way remain visible as do occasional bridge abutments and partially buried rails in city streets. Some rights-of-way can be identified because an electric power company uses the abandoned interurban route for its pole lines. A few former roads have become hiking, biking or nature trails; most roadbeds that survive, though, are choked with weeds and brush. And some old interurban buildings stand. From time-to-time a knowledgeable observer can spot a former interurban depot or shelter or electrical substation. As with canals, however, the *historical* record for interurbans is usually much more substantial.

COMPANY HISTORIES

A logical first step in exploring a local interurban company is to learn about its corporate identity. Since the industry has virtually disappeared—only the Chicago, South Shore & South Bend survives as a bonafide interurban (passenger service is presently operated by the Northern Indiana Commuter Transportation District)—traditional historical techniques must be employed to trace a particular road. These include both secondary and primary sources.

An excellent place to start is the encyclopedic study of the interurban industry, *The Electric Interurban Railways in America* by George W. Hilton and John F. Due (Stanford, CA: Stanford University Press, 1960). Four years after this bible for interurban students appeared, the authors made minor revisions and in 1999 Stanford University Press released an inexpensive paperback of the revised edition. In addition to examining the electric railway phenomenon, Hilton and Due present an extensive section on "The Individual Interurbans." Organized by geographical regions (with coverage of Canada's interurbans), the book provides thumbnail sketches of about 900 companies. Each entry contains a construction history, years of operations, names of predecessor and/or successor firms, and pertinent remarks about the road's overall operations. Here is how Hilton and Due treat the Willamette Valley Southern Railway in Oregon:

> The Portland Electric Power system had one subsidiary road, the Willamette Valley Southern, which extended southeastward from a connection with PEPCO at Oregon City through Robbins, Mulino, and Mollala to Mount Angel (32 miles). This line was well to the east of the Oregon Electric and Southern Pacific main lines, especially at Mollala; the line swung back westward south of it. Mollala and Mount Angel were served by SP branches, but the rest of the towns on the line had no other rail service. The country, however, was a thinly settled lumber and farming area, and none of the towns served (except Oregon City) had a population of more than 1,000. The line was completed and placed in service in 1915, designed more to handle freight (forest products) than passengers, although typical interurban cars were operated, the three daily runs connecting with PEPCO trains at Oregon City. The road made a small operating profit in its earlier years, although the revenue per mile never exceeded $4,000; its freight business, however, was hit very hard by the depression (which shut down lumber mills), and by 1935 gross revenue was less than one fifth of the 1929 figure. The weakest section, from south of Kayler (near Mollala) to Mount Angel (11 miles), had been abandoned in 1926. The passenger service on the remainder of the line was discontinued on April 9, 1933. The freight revenue continued to decline, and finally, in 1938, virtually all revenue vanished when the last of the logging camps serviced by the line closed down. Consequently, the line was abandoned on September 30; it had incurred operating losses in 7 of the last 8 years.

If a weakness exists in the Hilton and Due tome, it involves limited coverage of Massachusetts. The Bay State had the densest network of intercity electric railways, relative to size and population. But a researcher interested in the state's plethora of carriers, ranging from the Grafton & Upton Railroad to the Worcester Consolidated Street Railway, should consult *The Street Railway in Massachusetts* by Edward S. Mason (Cambridge, MA: Harvard University Press, 1932).

The Intercity Railway Industry in Canada by James F. Due (Toronto: University of Toronto Press, 1966), is a companion reference to *The Electric Interurban Railways in America* and *The Street Railway in Massachusetts*. Due expands coverage of materials originally presented in his earlier co-authored volume with George W. Hilton, giving a detailed examination of the more than a score of interurban roads that once operated north of the U.S.-Canadian border. Coverage of individual carriers is extensive, offering more than thumbnail sketches. Superb maps complement the text.

An equally logical beginning point is to consult directories of interurban companies. The best known (reprinted and readily available) is the *McGraw Electric Railway List*, published annually by McGraw-Hill from shortly after the turn of the twentieth century until the early 1920s. Organized by American state and Canadian province, each entry notes the official company name; lists principal communities served; indicates officials and their addresses; describes the power system; and reveals locations of generating stations and repair shops. Mileage and quantity and type of rolling stock are also included. Significantly the *List* contains data for street railways, most of which by 1900 were electric powered.

McGraw-Hill also produced another valuable resource for the researcher of an interurban, the *Electric Railway Journal* (1908–1927). This publication served as the industry's leading trade organ and succeeded the *Street Railway Journal* (1890–1907). These monthly issues give detailed information on specific companies and commonly feature a carrier's history, especially in light of an opening, merger or some other newsworthy event. Both journals printed annual lists of companies by states, and for years noted in special columns interurbans that were planned and those that were being built (many, of course, never opened). Thus "paper" or "hot-air" projects can be traced. Both publications include semiannual indexes, a useful finding aid for such a massive reference source. Generally, the *McGraw Electric Railway Guide* and trade-press publications are vastly superior to either *Moody's Manual* (1901–1924) or *Poor's Manual of Public Utilities* (1913–1938) or their successor publications for identifying and describing individual firms.

Moreover, county histories, and in some cases city ones, can be consulted profitably. These works, especially those published during the first two decades of the twentieth century, inevitably contain accounts of area interurbans, just as they nearly always review canals and steam railroads. Fortunately, there is a guide to the coverage of interurbans by local histories: *Street, Interurban and Rapid Transit Railways of the United States: A Selective Historical Bibliography*, compiled by Thomas R. Bullard. Published privately in Oak Park, Illinois, in 1984, but available in some libraries and through interlibrary loan, this comprehensive and carefully researched volume indexes local histories and the trade press, state and national historical journals and railroad enthusiast and scholarly publications. Organized by state, this guide lists both communities and companies.

Another source of materials on individual interurban companies is the rich variety of monographic publications. The best known are the works of the Central Electric Railfans' Association (CERA). This Chicago-based group, formed in 1938, has produced numerous tomes on individual Midwestern interurbans. An outstanding feature of most CERA books is inclusion of a set of detailed trackage maps, either as an insert or as part of the appendix. Routes through major communities are pinpointed as are stations, carbarns and other interurban-related properties, including amusement parks, dance halls and cemeteries. Two representative examples are *Iowa Trolleys* (1975) and *Fort Wayne and Wabash Valley Trolleys* (1983). Another important series, a remarkable enterprise called Interurban Press, located in Los Angeles, California, began in 1943. Ultimately this fan-driven enterprise produced scores of illustrated monographs, including numerous ones on the Pacific Electric, America's largest interurban. While not every juice road has been subject of a book or even a pamphlet-length study, virtually all important ones have been covered.

Just as CERA and Interurban Press books are geared toward traction enthusiasts, several commercial railfan-oriented film companies, most notably Pentrex of Pasadena, California, sell videos of historic interurbans. It is possible to acquire movies made by both amateur and professional photographers of such diverse electric roads as the Cedar Rapids & Iowa City (CRANDIC); Chicago, North Shore & Milwaukee; Illinois Terminal; Indiana Railroad and Piedmont & Northern. Pentrex and other firms advertise widely in enthusiast publications, including regular advertisements in *Trains* and *Classic Trains*.

Histories of individual interurbans can be pieced together in other ways. In scattered cases the corporate archive of a company exists. The Ohio Historical Society in Columbus, for instance, possesses records from several firms, including the Dayton, Covington & Piqua Traction Company (1902–1928) and the Scioto Valley Traction Company (1899–1930). One can expect to find in such collections financial records, stock certificates, minute books, annual reports and general correspondence.

Contemporary local newspapers, especially those published during the promotion and construction periods, are frequently rich with detail. Since interurbans were subject to public regulation, annual reports and occasional special investigations made by authorities, including the Interstate Commerce Commission, are potentially helpful. Similarly, there are other primary sources of value, particularly for economic and statistical data. *The Special Reports: Street and Electric Railways*, produced in 1902 and 1907 by the U.S. Bureau of the Census, are standard references.

Other possibilities for pertinent information exist. Interurban companies issued a variety of publications. These include both operating (for employees) and public timetables. Most of the larger concerns distributed promotional folders and booklets, occasionally with panoramic maps, especially during their halcyon years. At times companies produced magazines and newsletters. Museums and libraries of all types may own this paper ephemera, as do private collectors, some of whom belong to the National Association of Timetable Collectors (P.O. Box 217, Bethpage, NY 11714-0217). Arguably, the leading depository for these general traction items is the Midwest Railroad Research Center, part of the William Henry Smith Memorial Library, at the Indiana Historical Society, 450 West Ohio Street in Indianapolis, Indiana 46202.

Historical societies, both state and local, museums and enthusiasts are potential sources of photographic evidence. Pictures of interurbans (rolling stock, structures and the like) abound, whether commercial portraits, "real-photo" postal cards, or simple "Kodak" snap shots. Several nationally recognized traction fans have carefully organized their images, planning to present them to public institutions, including the Indiana Historical Society, after their deaths.

STATIONS AND BUILDINGS

Physical remains of electric interurbans are much less common than those of their steam-road counterparts. There were fewer interurbans and most closed six or seven decades ago. Since juice lines frequently paralleled intercity public roads, either on their edge or on adjoining rights-of-way, vestiges of interurbans, including depots and electric substations, disappeared when governmental authorities widened these roadways or commercial roadside development occurred.

Still, some structures remain. Former interurban depots, however, might be more difficult to identify than those used by steam roads. Companies relied heavily on *existing* buildings, most often commercial

AURORA, ELGIN & FOX RIVER ELECTRIC CO.

PUBLIC TIME TABLE—EFFECTIVE NOVEMBER 17, 1929

SUBJECT TO CHANGE WITHOUT NOTICE

Daily Schedule—Aurora and Elgin Line

J. W. GUNDERSON, General Manager

W. H. EISSLER, Div. Supt. Aurora, Ill.

E. S. ACKERMAN, Div. Supt. Elgin, Ill.

ELGIN - CARPENTERSVILLE DAILY SCHEDULE—Effective November 17th, 1929

Subject to Change Without Notice

DAILY BUS SCHEDULE—BET. AURORA-ST. CHARLES

AURORA CITY LINES

ELGIN CITY LINES

5.2 A public timetable from an interurban company can be revealing. This schedule of the Aurora, Elgin & Fox River Electric Company, which dates from near the end of its corporate life, provides exact information about where this "juice" road operated. Since the firm ran the local streetcar lines in Aurora and Elgin, similar data is supplied.

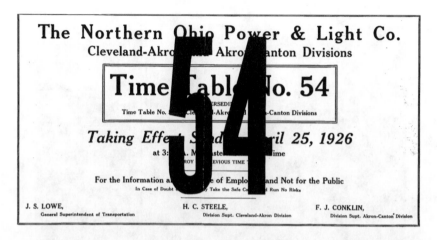

The Northern Ohio Power & Light Co.
Cleveland-Akron and Akron-Canton Divisions

Time Table No. 54

Time Table No. SUPERSEDING Cleveland-Akron and Akron-Canton Divisions

Taking Effect Sunday April 25, 1926

at 3:00 A. M. Eastern Standard Time

TROY PREVIOUS TIME

For the Information and Guidance of Employes and Not for the Public

In Case of Doubt Always Take the Safe Course and Run No Risks

J. S. LOWE,
General Superintendent of Transportation

H. C. STEELE,
Division Supt. Cleveland-Akron Division

F. J. CONKLIN,
Division Supt. Akron-Canton Division

A-B-C DIVISION—NORTH BOUND

[Tabular timetable, Read Up — columns numbered 2, 4, 6, 8, 10, 12, 14, 16, 18, 20, 22, 24, 26, 28, 30, 32, 34, 36, 38, 40, 42, 44, 46, 48, 50, 52, 54, 56, 58; stations include Cleveland, Miles Avenue, Newburg Terminal, Henry, Dunham, Osborn, Bedford North, Bedford South, Interstate, 28 Way, Macon, Pella Terminal, Little York Cross O., Chippendana Cross O., Sununa Cross O., Silver Lake Junction, Akron. Detailed time values not legibly reproducible.]

5.3 The employee timetable is likely more difficult to find than a public timetable. As with comparable schedules for steam railroads, detailed operating information is provided, including exact locations for every scheduled and often flag stops.

stores on main streets and occasionally former private houses. These places generally worked well since interurbans almost always entered the heart of a community, providing riders and shippers with down-town-to-downtown service. These structures might have survived the interurban era, perhaps retaining their commercial functions. (This is where pictorial sources, newspapers, city directories and fire insurance maps can help to pinpoint locations.)

PUB. BY DEAN HOUSE.

MAIN STREET, CAMBRIDGE CITY, IND.

5.4   Fortunately, the electric interurban era coincided with the national picture postcard craze. This view shows a large, wooden interurban car stopped on the main street of Cambridge City, Indiana. If the image is carefully studied, it is apparent that the traction company used a storefront building (left) as its local depot. By checking an interurban guide or a secondary source it is possible to identify the firm, the Terre Haute, Indianapolis & Eastern Traction Company.

Much easier to identify, yet somewhat less likely to have survived are company-built depots. An interurban, probably in its principal terminals, may have erected a substantial station, even including a freight depot, or maybe joined other electric roads in construction of a "union" depot, complete with trainsheds and adjoining freight and package express facilities. In medium and smaller-sized communities, companies sometimes put up their own stations, often with attached electrical substations, that were usually constructed of brick to lessen risk of fire. Some included apartment space for operators who supervised the electrical equipment and acted as agents—serving patrons and reporting train movements to dispatchers or other operating personnel. Early on there were those interurban companies that employed traditional combination depots, usually of frame construction with utilitarian designs. Additional interurban stations, mere "throw-away" trackside shelters, were likely to disappear with abandonment of the line. A few, though, found adaptive use as bus shelters or renewed life as privately owned storage sheds, chicken coops and children's playhouses. Similarly, some depots may have had an extended life, ending up as offices, beauty shops or cafes. And those dozens of interurbans that owned bus subsidiaries usually maintained their depots after they stopped running their electric cars. In time usually national bus systems, most notably Continental Trailways, absorbed many of these operations. Therefore, bus patrons continued to use these original interurban facilities now maintained by their new owners.

The best sources for gleaning information about interurban stations and auxiliary buildings are local newspapers, land and tax records and fire maps. Often by learning when the electric road opened, the date of a structure can be roughly determined, usually to the year. In contrast to steam carriers, collapse of the interurbans came too swiftly to permit the appearance of many replacement or remodeled structures, a phenomenon that makes dating more difficult. Of course, if corporate records exist, as in the case of the Scioto Valley Traction Company, the task may be considerably simplified.

ROLLING STOCK AND EQUIPMENT

Even less likely to have survived interurban buildings is electric railway rolling stock. Occasionally, the long-discarded body of a passenger car or box motor is discovered. More and better preserved pieces of equipment, however, are found in museums, usually railway oriented, or occasionally in the hands of traction "buffs." Some of the best collections of interurban rolling stock can be viewed at the East Troy Electric Railroad and Wisconsin Trolley Museum in East Troy, Wisconsin; Fox River Trolley Museum in South Elgin, Illinois; Illinois Railway Museum in Union, Illinois; Ohio Railway Museum in Worthington, Ohio; Orange Empire Railway Museum in Perris, California; Seashore Trolley Museum in Kennebunkport, Maine; Shore Line Trolley Museum in East Haven, Connecticut, and Trolleyville, U.S.A. in Olmsted Township, Ohio (near Cleveland).

Identifying a car builder can be challenging. This is especially so for those firms that produced only a few pieces of interurban rolling stock. Fortunately, more than a dozen builders remained active throughout the interurban era. These include American Car Company (1891–1931) of St. Louis, Missouri; Barney and Smith Car Company (1849–1923) of Dayton, Ohio; J. C. Brill Company (1868–1941) of Philadelphia, Pennsylvania; Cincinnati Car Company (1903–1931) of Cincinnati, Ohio; Jewett Car Company (1894–1918) of Newark Ohio; G. C. Kuhlman Car

THE OLD WAY

TRIPS BY TROLLEY
ALONG
BAY STATE STREET RAILWAY CO.
LINES AND CONNECTIONS

THE NEW WAY

PASSENGER DEPARTMENT
AND
FREE TROLLEY INFORMATION BUREAU

309 Washington St., Boston, Mass.

Telephone Main 4559

JUST ACROSS
THE STREET

OLD SOUTH CHURCH

INTRODUCTORY

New England has aptly been termed "The Summer Playground of America." Great stretches of sandy beaches, picturesque rocky shores, charming lakes and rivers, the most famous of all historical and educational centers, busy cities and peaceful towns of natural and industrial interest secure to it this reputation.

The American dearly loves to travel. Unfortunately all cannot afford time or money for long ocean or steam road trips to foreign lands or distant parts of this great country. Fortunately, however, the recent vast development of trolley facilities is furnishing a worthy substitute. The trolley at small expense, at one's own convenience, whirls one by pleasant ways on long or short trips as circumstances permit, or desire dictates.

The Bay State Street Railway Co., with its 940 miles of lines, which makes it the largest street railway company in the world, operates throughout this territory and provides a convenient, healthful and non-expensive way of attaining by trolley trips health, pleasure and education.

PURPOSE OF THIS FOLDER

This Folder is issued to facilitate trolley traveling throughout this section.

Pages 2 to 18, inclusive, are devoted to specific trips which are unusually attractive, and which are offered to you in the way of suggestions. Due to the fact that our tracks form a perfect network of lines, the variations which can be made from the special trips as outlined are practically unlimited.

Pages 19 to 26, inclusive, give in alphabetical order the most prominent and interesting points which can be reached from Boston by trolley. Under such listing the mileage, the fare, the running time and directions for making the trip are shown.

The fares and schedules in this Folder are those in effect May 15, 1913, and are subject to change without notice.

ADDITIONAL INFORMATION

If you wish more trolley information, if you wish to have pleasant trips suggested or planned, if you wish to learn how to spend hours or days in seeing the beautiful scenery, the busy cities and towns, the famous beaches, shore and inland resorts and historic places of New England in the most interesting, comfortable, convenient, easiest, lowest-cost way, don't hesitate to call, phone or write the Passenger Department and Free Trolley Information Bureau which the Company maintains at 309 Washington St., Boston. Telephone Main 4559. Maps, time tables, and other descriptive matter also furnished upon request.

5.5 Resembling their steam road counterparts, electric interurbans distributed promotional booklets. In 1913 the Bay State Street Railway Company, a leading New England rural trolley, produced a descriptive folder, highlighted by detailed maps, that conveys a good sense of its role in the region's intercity electric transport.

Company (1892–1932) of Cleveland, Ohio; Niles Car and Manufacturing Company (1901–1917) of Niles, Ohio; Ottawa Car Manufacturing Company (1891–1957) of Ottawa, Ontario; and the St. Louis Car Company (1887–1980) of St. Louis, Missouri. A helpful aid in studying equipment, both passenger and other types of rolling stock, is E. Harper Charlton's richly illustrated work, *Railway Car Builders of the United States & Canada* (Los Angeles: Interurban Special # 24, 1957). Charlton covers leading American and Canadian manufactures and such minor ones as James St. Charles Omnibus Company of Bowmanville, Ontario; J. S. Hammond & Company of San Francisco, California, and Twin Coach Company of Kent, Ohio.

Although records of most builders of interurban rolling stock have either been lost or destroyed, some catalogs and promotional literature, especially for the larger firms, survive. Research libraries, special transportation centers such as the Department of Science and Technology at the National Museum of American History (Smithsonian Institution), and private collectors are likely sources. Since some model railroaders specialize in traction layouts, periodicals oriented toward them, particularly *Model Railroader*, at times provide coverage of cars and related equipment. Also of value are publications produced by major suppliers, most of all General Electric and Westinghouse. One interurban car builder, the J. C. Brill Company, which controlled the American Car Company, G. C. Kuhlman Car Company and Wason Manufacturing Company of Springfield, Massachusetts, issued a smart monthly publication, *Brill Magazine*. Launched in 1907, this lavishly illustrated organ continued until 1928. Its articles commonly provided details on rolling stock, including interior and exterior photographs, car diagrams and statistical data. This publication readily identified carriers that acquired Brill products.

Not to be forgotten are documents, records and other materials gathered and retained by railfan organizations. They may contain data on particular pieces of rolling stock. Such an archive may also yield reminiscences about a specific piece of equipment, helping to place it in useful context. Take these written comments in possession of the Akron (Ohio) Railroad Club made by Robert "Bob" Richardson about interurban car No. 21 of the Ohio Public Service Company, today owned by the Ohio Railway Museum in Worthington, Ohio:

> One Saturday in April 1941, I boarded the 8:00 a.m. Big Four [Railroad] train at Columbus and right on time arrived after a fast 137 mile trip at Cleveland Union Terminal at 11:10 a.m. I hustled to the offices of the Ohio Public Service Company to meet the company lawyer. He'd agreed to meet me to discuss our [Akron Railroad] Club project to preserve one of their interurban cars then in storage at the Oak Harbor shop.
>
> He explained that his company could not allow sentiment to rule in the matter. The best he could do was to sell us a car for the sum already bid by the Alliance [Ohio] firm of Kulka, $300.00 each for the seven passenger cars.
>
> We'd had several fan trips using one or the other of the two oldest cars, the last remaining in Ohio of the typical early-1900's type with arch-transomed windows, Niles built. #6 was a straight passenger car,

#21 was a combination baggage-passenger car. Our members and the fans generally favored the #21, perhaps because many could congregate in that forward compartment. Built in 1905 by Niles, it weighted 27 tons and was typical of hundreds of such cars rolling on electric lines in the early part of the century.

Our last fan trip had been on Sunday, July 3, 1939, the last Sunday of passenger service. Supt. Lester E. Bennet heartily approved of our trips. When I asked him what it would cost on that day to replace the two light-weight cars then in use with the #6 and #21, he figured the extra cost to do so would be no more than $100.00. If we paid that, he could get the two ready and use them that day. Our treasury was slim, but it managed the sum.

For the time being, the cars were stored in the barn at Oak Harbor. Many urged that we should save at least one of the two. But our Club was small, barely 25 members, and we really functioned as a sort of committee, organizing fan trips to which enthusiasts came to from scattered locations in Ohio and adjoining states.

We never had much in our treasury, for it seemed that one trip would be profitable and then we'd lose on the next one.

What to do with the car was a problem. We thought we had an excellent solution when Mr. Shelter of Inter City Rapid Transit offered space at their carbarn in Reedurban. He proposed in return that he occasionally be allowed to take it out on his ten mile line from Canton to Massillon. We could have it operated on specials for a modest fee.

These plans were ended when Massillon's City Council demanded that the little company replace its tracks. Ohio laws required electric lines to pave not only between their rails, but some additional footage as well. If it were possible for the traction line to finance this, almost the entirety of Massillon's main streets would be repaved by the trolley company. That was impossible so the Inter City converted to busses. Now we had a homeless 27-ton interurban.

We searched everywhere for a suitable safe place for the car. Meantime our members, mostly young men, were vanishing into the armed forces, scattered over the globe. Supt. Bennet was helpful. To meet legal requirements the OPS billed us ten dollars a month for storage. As we worried over this mounting sum, he advised us that it was just a formality, to ignore the bills, and keep hunting for a place for the car.

The war over, the fellows gradually returning—for the most part— we finally sadly admitted an insoluble problem. My company had me in Texas when it was voted to give the car to the Central Ohio Railfans Association who had museum plans in mind. So the deed was notarized one spring day in Dallas and they moved the car to a field near the fairgrounds in Columbus. Here it was promptly and totally vandalized. One neighbor even took the steps.

The Columbus group seriously considered burning it for scrap. But they calmed down and with the great help of George Silcott who as a 14 year old fan had ridden the car, they found a site for a museum adjacent to his family's coal yard in Worthington. George had become a dealer in diesel locomotives, a result of his railfan interest.

The new Ohio Railway Museum rebuilt the car, and it became a star attraction. Their track was on the grade of the former Columbus, Delaware & Marion [inteurban] line. The most notable change was to replace the fender required by Toledo ordinance with a nice wooden pilot, and equip the car with a front end trolley pole to make backing easier.

EMPLOYEES

Finding information about interurban employees is difficult, much more so than with steam railroads. Since virtually all of these traction companies have folded, the likelihood of locating personnel records is at best chancy. Those interurbans, such as the Akron, Ohio-based Northern Ohio Traction and Light and the Centerville, Iowa-based Iowa Southern Utilities, which survived in various corporate forms as independent electric utilities, may have kept data on employees. "These power companies had so many old brick interurban structures—car barns and sub-stations—that they had ideal places to stash records of all types," noted interurban historian William D. Middleton. "[These places] were dry and safe and out-of-mind, except to some company clerk or secretary." Luckily some of these records have been transferred to public archives, historical societies and other depositories.

Another possible source, although also unpredictable, is labor union records. Although a majority of interurban workers never joined such groups, those who did commonly affiliated with steam railroad brotherhoods, often the Brotherhood of Railway Trainmen and the Order of Railway Conductors of America. Some, too, belonged to craft unions, usually the Brotherhood of Electrical Workers. Local records are scattered in state historical societies, libraries and railway museums. National records, namely membership lists, exist occasionally in the general headquarters of the United Transportation Union (successor to the trainmen and conductors' union) in Cleveland, Ohio, and in contemporary monthly labor publications.

Federally generated records are a possible source for locating inter-

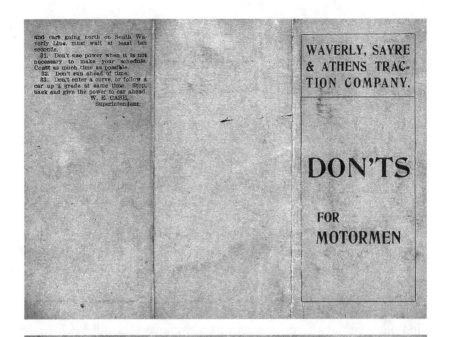

Don'ts for the Motorman

1. Don't forget that you are serving the public and that the Company look to you to be their representative. Treat every one with courtesy; answer all questions civilly; help old and infirm people and ladies with children or packages, on and off your car.
2. Don't gossip in and around your car, while you are on duty or in uniform. This refers to religious, political or other subjects which might be taken in an offensive manner by passengers who are patrons of our cars.
3. Don't smoke while you are on duty. This means at all times when you are under pay.
4. Don't allow passengers to ride on platform when there is plenty of room inside of car. Don't allow any one to ride on front platform of car, either passenger or employee, except E. L. Pickley, D. Splanne, L. Vought, E. James, and W. E. Case; also one man who is in charge of freight. If there is more than one man in charge of the freight, only one will be allowed on platform, except when unloading. The curve greaser will also be allowed to ride on front platform.
5. Don't keep the door open between the vestibule and inside of car. By observing this, you will offer no inducements for passengers to step outside.
6. Don't keep your front vestibule doors open, as it only invites passengers to enter and leave car by that way.
7. Don't run your car without the tail lights and signs which designate the destination of your car, being in place. Tail lights should be in position on back end of car at least 30 minutes before dusk and it is up to the conductor and motorman to see that these important details are attended to, as both will be held responsible.
8. Don't pass by a regular stopping place. Bring your car to a full stop.
9. Don't fail to slow up at the sign "SLOW."
10. Don't put your power on but one point at a time.
11. Don't handle your car roughly.
12. Don't fail to sound your gong at all street intersections and corners.
13. Don't talk to passengers; refer them to the conductor for any information they might desire.
14. Don't allow your car to coast down grade. Keep same well under control on all grades.
15. Don't pass through switch point without switch plug being removed.
16. Don't run your car after it becomes dark without motorman's curtains being drawn.
17. Don't fail to report any defects in your car to the car barn.
18. Don't run too close to car ahead. Keep five hundred feet apart.
19. Don't fail to inform car ahead that you are following them and to what point you are going.
20. Don't fail to report any accident you may notice, however large or small, on, around or about your car. Obtain the names of all witnesses and all other information that you can obtain.
21. Don't run past or over a ditch or other work being carried on in street near track, without bringing your car to a full stop; then proceed over same very slow, sounding your gong at the same time.
22. Don't neglect to change your signs on car if for any reason you are obliged to change car at Car Barn, or any other point on road. This is up to the Crew and not the barn men.
23. Don't fail to run slow around curves and through switches, so that your trolley will not leave wire.
24. Don't start your car without receiving proper bell signal from the conductor.
25. Don't back your car through switch or around curves. Change your tools and run same from head end. If your car becomes disabled, run same from rear end. Place your conductor on front end and he will operate brakes and gong. In this case, run very slow.
26. Don't enter a saloon while on duty or in uniform.
27. Don't run by passengers, except when you are running in sections, then inform passengers to take car following. In case car following has more of a load than you have, then you can make all stops necessary.
28. Don't allow your car to run after dark when power leaves same. Stop at once.
29. Don't go on duty without full uniform. This includes cap, badge and number. Extra men must have cap and coat. Keep your uniforms neat and clean at all times.
30. Don't apply power to your car immediately after it comes on after being off line. The cars going south on South Waverly Line and cars north at Sayre on Main Line may turn on power at once. The cars on Main Line south of Sayre, Clinton Ave. Car and cars going north on South Waverly Line, must wait at least ten seconds.
31. Don't use power when it is not necessary to make your schedule. Coast as much time as possible.
32. Don't run ahead of time.
33. Don't enter a curve, or follow a car up a grade at same time. Stop, back and give the power to car ahead.

W. E. Case,
Superintendent.

5.6 Except for trade journal articles and the occasional book of operating rules, it is hard to learn specific information about the duties of electric interurban employees. Yet, a small New York juice road, the Waverly, Sayre & Athens Traction Company, about 1910 published *Don'ts for Motormen*," revealing insights into the human side of the interurban business.

urban employees. Although the Railroad Retirement Act, which became effective on March 1, 1936, technically included only railroad and not interurban personnel, some were covered, including those who worked for two Ohio interurban giants, Cincinnati & Lake Erie and Lake Shore Electric. (See Chapter 4.) Of course, before the mid-1930s the majority of interurban companies had already ceased operations.

Often the best means to learn about interurban employees is through local newspapers, city directories, and manuscript federal censuses for 1900, 1910, 1920 and 1930, and similar censuses conducted by various states during this general time period. A few former interurban workers remain alive, although their numbers are dwindling rapidly. For instance, a reunion in the mid-1990s of one-time employees of the once-mighty Indiana Railroad System, which ceased its rail operations in January 1941, drew only five veterans. Naturally, family members and acquaintances can be found. Often they have memories and perhaps photographs and other documents to share.

INTERURBANS AND THE COMMUNITY

For those interested in the physical, bricks and mortar impact of the interurban on a community, it makes sense to explore the particular traction environment. After examining municipal, county and other maps to determine the location of these rail routes, a local inspection can begin. With knowledge of the exact or even approximate locations, a "windshield" survey by automobile or perhaps a walking tour may reveal much more than sites of former depots, substations and auxiliary facilities. In some places electric railways spawned construction of apartment houses and other dwellings, even entire residential subdivisions, that catered to traction patrons.

A fine illustration of "interurban architecture" is "The Willdred Flats," located in Sandusky, Ohio. Constructed in 1906–1907, at the height of traction fever, this three-story brick structure of neoclassical styling, situated at 1116 Columbus Avenue, was built by a local businessman who occupied one apartment and rented out the other three to traveling men. Indeed, not long after its completion a salesman, who liked these flats, purchased the property because of the convenient location to the fast and frequent interurban cars of the Lake Shore Electric Railway. It would not be until the era of World War I that the owner felt it necessary to add a detached garage, responding to the advent of the automobile age and the not-so-distant end of the interurban era.

A windshield survey may also reveal a variety of either abandoned or ongoing public places created by interurbans. After all, electric roads were responsible for scores of amusement parks and other centers of entertainment, and occasionally cemeteries and formal gardens. Before such an expedition is launched, a check of newspapers, area histories and related resources would be advisable. If available, a valuable tool would be the once popular "trolley guide." Usually a local entrepreneur rather than a traction company would create this sort of heavily illustrated publication loaded with local advertisements. *Trolley Trips Around Scranton, Wilkes-Barre and Hazleton* is representative of this genre. One edition, published in 1913, contains a *Foreword* by the Scranton, Pennsylvania, businessman who produced it, explaining nicely why "trolley touring" enjoyed widespread popularity early in the twentieth century. "It is now possible to travel long distances by 'Trolley' [interurban], and splendid opportunities are thus open to all persons desiring to see both town and country—a thing that is practically impossible when traveling by [steam] train." And he specifically noted, "It has an advantage over the railroad trip in that a passenger can alight where his fancy directs. He can stop off at convenient places to ramble in the woods or fields, or perhaps explore some picturesque or historic spot, and then, when tired, he can make his way back to the highway with the assurance that within a few minutes there will be a car to convey him in which ever direction he desires to go." In this guide readers learned about "Places Of Interest—How Reached By Trolley," including "ROCKY GLEN PARK: One of nature's beauty spots, resplendent with pretty flower beds, grassy slopes, and plenty of shade. Its amusements are varied, including roller coaster, merry-go-round, boating, and Crystal Palace, the finest dancing pavilion in Pennsylvania." A combination of maps, illustrations and text would surely aid anyone who sought to locate this once income-generating stop on the Lehigh Traction Company, the "Laurel Line," one of America's most profitable and enduring interurbans.

Alas, anyone who wishes to discover more about a community's long ago interurban must be determined and use imagination. Materials about individual roads, structures, rolling stock, employees and related nearby-history dimensions, of course, can be found. Yet as one historian has put it: "Dealing with interurbans can take on the character of a treasure hunt with usually unpredictable results."

ॐ ॐ ॐ ॐ ॐ

In what was unquestionably a true interurban odyssey, J. S. Moulton, a curious and resourceful employee of the Interborough Rapid Transit

Company in New York City, decided to show the extensive nature of America's evolving network of intercity electric railway lines. In an August 1909 letter to Henry W. Blake, editor of the *Electric Railway Journal*, the industry's leading trade publication, Moulton immodestly claims to have been the first person to use traction for most of the way from New York City to Chicago. Although Moulton's exact motives for publicizing his travels are not known, it is easy to speculate about them. In writing to a prominent and presumably influential electric railway spokesman, he surely sought to underscore the obvious possibilities of long-distance electric-powered transportation. And he likely wanted to propose that extensive traction treks could be greatly facilitated if better connections were made at junctions and if carriers would offer complete information regarding times and costs to potential patrons. Anyone researching a local interurban must realize that it cannot be understood in a historical vacuum. The connections between many firms indicate that interurbans frequently enjoyed interrelationships, even though they usually retained their corporate independence.

Leaving New York City at 12:30 a.m. by the New York Central road, I arrived at Hudson at 4:47 a.m., which gave me a full hour before taking the car of the Albany & Hudson Traction Company at 6 o'clock. I had breakfast at Electric Park on the line of this road and shortly after leaving there A.P. Deeds, general freight and passenger agent of the company, joined me and traveled as far as Albany. I took there the car of the Schenectady Railway at 8 a.m. and arrived at Schenectady, a distance of 16 miles, at 8:45. At 9 o'clock I took the car of the Fonda, Johnstown & Gloversville Railroad for Amsterdam. . . . Arriving at Amsterdam at 9:41 a.m., it is possible to go to Fonda by electric line, but the distance gained is so small that I took the New York Central road to Little Falls, a distance of 39 miles between Amsterdam and Little Falls. Leaving Little Falls at 12:30 p.m. on the Utica & Mohawk Valley Railway, the entire route of 23 miles to Utica was a trip that was made beautiful by the scenery. This trip was made in an hour. At 2:05 p.m. I took the limited car for Syracuse, a distance of 49 miles, which we traveled in one hour and 28 minutes. The country is fully as interesting as that between Little Falls and Utica. At 4:30 p.m. I took the car of the Auburn & Syracuse Electric Railroad for Auburn, 26 miles away, and a wait of 30 minutes gave me time for supper and to see a little of the city.

I left Auburn at 6:30 p.m., taking the Auburn & Northern road and the Rochester, Syracuse & Eastern Railroad, by way of Port Byron for Rochester, a distance of 66 miles. The train was on time at Rochester and, getting there at 9:45 p.m., I found I had traveled 387 miles, of which 233 miles were on electric roads. I was not fatigued in the least and, after going to the hotel, went out and walked about the city for an hour. Remaining at Rochester all night, I started at 9:50 o'clock the next morning, taking a local car to the city line, where the car of the Buffalo, Lockport & Rochester Railway started for Lockport at 10:20 a.m. J. M, Campbell, general manager of this road, met me at the Rochester end of the line and went with me to Lockport, a distance of 56 miles, and made my ride very enjoyable by explaining the signal system and the interesting points of the country through which we passed. Riding in the motorman's cab gives a much better view of the country. I arrived at Lockport at 12:18 p.m. within a few steps of the car of the International Railway, which leaves there at 12:20 p.m. for Buffalo, 25 miles distant. I reached the latter city at 1:25 p.m. It was remarkable to find that the electric lines, with their long runs and many stops in the difference cities and villages, made almost exact schedule time. At Buffalo I called on J.C. Calisch, of the Buffalo & Lake Erie Traction Company. Mr. Calisch said he was glad to meet a man brave enough to undertake so unique a trip. He was wrong in suggesting that bravery was needed, because the trip affords pleasure all the time. At Buffalo I went through the city on a local car to the city line, now called Lackawanna City, where the Buffalo & Lake Erie Traction Company has its terminal. In this trip of 88 miles on the lines of this road to Erie, Pa., the cars pass through a great grape belt. After a beautiful ride of six hours, I reached Erie at 9 p.m., where I remained all night, having covered that day 169 miles entirely on electric roads.

At 7 o'clock the following morning I started over the road of the Conneaut & Erie Traction Company for Conneaut, a distance of 33 miles, arriving there at 8:55 a.m. A wait of 30 minutes gave me time to set back my watch one hour, as I was traveling then on western [Central] time. Leaving Conneaut at 9:30 a.m. on the Pennsylvania & Ohio Railway, I traveled to Ashtabula and there took a car of the Cleveland, Painesville & Eastern Railroad via Painesville, for Cleveland. The distance from Conneaut to Cleveland is 73 miles. Cleveland was reached at 12:50 p.m. and after lunch I left at 1:30 p.m. on a limited car of the Lake Shore Electric Railway for Toledo, a distance of 120 miles, via Sandusky, which was made in four hours and 20 minutes without change. After supper at Toledo, I went to the terminal of the Ohio Electric Railway and took the 8 p.m. car of that company for Fort Wayne, Ind., via Lima, Ohio. As I did not leave Toledo until so late, I did not stay on the car until Fort Wayne was reached, but thought it better to stop at Lima, where I arrived at 10:55 p.m.

On the following morning . . . [I] took the 10:15 a.m. [Ohio Electric] car . . . a distance of 60 miles to Fort Wayne, which was reached at 12:10 p.m. At Van Wert, Ohio, the Manhattan Limited of the Pennsylvania Railroad, which parallels the electric line at this point, came up, but we passed the stream train and kept ahead of it. At Fort Wayne I had dinner. . . . After supper [I] took one of the cars of the Fort Wayne & Wabash Valley Road to Wabash. . . . I remained at Wabash that night and started for Warsaw at 8:55 a.m. on the Cleveland, Cincinnati, Chicago & St. Louis ["Big Four"] steam road. After traveling a distance of 33 miles between these points I reached Warsaw at 11:36 a.m.[,] 30 minutes late. By this fall [1909] the road will be from Fort Wayne to Peru, Ind., on the Fort Wayne & Wabash Valley Traction Company road and thence to Warsaw by electric line, as the road now under construction will make the electric line route complete at that point, and therefore complete in the west.

I left Warsaw at 1:30 p.m. for South Bend, Ind., over the lines of the Winona Interurban Railway and the Chicago, South Bend & Northern Indiana Railway, reaching South Bend at 3:40 p.m. I remained there until 5:30 p.m. taking a limited car on the Chicago, Lake Shore & South Bend Railway for Chicago, a distance of 90 miles, passing through the industrial settlements of Michigan City, Gary, and Hammond and reaching Pullman [Illinois] at 8:15 p.m. I took the suburban line of the [steam] Illinois Central Railroad to the central district of Chicago.

It took me three full days and 21 hours from the time I left New York to get to the central [business] district of Chicago. The actual running time was 45 hours and 24 minutes. I traveled 1143 miles, 956 miles on electric cars and 187 miles on steam roads. In one day of a little over 15 hours I traveled 298 miles on electric lines and the best of it all was that I saw the country pretty generally as well as the cities, towns and villages. These places are not seen by the traveler on steam roads. The electric lines pierce these places, the steam roads skirt them. About a year ago I made the trip by electric line to Philadelphia from New York, a distance of a little over 90 miles, and I thought I did well to cover it in nine hours.

The actual traveling time could be reduced several hours and as soon as I finished the trip and returned home I made a careful calculation and found that the actual traveling time could be reduced to 31 hours and 10 minutes. I had a fine and comfortable trip and shall certainly repeat it at the earliest practicable time.

ॐ ॐ ॐ ॐ ॐ

Chapter 6

URBAN TRANSIT

A vital part of getting around in America involves urban transport. Although knowing how to explore the legacy of steam and electric interurban railways provides useful tools for learning more about a municipal traction operation or related form of surface transport, there are situations that make city transit different, if not unique.

During the colonial period and for a time threafter, nearly all residents of urban areas walked to work, walked to shop and walked to most everywhere else unless they were wealthy enough to own or hire a team and carriage. These citizens were part of the pedestrian or "walking" city. But eventually major changes occurred. As suburban areas developed in the nineteenth century, the central walking city began to fade. Crowding, pollution and crime made living away from the urban core more attractive. In some places frequent stagecoach service developed; for example, it appeared by the 1820s between the tightly packed seaport of Boston and the nearby community of South Boston. Yet, these coaches could handle only a few riders and fares were high. In scattered locales it was possible to employ steamboats as an practical means of commuting between a suburban residential area and the work place. By the 1830s, for example, residents of Hoboken and Weehawken, New Jersey, made weekday ferry trips to the City of New York on Manhattan Island. Some of the first steam railroads also provided commuter service, but fares were often too expensive for most wage earners. Moreover, trains made infrequent stops and the urban terminal was often situated far from most riders' destinations.

Early on urbanites thought that the omnibus might solve their local transport problems. This type of vehicle was essentially a stagecoach, modified to carry additional passengers, and was usually pulled by a team of spirited horses. Unlike liverymen, who provided "hack" service on call, omnibus owners operated their conveyances or "accommodations" over dedicated routes with announced schedules. But these slow-moving vehicles offered a public transport alternative that was only slightly better than walking. The typical omnibus consisted of a small passenger compartment that was unheated in cold weather. Seats were wooden and artificial lighting non-existent. Furthermore, these conveyances had difficulty negotiating heavy mud or deep snow, and the strain on animals, not only with bad road conditions but on hills, hampered, even prevented operations.

As with all other forms of transportation, creative entrepreneurs engineered a replacement to the omnibus. By the mid-nineteenth century a number of American communities, ranging from Troy, New York, and Cleveland, Ohio, to New Orleans, Louisiana, took pride in their animal-car lines. The better idea involved using horses (and often mules in hot and humid climes) hitched to street *railway* vehicles. These operations employed an omnibus-like car, albeit a somewhat larger one, that traveled on iron wheels rolling over metal strap or iron rails laid in public streets. In some communities, for example Lake Charles, Louisiana, where streets were not paved with cobblestone or brick, companies installed a wooden walkway for the animals in order to solve the mud problem. The relative ease of movement on these street railways permitted faster speeds, four to six miles an hour, and much less stress on horses. Patrons, too, experienced a somewhat more comfortable ride, although cars were usually diminutive affairs that lacked heat, featured hard wooden seats and provided minimal lighting. By the early 1880s this urban transit phenomenon had evolved into 415 firms that ran approximately 18,000 cars over 3,000 miles of urban track.

The animal-powered railway, like the omnibus, possessed distinct negatives. As a major part of a firm's investment, horses were expensive by contemporary standards. They cost about $200 each and were good for an average of only four or five years of active service. Furthermore, these animals had voracious and expensive appetites, devouring by the 1880s approximately 150,000 tons of hay and 11 million bushels of grain annually. Moreover, they were susceptible to injury and disease. Then there was the nuisance of animals crowding and dropping large amounts of organic waste on public thoroughfares, with the latter posing serious health risks. Since companies also maintained extensive stable facilities, there was an ongoing problem with manure. The noxious smell that wafted from the collection pits constantly brought complaints from nearby residents. Despite the use of various disinfectants, the problem was never solved.

Fear of recurrent diseases and the other troubling aspects of animal propulsion promoted street railway executives to seek replacement technologies. In their quest they experimented with the method of overland transportation: steam. After the Civil War several major rail-

Street Car, Brownstown, Ind.   889

6.1   A researcher needs to sense visually the nature of every form of transport, including the once popular animal-car line. This picture postcard makes it is easy to understand how such operations could be found in small communities like Brownstown, Indiana. The animals, rolling stock and rails did not represent a sizable capital investment. Labor costs, too, were modest since the driver also served as conductor. This view suggests that once a car ended its life as a transit vehicle, it could readily become a storage shed, summer lake cottage or something else.

road locomotive manufactures, including the giant Baldwin Locomotive Works of Philadelphia, produced motive power for the metropolitan market. These "steam dummies" were dramatically downsized versions of standard road locomotives, cleverly disguised as horse cars (and hence the common nickname). They either pulled powerless trailers or occasionally were part of a combined engine-coach unit. Not withstanding their generally nonthreatening, albeit odd appearance the public fretted that these hissing contraptions would scare horses and cause uncontrollable mayhem, surely explaining why by 1890 dummy lines made up only about 200 miles or approximately seven percent of the national street railway mileage.

"Elevated" railways became a much more successful application of steam. Specifically, these were lines that ran above city streets on metal "stilts." Use of anthracite or "hard" coal reduced the smoke problem significantly and operating these steam-powered trains above the street

Copyright 1905 by the Rotograph Co.

A 111a 8th Ave., 116th Street North, N. Y. City.

6.2 By the turn of the twentieth century major American cities might have more than public surface conveyances such as the electric trolley. Some of the largest ones, including New York City, boasted elevated railways that shunted urbanites between major local stops at speeds far faster than those who traveled along congested streets.

level virtually eliminated problems with "spooked" horses and urban congestion in a time before modern traffic signals. These expensive forms of urban transit most often appeared in large cities with heavy population densities, with Chicago and New York City having the most elaborate systems. Yet, Sioux City, Iowa, had an "el" that operated for a few years in the 1890s.

Admittedly steam-powered "els" (in Chicago it was the "L") functioned reasonably well where traffic warranted such complex and costly operations. But in the 1870s urban transit operators began to use steam in another way. Instead of moving vehicles, powerful stationary steam engines propeled wire-rope cables that traveled in cement conduits under streets. Cable or "grip" cars, not dissimilar from animal cars, were attached by retractable mechanical devices to the steadily moving cable, allowing for constant speeds of roughly ten miles per hour. Introduced in 1873 to conquer the steep hills of San Francisco, within two decades cable lines appeared in most major American cities. The leader was Chicago, which claimed three companies, collectively owning eighty-two miles of track, several power plants and more than seven hundred grip cars.

Generally speaking, cable cars were superior to animal-car and steam-dummy lines. Still, an even better way to move the rapidly increasing urban population was the electric streetcar or trolley. Introduced in the late 1880s the trolley was faster, less expensive to build, more versatile and easier and less costly to maintain than its predecessors, including the cable car. After the trolley-era dawned, this new public conveyance spread quickly. The rapidity with which the conversion process occurred was breathtaking. By 1900 intracity steam dummy lines had disappeared and there were few remaining animal-car or cable-car operations. The trolley became ubiquitous, the new backbone of urban transit systems. Even small county-seat towns such as Anderson, South Carolina; Biloxi, Mississippi; and Oskaloosa, Iowa, proudly claimed to have electric cars.

As with most other forms of urban transit, the day of the trolley did not last forever. With increased automobile ownership, especially after World War I, and introduction of regularly scheduled motor buses and electric buses ("trackless trolleys," "trolley buses" or "curbliners"), streetcars began to disappear. The Great Depression caused scores of trolley firms to fold. In larger communities more flexible buses nearly always replaced electric traction. In smaller places, however, residents either drove their cars, took taxicabs, rode with others or walked. Those traction operations that survived until the eve of World War II commonly lasted until war's end; after all, severe tire, fuel and parts rationing gave renewed, even patriotic value to trolleys "for the duration."

At the time when trolleys had become the darlings of urban transit builders, another, albeit limited type of public convenience made its debut, the subway. Inspired by the success of underground projects in Europe, most notably in London, England, and dramatic improvements in electric propulsion, promoters and others realized that physical difficulties prevented them from increasing the volume of streetcar usage on some routes in major cities. During rush periods gridlock ensued. In the 1890s traffic snarls in downtown Boston, noted an observer, became endemic. "On Tremont Street during the afternoon rush hour the [street]cars were packed so close together that one could almost walk from Scollay Square to Boylston Street on the car roofs." However, before the end of the century Bostonians received considerable relief from their downtown congestion. The Tremont Street Subway, which was about one and two-thirds miles in length, encouraged other cities to build subways, including New York City, Philadelphia and Chicago. Eventually one even appeared in Rochester, New York.

Virtually all subways have endured, attesting to their value in the annals of urban transit. In fact, transit builders have updated the sub-

6.3   This "real photo" postcard of main street in Mount Vernon, Ohio, graphically shows the variety of local transport available by the first decade of the twentieth century: walking, horse and buggy, electric streetcar and automobile.

way concept. In the early 1970s a renaissance of sorts came with the opening of the publicly financed Bay Area Transit System (BART), a network of three lines linking the East Bay area with the Market Street District in the commercial heart of San Francisco. Technological betterments, including automated cars, are part of BART. Yet, the system sports traditional subway features. Sections of the rail line, most obviously the 4 ½ mile trans-bay tunnel, operate below the surface. The subsequent MARTA in Atlanta, Georgia, and METRO in Washington, D.C. possess even more subway-like characteristics, with downtown stations that are below ground level.

Moreover, not only have a few trackless-trolley operations remained, notably in Dayton, Ohio; San Francisco, California, and Seattle, Washington, but those trolleys that still operated by the 1960s continue to roll. In fact, by the 1980s a renewed interest in electric traction, renamed "light rail," sprang up in numerous cities, ranging from Buffalo, New York, to Portland, Oregon. The first modern light-rail trolley operation in North America opened in 1978 in Edmonton, Alberta, and three years later the initial one in the United States began in San Diego, California. Existing systems have been modernized and frequently extended. Even the venerable St. Charles Street Car line in New Orleans, a popular tourist attraction which runs through the upscale Garden District, has been rebuilt and its circa 1925 900-series cars rehabilitated.

Just as subway and some trolley lines remain active, nearly all "heavy traction" commuter train operations have also continued. Before World War I several steam roads electrified portions of their busiest commuter routes to offer high-speed, high-capacity service. The New York, New Haven & Hartford Railroad (New Haven), for example, installed a twenty-five cycle, 11,000 volt overhead trolley system on its mainline between New York City and New Haven, Connecticut. Similarly, most steam, later diesel-powered, commuter trains, including some of the "push-pull" variety, endured, even thrived in various major metropolitan areas, notably in "Chicagoland" where throughout the workweek roads like the Milwaukee, North Western and Rock Island (now METRA) transported tens of thousands of riders.

Urban bus systems, today's most dominant form of mass transit, evolved rather quickly. The motor bus, which first appeared on the American scene in 1907 in New York City, almost immediately appealed to transit operators. Not only could a bus maneuver through ever-increasing automobile traffic but it traveled over "free" public thoroughfares. "Motor bus routes involve no construction costs," explained a spokesperson for the American Transit Association in the 1920s, "and may be extended or contracted as circumstances dictate with little or no sacrifice of financial investment. Street railway track, however, requires heavy expenditure." This reasoning goes far to explain why by the 1930s and 1940s buses repeatedly replaced trolleys on city streets.

Buses, like transit vehicles, have changed. Equipment has evolved from small capacity gasoline vehicles to large, even articulated or multi-unit diesel-powered ones. Modern buses are universally air-conditioned and the newest ones have capabilities to meet needs of handicapped riders with wheelchair lifts and grab bars.

But the evolution of motor buses has involved more than replacement technologies. These popular vehicles belong to systems that by the twenty-first century are almost exclusively the responsibilities of municipal or regional transit authorities. Since the closing decade of the nineteenth century, the trend in urban transit has been toward public ownership. During the long-lasting depression of the 1890s, private sector operations for the first time faced the possibility of government take over. Trolley owners commonly encountered intensive grass-roots pressure to behave as model corporate citizens. Consumers demanded good, cheap and safe service. And the public at large cried out for an equitable rate of taxation on *all* traction properties, including rolling stock and electric-generating plants. They blasted low franchise taxes and other special tax exemptions that had been widespread before the Panic of 1893, and made it clear that "tax-dodging" would not be tolerated. In some localities these feelings resulted in municipal ownership, although usually not until hard times had passed and municipal "home rule" had occurred.

Even though transit company investors strongly opposed what they called "gas and water" socialism, by the post-World War II era the negative impact of the automobile on fare-box revenues caused many to drop their opposition. Owners often embraced what in reality was "lemon" socialism; namely, they wanted taxpayers to acquire their equity and to absorb their debt. In time some were successful; "bailouts" occurred in Cleveland, Detroit and San Francisco. If the private sector no longer cared to provide what citizens considered an essential service, the only option became public ownership.

Following World War II those private sector operators who had held on usually had replaced their trolleys with buses or proceeded to do so. This was hardly a panacea; they repeatedly encountered troubling financial challenges. A growing number of patrons had moved to suburbia and now drove their cars to work, destinations increasingly outside the central city or older suburban communities. In northern cities, especially, large factories and mills closed, further damaging transit revenues. By the 1960s, for example, the for-profit Akron (Ohio) Transportation Company shut down, leaving its riders to fend for themselves. In time public officials were forced to launch a takeover operation, creating the Akron Metropolitan Transit Authority. Still, this enterprise, like so many others that have become publicly financed, found itself left with a ridership that had limited financial means. In recent years, however, federal and state aid, together with growing problems with parking, fuel costs, air pollution and other considerations have stabilized, even revived numerous urban transit systems, including the now expanded Akron Metro Regional Transit Authority.

Often overlooked in the story of urban transit is the taxi cab. Shortly before World War I motorized cabs emerged usually as "jitneys." Freewheeling entrepreneurs, driving touring cars, picked up riders at trolley stops along busy main roads, charging a nickel fare. These fly-by-night operators siphoned off revenues from trolleys, prompting many communities to take legal action against them. Locally licensed cab companies then became the norm. After the war the industry grew dramatically, and by 1930 there were thousands of firms dispatching cabs on the streets of communities large and small. During the 1930s consolidations became common, often promopted by the hard times. Always mindful of potential business, companies frequently expanded service, especially to airports and other new and popular destinations. But starting in the 1970s competition from car rental agencies, limousine companies and hotel service vans coupled with rising vehicle, labor and operating costs, especially fuel, promoted cab operations in some places to decrease. And in smaller localities service even disappeared.

What took place in Cleveland, Ohio, is fairly typical of taxi cab operations in a major urban area. In 1923 a Yellow Cab Company, inspired by one launched in Chicago, Illinois, in 1915 by John Hertz, was organized, serving mostly downtown customers. Three years later this operation merged with its rival, the Red Top Cab Company, and expanded its basic service. More mergers and reorganizations followed, and in 1934 City Council gave the firm, officially The Yellow Cab Company, a monopoly within Cleveland. About this time another carrier that served the Greater Cleveland area, Zone Cab Company, entered the Yellow orbit following a nasty strike by the latter's drivers. Unlike in several major communities, Cleveland officials rejected a proposed start-up car company organized by World War II veterans. No "G.I. Cabs" ever traveled city streets. While Clevelanders for several decades experienced stable cab service, by the 1970s the business declined (except for Yellow Cab limousine service between Hopkins International Airport and downtown hotels), in part because of relatively poor service and rising costs for equipment, fuel and labor. A similar tale was repeated in such cities as Atlanta, Buffalo, Dallas, Pittsburgh and Omaha.

The quest for information on a local transit operation generally should follow strategies previously employed. An appropriate starting point is the "overview" book. The most useful studies are *Fares, Please!* by John A. Miller (New York: Appleton, 1941, Dover reprint, 1969) and *Cash, Tokens and Transfers: A History of Urban Mass Transit in North America* by Brian J. Cudahy (New York: Fordham University Press, 1990). Also of value are *Horse Cars, Cable Cars and Omnibuses* by John H. White, Jr. (New York: Dover, 1974); *Urban Rail in America: An Exploration of Criteria for Fixed-Guideway Transit* (Bloomington: Indiana University Press, 1982), and *The Time of the Trolley: The Street Railway from Horsecar to Light Rail* by William D. Middleton (San Marino, CA: Golden West Books, 1987).

Over the years the federal government has produced publications that help anyone to understand the context of urban transit. Of particular note are *Street Railroads, 1902: A Special Report* (Washington, D.C.: U.S. Government Printing Office, 1902); *Electric Railways and Affiliated Motorbus Lines* (Washington, D.C.: U.S. Government Printing Office,

1932), and *Street Railways and Trolley-bus and Motorbus Operations* (Washington, D.C.: U.S. Government Printing Office, 1937). Specifics on individuals transit operation require much more digging.

COMPANIES

Since urban transit in America involves distinct phases, the type of available information about individual operating companies varies. Surely the most difficult ones to learn about are the earliest. Omnibus firms were modest, privately owned operations. Since most disappeared by the Civil War, an examination of local newspapers, if available, is the best approach for news coverage. If nothing else, an omnibus company may have taken out a small block "notice" or advertisement. While its routes may not be clearly described, the corporate name and termini likely will be. A probable path of service would be from the point of connection with intercity travel, usually a railroad depot or steamboat wharf, to the commercial center, mostly commonly the community's leading hotel.

Although animal-car railway companies resembled omnibus firms, they were larger operations, lasted longer and encountered greater public scrutiny. Once again contemporary newspapers hold value as do city directories and regional or local guidebooks. The latter developed simultaneously with published railroad guides, designed principally to serve the "commercial traveler," the traveling salesman. Formed in 1882, the Street Railway Association, a national professional organization of mostly horsecar operators, two years later launched its widely circulated trade organ, *The Street Railway Journal*, an appropriate source to seek information on an individual carrier. Since public authorities required that a street railway firm obtain a corporate franchise, a city archive may possess such a document. Some municipalities issued annual reports and they may contain franchise-related information. And newspapers probably reported such a business action.

A comparable approach can be followed to learn more about cable car companies. Yet in sharp contrast to omnibus and animal-car firms, the American cable car enterprise has generated an encyclopedia work. George W. Hilton, who has written similar books on electric interurbans and narrow-gauge steam railroads, produced *The Cable Car in America* (Stanford, CA: Stanford University Press, 1982; revised paperback edition, 1997). In a format like that employed in the other two publications, Hilton provides a section on specific companies. "Part

Two: The Individual Cable Lines" consists of a city-by-city account of cable car activities, detailing the one or more companies involved. Each community entry features a particularized map that shows principal streets, power houses and other pertinent data.

Even though a Hilton-like volume is missing for either steam dummy railways (although one transit enthusiast is preparing such a study) or the electric trolley industry, a combination of previously mentioned sources and such works as the *McGraw Electric Railway List* and *Poor's Manual of Public Utilities* (see Chapter 5) allow one to identify the vast array of companies that flourished for nearly a half century. If the researcher seeks knowledge about the street railway story in Natchez, Mississippi, and consults the *List* (August 1918), the following information is found:

Natchez, 11,791

Southern Ry. & Lt. Co.—(Owns and operates the electric and gas plants in Natchez.)

Pres. & Gen. Mgr. Frank J. Duffy, Natchez

V. Pres. E. H. Ratcuff, Natchez

Sec. & Treas. J. W. Billingsley, New Orleans, La.

Elecl. and Ch. Engr. William F. Cox, Natchez

Power sta. Equip. 2 d.c. G.E. tot. 400 kw, hp.e. R&F, Nord. Uniflour. F&S, 800 hp. B. Bab.&W., trolley volt. 500v.

Powersta. and repair shop at St. Catherine St.

Reaches Concord Park

4 miles; 4–8 ½ g. 3 cars. (Furnishes power and lighting.) [A key explains abbreviations]

In pursuit of information on more recent urban transit concerns, research techniques mentioned earlier remain applicable. For one thing, trade journals enable a researcher to pinpoint particular operations. (See Chapter 5.) With the widespread triumph of grass-roots crusades for public ownership of electric trolley and then bus companies, municipal governments maintained their own copious files of transit activities. The *process* of municipalization itself generated a variety of reports on the to-be-acquired unit, including engineering studies and operating data, often the work of national transit consulting firms. Once established the transit authority produced annual reports and other documents, both published and unpublished. Occasionally, individuals and groups who spearheaded public ownership drives have had their papers preserved, housed most commonly in local and state historical societies. The proceedings of a city council likewise may re-

6.4   The researcher always needs to be cautious about source materials. Although the picture postcard can aid in reconstructing transport history in a community, there are examples of fakery. The village of Goggan, Iowa, never had electric trolleys, even though residents probably wanted them. If "real" traction was not achievable, the next-best-thing was a picture postcard depicting it. Fakes usually can be identified by checking guides of trolley operations and by consulting local transportation enthusiasts.

sult in worthwhile information. The latter, too, will contain information about the licensing of taxi cab companies and perhaps customer complaints about service and safety issues.

Vastly different from the secondary literature on steam railroads and electric interurbans the urban transit bibliography is at best spotty. Nevertheless, several excellent regionalized or specialized studies exist and include *Horse Trails to Regional Trails: The Story of Public Transit in Greater Cleveland* by James A. Toman and Blaine S. Hays (Kent, OH: Kent State University Press, 1996), *Street Railways and the Growth of Los Angeles: Horse, Cable, Electric Lines* by Robert C. Post (San Marino, CA: Golden West Books, 1989), and *Chicago Transit* by David M. Young (DeKalb: Northern Illinois University Press, 1998). *When Fresno Rode the Rails* by Edward Hamm, Jr. (Los Angeles: Interurban Publications, 1979) is representative of the detailed works of enthusiasts, universally highlighted by photographs, maps and equipment rosters.

EQUIPMENT

For decades the trolley car has generated strong feelings of nostalgia, much more so than most other transport vehicles. Even today, historic and replica trolley cars are being added to existing light-rail and special "old timey" electric lines. Examples include the Main Street Trolley in Memphis, Tennessee, and the McKinney Avenue Transit Authority in Dallas, Texas. "People who wouldn't ride a bus," observed the General Manager of the San Francisco Municipal Railway (MUNI), "will ride a streetcar."

Although private collectors, museums and other individuals and organizations may possess a variety of pieces, ranging from omnibuses to trolley buses, the total pales in comparison to the number of electric trolleys that have been saved. But the charms of the trolley do not fully explain their widespread presence. Since thousands once rumbled down the streets of America, there have been more opportunities to preserve them. As with other boxy pieces of rolling stock, adaptive uses were plentiful for old trolley bodies, whether as chicken coops, fishing cottages or tool sheds. Occasionally, one is located and these questions logically arise: "Who built this trolley?" "When was it constructed?" "Who operated it and when?" As with other types of transportation equipment, contacting local traction enthusiasts and amateur historians is a wise initial step. If a transit museum is convenient, then a representative, whether a professional or volunteer, may be employed. If not, photographs might be mailed or sent by facsimile to such transit experts.

The process of learning details about the retired car might involve examination of printed rosters. The Hamm book on the Fresno Traction Company, for example, offers an annotated roster of its equipment. Scores of individuals histories of street railways include such compilations. Studies, too, of particular car builders may be helpful. An illustration is *The Barney & Smith Car Company: Car Builders, Dayton, Ohio* by Scott D. Trostel (Fletcher, OH: Cam-Tech Publishing, 1993), which lists this firm's urban transit equipment. Industry-generated publications also might provide answers, particularly the *Brill Magazine* (many issues of which were reprinted in the 1960s). *The Car Builders Directory*, an annually published serial, is a useful source. If the street railway that operated the car can be identified, roster checking might be relatively easy. Car builders kept records by names of customers. One caveat should be remembered. If the trolley car passed into the used-equipment market, tracing its lineage might be difficult, if not impossible. A local newspaper account could possibly be found that notes

VOL. 11   JUNE, 1921   No. 12

BRILL
MAGAZINE

Birney Safety Car.
Baltimore, Md.

New Gasoline Rail Car decsribed Page 362

6.5   Detailed information about urban transit equipment can be found in manufacturers' publications. A long-time producer of streetcars and other transit
conveyances was the Philadelphia, Pennsylvania-based Brill Company. The
issue for June 1921 of the *Brill Magazine* (which has been reprinted) contains
coverage of its "Birney Safety Car" operating in Baltimore, Maryland.

that "new" or replacement cars on the line recently came from city "x" or the "xy&z" railway. This, too, is the kind of information that transit enthusiasts likely remember or have recorded.

Although the secondary literature on taxi cab companies is virtually nonexistent, information about the taxis themselves is plentiful. Even though in recent years taxis have come in all makes and models; historically, however, in major cities the likelihood was great that it was a Checker, a roomy vehicle with leather upholstery and jump seats. A product of the Checker Cab Manufacturing Company, founded in 1922 in Joliet, Illinois, the firm soon relocated to an abandoned automobile body plant in Kalamazoo, Michigan. Thousands of these commercial cabs were produced, and they became almost synonymous with "taxi." But in 1982 Checker ended cab production, largely because fleet operators sought smaller, more fuel-efficient vehicles. Yet the Kalamazoo firm continues in operation, producing automobile parts for General Motors, and fortunately it maintains an archive of its taxi cab-making activities. And there exists an active enthusiasts' group, The Checker Car Club of America, whose knowledgeable members publish a newsletter that covers the history and other aspects of this once popular commercial vehicle (10530 West Alabama Avenue, Sun City, AZ 85351).

EMPLOYEES

Knowledge of who worked for the local transit company comes through several possible actions. One source would be city directories. Occupations are identified in most volumes. Another place to check would be "in-house" transit publications. Some of the larger firms issued newsletters, noting activities of employees and highlighting retirements, especially for those who had long work histories. The Rhode Island Company in Providence, Rhode Island, and its successor, Union Electric Railways, for example, provided personnel information in its corporate magazines, *Trollier* and *All Aboard*, both of which are available at the Rhode Island Historical Society (110 Benevolent Street, Providence, RI 02906).

Before the advent of modern bus, subway and light-rail systems the vast majority of companies did not have unionized workers. During the heyday of electric street car operations large firms were notorious for their anti-union activities, commonly hiring green country boys who worked cheaply and did not form unions. Without saying so directly, the *Street Railway Journal* stated the general policy of firms at the end of the nineteenth century: "In small cities and towns it is usually best to select the employees from among the residents of the place in which the road is located, and such as are favorably known and well-endorsed, but for lines in large cities it is claimed that the country-bred men make for the best employes."

Yet unions existed. The foremost one is today's Amalgamated Transit Union, which consists of more than 170,000 members in nearly 300 locals. It made its debut in 1892 as the Amalgamated Association of Street Railway Employes of America, changing its name in 1905 to the Amalgamated Association of Street and Electric Railway Employes of America, and later taking its present moniker. Over the decades the various publications of the Amalgamated Transit Union and its individual locals contained material about individual employees, including their retirements, deaths and insurance-benefit claims. Indeed, this transit union was the first major labor organization to establish a Funeral and Disability Fund for beneficiaries of deceased or disabled members. The initial publication, *The Street Railway Employes Gazette*, appeared in November 1892. Just over two years later, March 1895, the title changed to *The Motorman and Conductor*. In 1928 this monthly became *The Motorman, Conductor and Motor Coach Operator*, reflecting the national movement away from trolley cars to motor buses. Still later the publication took *In Transit* as its title.

There were other unions, too. An important one is the United Transit Workers Union of America, which beginning in the 1930s represented thousands of subway workers in New York City. Its principal publication, *Transport Workers Bulletin*, and assorted records about its members are found in the Robert F. Wagner Labor Archives at the Taminent Institute Library of New York University in New York City 10012. As previously suggested, transit operations attract a large number of enthusiasts, yet for some reason the intense interest that many people have in these systems fails to extend to the individuals who ran them.

Similarly, in cities it was common for taxi cabs drivers to unionize. These organizations were local or regional, like the short-lived Midwest Taxi Drivers Union, organized in 1937 and based in Chicago, and commonly affiliated with a major national union. The New York City Taxi Driver's Union, for example, is part of the AFL-CIO. Records are scattered, but ongoing locals may have membership records and other information and can provide contacts for interviews.

TRANSIT AND THE COMMUNITY

While arguably every form of transportation has had a profound impact on American communities, urban transit operations perhaps had
the greatest. Urban areas grew with construction of local car lines. Following the Civil War, Boston, for one, expanded in a series of concen-
tric circles, a process that after 1887 the electric trolley greatly accelerated. A wonderful account of what occured in Boston is found in
Streetcar Suburbs: The Process of Growth in Boston, 1870–1900 by Sam
Bass Warner (Cambridge, MA: Harvard University Press, 1962). Apartment houses, suburban cottages and an assortment of private and public structures appeared along these street railways or within an easy
walking distance. Buildings, streets and the overall urban landscape,

6.6 The photograph of a Birney car rolling along a commercial street in Lan-
caster, Ohio, helps the researcher pinpoint the location of this long-abandoned
transit company. It is extremely likely that most, perhaps even all of the buildings, including the three-story commercial/apartment structures, remain.

6.7 The Los Angeles Transit Lines and other large urban transit systems distributed a plethora of publications, including route maps. An excellent sense of the service provided after World War II by this firm in downtown Los Angeles comes from this 1946 folder.

including boulevards now grassy but once trolley rights-of-way, may remain largely intact. If one were to drive along 28th Street in South Lorain, Ohio, portions of the center boulevard, the former right-of-way of the Lorain Street Railway, remain visable. Historic photographs, picture postcards, fire-insurance maps and related documents coupled to a walking or driving tour of the neighborhood may reveal much, indeed showing the legacy of public transit on the built environment.

The impact of public transit can be measured in ways other than the physical landscape. Court records represent one source of potential insight. During the 1890s trolley cars annually killed hundreds of pedestrians, although the number of fatalities dropped significantly when companies installed safety fenders that literally caught pedestrians who came in contact with the fronts of these vehicles. While not every accident resulted in legal action, many did. Depositions and trial testimonies reveal detailed patterns of transit operations, describe equipment and explain the roles of employees.

ADDITIONAL POINTERS

The value of transit museums should never be underestimated. Although some operations overlap with interurban and steam railroads in terms of collecting, expertise and the like, there are approximately a score of institutions in the United States that call themselves "transit museums." Included in this group are the Baltimore Trolley Museum, New York City Transit Museum and the Museum of Bus Transportation. [See appendix] These facilities frequently possess reference collections; acquire, restore and display artifacts and have knowledgeable professional and/or volunteers. The holdings of these facilities will continue to expand. Unlike some forms of transportation, urban transit remains alive and constantly changing.

Chapter 7

AVIATION

When on December 17, 1903, Dayton, Ohio, bicycle-makers-turned-aeronauts Orville and Wilbur Wright made their historic flight at Kitty Hawk, North Carolina, no one expected that within a score of years the flying machine would become a form of commercial transport and by mid-century a major one. Even though aviation science early on made rapid advancements, it would be the Great War of 1917–1918 that stimulated enormous change. Lucrative contracts from the federal government spurred such technological improvements as streamlined designs, stronger structural components and more powerful engines. By 1920 thousands of planes had been produced for the military, although many remained unused in warehouses.

Both technological betterments and surplus equipment gave rise to commercial aviation. One entrepreneur, Inglis Uppercu, a New Jersey engineer, believed that the time was right for regularly scheduled passenger flights. Using ex-Navy seaplanes, with space for a dozen riders, Uppercu in 1920 formed Aeromarine Sightseeing and Navigation Company and set out to demonstrate the comfort, reliability and safety of air travel. Initially his firm shuttled passengers between New York City and nearby summer resorts, and shortly thereafter it entered the Cuban market. The Uppercu company scheduled flights between Key West, Florida, and Havana and subsequently expanded, linking Miami, Bimini and Nassau. The firm also inaugurated service between Cleveland and Detroit. Although prospects seemed bright, problems developed. In 1923 declining revenues, operational difficulties and two plane crashes forced Aeromarine to retrench. Then, in 1924, Uppercu liquidated his fledgling airline to pursue other business interests.

Inglis Uppercu might have experienced greater financial success in commercial aviation had the federal government provided subsidies. Since 1918 U.S. Army pilots, not private contract workers, flew air mail planes. They continued to do so until 1925 when Congress passed and President Calvin Coolidge signed the Contract Air Mail Act, popularly called the Kelly Act after its sponsor, Representative Clyde Kelly of Pennsylvania. This measure energized commercial air transport because it authorized the Postmaster General to select air routes and to pay operators to fly mail over them. No other *non*technological event so directly encouraged commercial aviation. Soon passengers were traveling in the same aircraft as sacks of U.S. mail.

As the 1920s continued, commercial aviation burgeoned. Not only did air-mail contracts help to generate black ink, but new companies like Kohler, Stout and Universal acquired airplanes with increased capacity for passengers, mail and express. The appearance of all-metal, enclosed cockpit, multi-engine, single-wing craft fully established aviation as a viable form of intercity transport.

Learning specifics about the pioneer phase of commercial aviation throughout the United States involves several approaches. Certainly a starting point would be to check newspapers. After all, the press, national, regional and local, gave considerable attention to airplanes and all things aviation, whether involving daredevil "barnstormers," building of a public or private airport or establishing scheduled airline service.

As with other transport forms, news-laden trade journals emerged, and in this case before World War I. One of the first, *Aircraft*, made its debut in March 1910, and even before the end of its initial year monthly circulation reached an impressive 14,000 copies. Although issues of this particular publication (1910–1914) are difficult to find, some of its articles and editorials later appeared in *Aircraft Industry Builder*. An even earlier journal, *Fly*, (1908–1909) has been reprinted in facsimile in a single-volume format, *The National Aeronautic Magazine, Fly, Volume 1, No's 1 to 10, November, 1908, through August, 1909* (Seattle, WA: Salisbury Press, 1971).

Just as the trade journal is a potentially rich source of information about commercial aviation for any large locality, at times the printed public timetable is even better for gleaning information about activities during the formative years of local aviation. The schedule for Stout Air Lines, Inc., for April 1, 1929 is representative. This early carrier, which operated two units ("Detroit–Cleveland Division" and the "Detroit–Chicago Division"), carefully informs readers about its terminal operations. In Cleveland, Ohio, for example, "Company car leaves Consolidated Air Travel ticket office, 712 Superior Ave., N.E. 35 minutes before departure of plane. [Offices:] Cleveland 308 Marshall Building. The terminal points for these flights are the Ford Airport at Dearborn, the Municipal Airport at Cleveland, and the Municipal Airport at Chicago—three of the most completely equipped airports in the country."

Commercial aviation grew, almost exponentially, in part because of improving equipment, best illustrated by larger and much more powerful airplanes. In 1934 Douglas Aircraft Company entered the commercial aircraft field with the revolutionary DC-2. American Airlines and other carriers placed these fourteen-passenger planes into service and two years later an expanded version, the DC-3, appeared. This type of airplane increased the likelihood that passenger revenues alone could underwrite much or even all of the cost of a flight and with mail and express contracts healthy profits were possible. By 1940 the DC-3 accounted for ninety percent of all domestic air transport. Better and safer aircraft meant that more citizens took to the skyways.

With growth came increased governmental supervision. In 1938 Congress passed and President Franklin Roosevelt signed the Civil Aeronautics Act, which created the Civil Aeronautical Authority. This federal agency, later reconstituted as the Civil Aeronautics Board (CAB), possessed extensive powers to regulate aviation, including routes, thus creating a remarkable degree of stability within this maturing industry.

Early commercial airline operations may be reconstructed through a variety of sources. Individual companies not only published descriptive public timetables but they also issued pamphlets, usually designed for self-promotion and to reduce the fears of potential patrons about leaving terra firma. Suppliers, too, produced a variety of publications about local, regional or national aviation. In 1929 the Standard Oil Company of Ohio, for example, distributed the *ABC Book of Flying*, which it called "a primer on aviation," and systematically described the location of all commercial and private airports in the Buckeye state. Similarly communities, which operated municipal airports, produced reports, commonly with detailed maps, and an array of other documents. The governmental body that created these materials may have retained them or deposited them in a public archive.

With congressional regulation the federal government began to generate a vast amount of materials that allow researchers to learn more about aviation in their communities. Although admittedly the 3,962 cubic feet of records belonging to the Civil Aeronautics Board (Record Group 197), held by the National Archives and Records Administration in Washington, D.C., contain documents of limited value for the nearby history sleuth, some do hold special interest. The most useful surely include records belonging to the Bureau of Air Operations and those of the Publications Service Division Office of Facilities and Operations. Since no other state has depended more on air transport than Alaska, records of the CAB's Alaska Office are essential for reconstructing its local aviation history. The existing case files, which cover operation of air carriers from 1940 through 1951, are especially valuable. If the subject involves an airline crash in or near the place studied, documents produced by the Air Safety Board should be consulted. And if there is interest in federal air mail operations, a researcher should explore the extensive archives of the U.S. Air Mail Service. These materials are located in the papers of the United States Post Office, Record Group 28, in the National Archives.

Federal deregulation of the aviation industry, which began in the administration of president Jimmy Carter, included passage in 1984 of the Civil Aeronautics Board Sunset Act. As with the subsequent dismantling of the Interstate Commerce Commission, various functions of the abolished Civil Aeronautics Board (CAB) moved to other federal agencies, most often to the Department of Transportation. These bodies retained records of industry activities that are either or will become available at the National Archives.

Some records of the Civil Aeronautics Board resulted from public policy decisions about the structure of the commercial airline business. The CAB quickly allowed a handful of "trunk" carriers to dominate the big-city, long-distance market. Later, the CAB decided that commercial aviation should be brought to smaller communities. "Local service" carriers, rather than major ones, provided these flights, operations that became "feeders" to metropolitan centers that then allowed passengers to connect with major lines. One such company was Wisconsin Central Airlines that in December 1946 received its regulatory certification and in February 1948 began flying. Three years later Wisconsin Central became North Central Airlines, still a "local service" concern.

In 1978 a monumental change in the structure of domestic commercial aviation history occurred. Congressional reform produced major deregulation, resulting in a reshuffling of routes for existing carriers and the appearance of hundreds of new airlines. When an entrenched airline decided to withdraw from a marginally profitable or money-losing community that previously the Civil Aeronautics Board had mandated be served, upstart companies, often with modest capital and few pieces of equipment, sought to fill the void. Some of these carriers survived; others failed, often quickly. The process of numerous carriers entering and exiting the skyways remains a distinguishing characteristic of this form of transport. Typical of the short-lived carriers was Liberty Airlines. In mid-1982 this Swanton (Toledo), Ohio-based firm began service between Toledo and Chicago and soon added Akron, Ohio, to its route. But then the company ceased operations for financial reasons and liquidated its assets, mostly through the sale of its two vintage Convair prop jets.

GEORGIA

ALBANY—Commercial; 2 mi. N.; wet; supplies; 2000 ft.x1050 ft.
AMERICUS—Government; 4 mi. N. E.; good wet; supplies.
ASHBURN—Municipal; 1 mi. N.; fair wet; supplies; 1200 ft.x1200 ft. N. & S. by E. & W.
ATHENS—Emergency; landing golf links S. W.
ATLANTA—Emergency; fair accommodations.
ATLANTA—Emergency; 7 mi. S.; 270 E. & W.x750 ft. N. & S.
AUGUSTA—Governmental; parade grounds, Camp Hancock; 5 mi. S. W.; road N.; ravine W.
BELLEVILLE—Emergency; supplies.
BLAKELY—Emergency; S. E.; supplies; fair roads; road N.; trees N., S. & W.; 750 ft. N. & S.x450 ft. E. & W.
BRUNSWICK—Naval Air Station; Navy seaplanes only.
BUENA VISTA—Emergency; possible landing.
CAMP GORDON (at Atlanta)—Emergency field; parade grounds.
COLUMBUS—Emergency; 1 mi. S. W.; soft wet; land E. or W. on S. side.
COLUMBUS—Governmental; 8 mi. S.; 2 canvas hangars; supplies; 1½ mi.x⅜ mi.
CORDELLE—Municipal; fair; poor field, narrow and small.
DAWSON—Municipal; ½ mi. S.; wet; supplies; 1350 ft. E. & W.x900 ft. N. & S.
DOUGLAS—Emergency; 2 mi. W.; 800 yds.x 800 yds.; supplies.
ELLAVILLE—Emergency; S.; soft wet; supplies; 400 sq. yds.
FITZGERALD—Municipal; 40 acres, 1 mi. S.; good wet; alt. 515 ft.; supplies; 900 ft. N. W. & S. E.x1500 ft. S. W. & N. E.
FORT VALLEY—Commercial; S. W.; soft wet; supplies; trees E.; 500 sq. yds.
GRACEWOOD—Emergency; runs N. & S.; poor condition.
GRIFFIN—Emergency; 2 mi. S. E.; supplies; 600 ft. E. & W.x1200 ft. N. & S.; road N.; bushes S.; trees W.
HAWKINSVILLE—Municipal; 2 mi. W.; fair wet; supplies; 750 ft. N. W. & S. E.x1200 ft. N. E. & S. W.
HELENA—Emergency; S. E.; small; landing N. & S.; sandy in take-off.
LA FAYETTE—Emergency; S. of town, W. of R. R.
MACON—Municipal; E.; good wet; alt. 324 ft.; oil and gasoline; ½ mi. runway.
MACON—Governmental; 5 mi. E.; alt. 324 ft.; supplies; 500 ft.x200 yds.
McRAE—Municipal; S. W.; soft wet; alt. 150 ft.; supplies.
MARSHALLVILLE—Municipal; 2 mi. S. E.; good wet; supplies; 600 ft. E. & W.x1200 ft. N. & S.
MILLEDGEVILLE—Emergency; golf course.
MONTEZUMA—Commercial; 1½ mi. S. E.; supplies; sq.; 900 ft. E. & W.x1500 ft. N. & S.
MOULTRIE—Emergency; 2 mi. S. W.; golf course; 1800 ft. E. & W.x750 ft. N. & S.
OGLETHORPE—Emergency; 5 mi. W.; supplies; 1200 ft. E. & W.x900 ft. N. & S.; good dry.
OMAHA—Emergency; N.; supplies; 1500 ft. E. & W.x1500 ft. N. & S.; trees; road S.
PLAINS—Emergency; 2 mi. E.; good wet; supplies; 1200 ft. E. & W.x450 ft. N. & S.; trees N.; R. R. on S.
REYNOLDS—Emergency; S. E.
RICHLAND—Emergency; good small field.
ROME—Emergency; N. of town, W. of R. R.
SAVANNAH—Municipal; N. E.; supplies; obstacles; slow landing N. & S. only; 470 ft.x2000 ft.
SHELLMAN—Emergency; S. E.; soft wet; gas and oil; 900 ft. E. & W.x750 ft. N. & S. wires south.
SUGAR VALLEY—Emergency; ½ mi. N.; soft; supplies; woods 4 sides.
SYLVANIA—Emergency; landing possible.
SYLVESTER—Emergency; N.; soft wet; gas and oil; wires W.; 792 ft. E. & W.x1485 ft; N. & S.
THOMASTON—Municipal; 1 mi. N.; soft wet; 1800 ft. N. & S.x900 ft. N. & S.x2700 ft. E. & W.
TIPTON—Emergency; 2 mi. N.; fair wet; gas; marked by "X"; 4500 ft. E. & W.x4800 ft. N. & S.
VIDALIA—Emergency; ¾ mi. out; 900 ft. E. & W.x225 ft. N. & S.; supplies.
VALDOSTA—Municipal; alt. 300 ft.; good wet; supplies; white "X" center; approach E.; slow landing.
WASHINGTON—Municipal; good wet; alt. 640 ft.; supplies; 1200 ft. N. of tank.
WAYCROSS—Municipal; S.; good wet; supplies.
WAYNESBORO—Emergency; very good landing E.

7.1 The National Aeronautic Association of the United States in 1923 produced *The Complete Camp Site Guide Including All Airplane Lands in the U.S.A.*, a strange combination of listings. Yet for anyone who seeks to locate an early airport or landing strip this compendium holds value.

If a researcher wishes to identify which commercial airline companies served a particular community, an easy way would be to consult copies of *The Official Airline Guide* or its predecessor publications. Admittedly, old issues usually have not been retained by local libraries or historical societies, but state, national and transportation-oriented history centers may have them available. When an appropriate copy is located, it is a simple matter to determine what airline offered service; if, in fact, a commercial carrier paid daily calls. In the index to the October 1933 edition of *The Official Aviation Guide of the Airways,* for example, service is listed for Fort Wayne, Indiana, as being provided by Transcontinental & Western Air Line. Santa Barbara, California, welcomed planes belonging to Pacific Seaboard Air Lines. And Portland, Maine, received aircraft that linked it to Boston and Bangor on the "Flying Yankee of the Air," Boston-Maine Airways.

If airline guides are not easily obtainable, a perusal of local newspapers is in order. Undoubtedly they are *daily* publications because historically virtually no small community or town enjoyed commercial air service. Since these daily newspapers commonly lack indexes, research may be time-consuming. Yet, more than most contemporary railroads, airlines advertised extensively. For decades companies catered to the upper and upper-middle classes, especially corporate executives, and expensive ad space became just another cost of doing business. Fortunately, these advertisements can usually be spotted quickly and can offer information on service, equipment and the like. News stories, too, may be found.

Learning about a company that served a particular community either prior to or after federal deregulation involves several strategies. An excellent point of beginning would be consulting the best single-volume history of the industry, *Airlines of the United States since 1914,* by R. E. G. Davies (London: Putnam, 1972). This encyclopedic study contains succinct commentaries about the histories of carriers and reveals corporate genealogies. In a series of appendices Davies offers such useful data as a "Summary of Pioneer Airlines, 1914–1924;" "Domestic Airlines, 1925–April 1927;" "Local Service Operators," and "Freight Airlines, 1946–1947." The principal limitation with the Davies book is its age. An updated edition of this talented historian's work has not been produced.

Yet, there exists a type of companion volume to *Airlines of the United States since 1914.* It is *The Airline Bibliography: The Salem College Guide to Sources on Commercial Aviation, Volume I: The United States,* which appeared in 1986. One part is especially helpful in learning about a particular carrier: "Individual Passenger Airlines, 1914——." This section offers a listing of secondary literature and thumbnail sketches of a raft of companies, some of which developed following publication of the Davies book. For example, there is an account of Air Atlanta, which began service in 1981, and an inclusion of citations, mostly from the aviation trade press, on its activities. Air Atlanta ceased operations after publication of *The Airline Bibliography*, reflecting the rather ephemeral nature of many new companies.

Another basic and readily available reference work that complements both *Airlines of the United States since 1914* and *The Airline Bibliography* is *Commuter Airlines of the United States* by R. E. G. Davies and I. E. Quastler (Washington, D.C.: Smithsonian Institution Press, 1995). The format of this exhaustive book resembles the one Davies employed in his *Airlines of the United States since 1914*, particularly tabulations of carriers. Specifically Davies and Quastler list thirteen regions (Alaska, Hawaii, Northwest, Pacific, Rocky Mountains, North Central, Central, Texas and Louisiana, Midwest, Southeast, Northeast, Mid-Atlantic and Caribbean), providing overview commentaries and thumbnail histories of scores of commuter carriers.

By consulting the Davies and Quastler book it is easy to learn the scope of service to a particular area and often to a specific community If a researcher wishes to learn about commuter air service to Ottumwa, Iowa, a small industrial city in the southern part of the Hawkeye state, the section on the North Central region reveals two carriers, both of which were short-lived. They include Central Iowa Airlines, with service to Davenport, Iowa, and Minneapolis and Hawkeye Airlines, with links to Marshalltown, Iowa, Des Moines, Omaha and Sioux City. The former flew DC-3's and closed in October 1973, less than a year after its first flight, and the latter, which also used DC-3's, operated only for several months in 1974.

When an airline company under investigation has been identified, a review of the modern trade press can also be undertaken. *Aviation Week and Space Technology* (1916–) provides news and information about the industry, including commentary on individual carriers and service. This serial is the product of various mergers and name changes. For example, the core publication in 1943 united with *Aviation News*, in 1948 absorbed *Air Transport* and in 1960 took its present name.

Unlike railroads, the number of corporate histories of commercial aviation enterprises is limited. Yet, students of aviation have examined several firms, and their contributions offer helpful information and insight. Arguably the best comprehensive study of a large company is *Delta: The History of an Airline* by W. David Lewis and Wesley Phillips Newton (Athens: University of Georgia Press, 1979). Since publication

BOSTON-MAINE AIRWAYS, Inc.

The "Flying Yankee" of the Air

Daily Service To and From Northern New England

(Airway subsidiary of the Boston and Maine Railroad and the Maine Central Railroad)

General Offices: Boston-Maine Airways, Inc., Boston, Mass.

BOSTON-MAINE AIRWAYS, INC.

Philips M. Payson, President
    Laurence F. Whittemore, Vice President
        Arthur B. Nichols, Clerk of Corporation
            Walton O. Wright, Passenger Traffic Manager
                Herbert L. Baldwin, Publicity Manager

DAILY SERVICE

Between

Boston, Massachusetts

Portland, Maine

Waterville, Maine

Bangor, Maine

DIRECT CONNECTIONS

At

Boston Airport from and to planes

for New York and points south,

and Albany, Chicago and

the west

GENERAL INFORMATION

Baggage—Thirty pounds will be carried free on each ticket. Baggage in excess thereof will be charged for at excess rates.

Equipment—10-Passenger tri-motored Stinson cabin planes. Heated and radio equipped.

Round Trip—Round trip tickets good for 30 days.

Stopovers—Stopovers not permitted on through tickets.

Children—Children under two years of age may be carried free. Over two years will be charged the full fare.

Operations by NATIONAL AIRWAYS, INC.

Paul F. Collins, President
        Amelia Earhart, Vice President
                S. J. Solomon, Vice President

RESERVATIONS and INFORMATION

Bangor, Maine—phone Bangor 7304
Boston, Massachusetts—North Station, phone Cap. 1400
Portland, Maine—Union Station, phone Portland 2-0104
Waterville, Maine—phone Waterville 42
    Any agent of the BOSTON and MAINE or MAINE CENTRAL railroads, all leading HOTELS and TRAVEL BUREAUS.

Boston-Portland-Waterville-Bangor

East—Read Down			Mls.	September 24, 1933 TABLE **21 B** Eastern Standard Time		West—Read Up		
†	*	*				*	*	†
4 30PM	3 00PM	10 20AM		Lv......Boston......Ar		4 45PM	10 30AM	9 10AM
5 20PM	3 50PM	11 10AM		Ar......Portland......Lv		3 55PM	9 40AM	8 20AM
......	4 00PM	11 20AM		Lv......Portland......Ar		3 45PM	9 30AM	......
......	4 40PM	12 00AM		Ar......Waterville......Lv		3 05PM	8 50AM	......
......	4 45PM	12 05PM		Lv......Waterville......Ar		3 00PM	8 45AM	......
......	5 15PM	12 35PM		Ar......Bangor......Lv		2 30PM	8 15AM	......

*—Daily.
†—Daily Except Sunday.

FARES

ONE WAY Fares (Light Face Type)   ROUND TRIP Fares (Dark Face Type)

	Bangor	Boston	Portland	Waterville
Bangor......	....	$23.00 13.00	$13.50 7.50	$ 7.50 4.00	....
Boston......	$23.00 13.00	....	9.50 5.50	17.00 9.50
Portland....	13.50 7.50	9.50 5.50	....	8.00 4.50
Waterville..	7.50 4.00	17.00 9.50	8.00 4.50	....

TRANSPORTATION TO and FROM AIRPORTS

Bangor—Between Airport and Maine Central Railroad Station and Bangor House. Kane's Taxi. Running Time 12 minutes. Fare $0.50.
    Taxis leave for Airport 20 minutes before scheduled plane departure and will pick up passengers anywhere within city limits. Simply phone Bangor 7304.

Boston—Between Airport and any Hotel in Boston's business section, also North or South Stations. Call any Checker Taxi. Running time 30 minutes. Fare $0.50.

Portland—Between Airport and Union Station and Eastland Hotel. Town Taxi. Running time 20 minutes. Fare $0.50.
    Taxis leave for Airport 30 minutes before scheduled plane departure.

Waterville—Between Airport and Railroad Station and 95 Main Street. Testa's Taxi Service. Running time 15 minutes. Fare $0.40.
    Taxis leave for Airport 30 minutes before scheduled departure and will pick up passengers anywhere within city limits. Simply phone Waterville 1822 or 42.

7.2   Learning about air service to a particular city at a particular time can be accomplished by examining *The Official Aviation Guide of the Airways* or other contemporary or subsequent collection of timetables. The *Guide* for October 1933 has entries for such carriers as Boston-Maine Airways, National Park Airways and U.S. Airways.

NATIONAL PARKS AIRWAYS, Inc.

General Offices—Municipal Airport, Salt Lake City, Utah—Tel. Wasatch 3631
Operating Office—Butte Airport, Butte, Montana.

OFFICERS

Alfred Frank, President
Walter C. Lewis, Vice President
Joel Nibley, Secretary
S. F. Baliff, Jr., Treasurer
Felix Steinle, General Operations Manager, Butte, Montana
W. G. Ferguson, Traffic Manager, Butte, Montana

OFFICES

Billings, Montana.......Northern Hotel, phone 2133; Municipal Airport, phone 30591.
Butte, Montana.......Municipal Airport, phone 6555; Finlen Hotel, phone 5461;
Intermountain Bus Depot, phone 4912.
Great Falls, Montana...Municipal Airport, phone 4271; Rainbow Hotel, phone 4311.
Havre, Montana.......Hotel Havre, phone 5.
Helena, Montana.......Municipal Airport, phone 396; Placer Hotel, phone 1330;
Commercial Club, phone 37.
Idaho Falls, Montana...Hotel Bonneville, phone 1040.
Livingston, Montana...Park Hotel, phone 657.
Ogden, Utah...........Ben Lomand Hotel, phone 4100; Utah Pacific Airways, phone
101-R-4.
Pocatello, Idaho........Municipal Airport, phone 2206; Bannock Hotel, phone 1700.
Salt Lake City, Utah...Municipal Airport, phone Wasatch 6160; Newhouse Hotel,
Wasatch 570; Hotel Utah, phone Wasatch 190.

Reservations may be made through any
POSTAL TELEGRAPH or WESTERN UNION office.

Havre-Great Falls-Butte-Billings-Salt Lake

South—Read Down					North—Read Up		
5	3	1	Mls.	TABLE 22 Mountain Standard Time	2	4	6
.....	.....	6 15AM	0	Lv.......Havre.......Ar	.....	.....	5 00PM
.....	3 00PM	7 15AM	0	Ar..Great Falls...Lv	.....	.....	4 00PM
.....	3 00PM	7 30AM	0	Lv...Great Falls...Ar	8 50AM	.....	1 20PM
.....	3 55PM	8 25AM	77	Lv......Helena......Ar	8 00AM	.....	12 30PM
.....	4 30PM	9 00AM	127	Ar......Butte......Lv	7 30AM	.....	12 00N
9 05AM				Lv Butte.........Ar			4 10PM
10 15AM	↓	↓		Lv Livingstone......Ar	↑	↑	3 05PM
11 10AM				Ar Billings........Lv			2 00PM
.....	4 30PM	9 00AM	127	Lv......Butte......Ar	7 30AM	12 00N	.....
.....	.....	10r50AM	313	Lv..Idaho Falls....Lv	.....	10r00AM	.....
.....	6 55PM	11 25AM	359	Lv.....Pocatello....Lv	.....	7 30AM	.....
.....	8 05PM	12 35PM	483	Lv......Ogden......Lv	.....	3 50AM	8 20AM
.....	8 35PM	1 05PM	509	Lv...Salt Lake City..Lv	.....	3 30AM	8 00AM

r—Flag Stop.

GENERAL INFORMATION

Baggage—Thirty pounds carried free on each ticket.

Cancellation—The company reserves the right to cancel reservations on account of weather or other conditions.

Connections—Passengers and mail make connections at Salt Lake City to all parts of the United States.

Express—Express is carried on all flights.

FARES
ONE WAY Fares Light Face Type   ROUND TRIP Fares Dark Face Type

	Billings	Butte	Great Falls	Havre	Helena	Idaho Falls	Livingston	Ogden	Pocatello	Salt Lake
Billings...	.....	22 70	34 56	45 60	27 00	40 60	12 90	57 00	45 35	59 70
	.....	12 60	19 20	25 35	15 00	22 55	7 15	31 70	25 20	33 15
Butte.....	22 70	.....	17 10	24 50	7 20	20 25	11 70	36 00	24 30	40 50
	12 60	.....	9 50	13 60	4 00	11 25	6 50	20 00	13 50	22 50
Great Falls	34 56	17 10	.....	12 50	10 80	35 10	23 70	49 50	40 50	54 00
	19 20	9 50	.....	7 00	6 00	19 50	13 15	27 50	22 50	30 00
Havre....	45 60	24 50	12 50	.....	19 80	43 20	34 40	59 50	47 90	62 20
	25 35	13 60	7 00	.....	11 00	24 00	19 10	33 00	26 00	34 55
Helena...	27 00	7 20	10 80	19 80	.....	25 65	16 20	43 20	31 50	47 25
	15 00	4 00	6 00	11 00	.....	14 25	9 00	24 00	17 50	26 25
Idaho Falls	40 60	20 25	35 10	43 20	25 65	.....	29 70	19 80	6 30	24 75
	22 55	11 25	19 50	24 00	14 25	.....	16 50	11 00	3 50	13 75
Livingston	12 90	11 70	23 70	34 40	16 20	29 70	.....	45 55	34 00	48 60
	7 15	6 50	13 15	19 10	9 00	16 50	.....	25 30	18 90	27 00
Ogden....	57 00	36 00	49 50	59 50	43 20	19 80	45 55	.....	14 85	7 00
	31 70	20 00	27 50	33 00	24 00	11 00	25 30	.....	8 25	4 00
Pocatello.	45 35	24 30	40 50	47 90	31 50	6 30	34 00	14 85	.....	18 90
	25 20	13 50	22 50	26 00	17 50	3 50	18 90	8 25	.....	10 50
Salt Lake.	59 70	40 50	54 00	62 20	47 25	24 75	48 60	7 00	18 90	.....
	33 15	22 50	30 00	34 55	26 25	13 75	27 00	4 00	10 50	.....

FLYING EQUIPMENT

2 Boeing 40-B-4, 4 passenger cabin plane, Hornet engine, 525 H. P.
5 Fokker Super Universal Mail and Passenger planes, cabin type, Pratt and Whitney "Wasp" engines, 425 H.P.

U. S. AIRWAYS, Inc.

Passengers   U. S. Mail

General Offices—Fairfax Airport, Kansas City, Kansas

W. A. Letson, President
F. A. Conway, Treasurer

D. C. Walbridge, Operations Manager
Hugh W. Coburn, Traffic Manager

OFFICES

Denver, Colo........Traffic Office 534 17th Street, phone Keystone 0771;
Municipal Airport, phone Franklin 6168.
Goodland, Kan.......Neu Hotel, phone 355; Municipal Airport, phone 6153.
Kansas City, Mo......Traffic Office, 1103 Baltimore Ave., phone HArrison 3445;
Municipal Airport, phone NOrclay 1750.
Salina, Kan.........Municipal Airport, phone 678.
Topeka, Kan.........Jayhawk Hotel, phone 4112; Topeka Airport, phone 197 K 1

ANY POSTAL TELEGRAPH OR WESTERN UNION OFFICE

Kansas City—Denver   Mail-Pass.-Exp.

West—Read Down		Mls.	Effective August 15, 1933 TABLE 22-A	East—Read Up	
	*21			*22	
.....	12 45PM	0	Lv...Kansas City (CT)...Ar	5 30PM	.....
.....	1 20PM	54	Lv...F....Topeka.....Lv	4 45PM	.....
.....	2 15PM	159	Ar......Salina......Lv	4 05PM	.....
.....	2 25PM	159	Lv....Salina (CT)....Ar	3 55PM	.....
.....	3 35PM	386	Lv...Goodland (MT)...Lv	12 55PM	.....
.....	5 10PM	557	Ar.....Denver (MT)...Lv	11 25AM	.....

r—Flag stop.   *—Daily.   (MT) Mountain time.   (CT)—Central time.

ONE WAY Fares—Light Face Type.   ROUND TRIP Fares—Dark Face Type

	Denver	Goodland	Kansas City	Salina	Topeka
Denver.....	.....	15 30	49 50	40 50	45 00
	.....	8 50	27 50	22 50	25 00
Goodland...	15 30	.....	40 50	25 20	40 50
	8 50	.....	22 50	14 00	22 50
Kansas City..	49 50	40 50	.....	18 90	9 45
	27 50	22 50	.....	10 50	5 25
Salina......	40 50	25 20	18 90	.....	18 90
	22.50	14 00	10 50	.....	10 50
Topeka.....	45 00	40 50	9 45	18 90	.....
	25 00	22 50	5 25	10 50	.....

Baggage—30 lbs. free. Excess up to 50 pounds at rate of 1/4 of 1% of fare per pound. Equipment—All-metal six passenger Flamingo cabin monoplanes powered with 425 H. P. engine.

TERMINAL FACILITIES

Kansas City, Mo.—Municipal Airport. 1 mile. Taxi fare 50c. Buses on 20 minute schedules. Fare 10c.
Salina, Kans.—Airport. 5 miles.
Goodland, Kan.—Goodland Airport. 1/2 mile. Taxi fare 25c.
Denver, Colo.—Municipal Airport. 6 miles. Taxi fare 50c.

CHICAGO—TULSA—DALLAS (Braniff Air Lines)

12 00N	8 30AM	Lv Chicago........	Ar	8 45PM	2 40PM
3 00PM	11 30AM	Ar Kansas City.....	Lv	6 00PM	11 55AM
3 15PM	12 00N	Lv Kansas City.....	Ar	5 35PM	11 45AM
4 45PM	1 30PM	Lv Bartlesville.....	Lv	4 20PM	10 30AM
5 00PM	1 45PM	Ar Tulsa..........	Lv	4 05PM	10 15AM
6 00PM	2 45PM	Ar Oklahoma City...	Lv	3 15PM	9 15AM
6 45PM	4 00PM	Lv Dallas.........	Lv	2 00PM	8 30AM
7 05PM	4 25PM	Ar Ft. Worth......	Lv	1 35PM	8 10AM

NEW YORK—ST. LOUIS (Transcontinental and Western Air)

11 15AM	12 01AM	Lv Kansas City.....	Ar	8 23PM	7 08AM
1 20PM	2 05AM	Lv St. Louis.......	Lv	6 12PM	4 57AM
6 18PM	6 58AM	Lv Columbus......	Lv	2 58PM	1 43AM
11 07PM	11 55AM	Ar New York......	Lv	9 30AM	8 10PM

NEW YORK—CLEVELAND—CHICAGO (United Air Lines)

12 30AM	Lv New York......	Ar	6 35AM	.....
4 37AM	Lv Cleveland......	Ar	3 46AM	.....
5 55AM	Lv Chicago.......	Lv	12 45AM	.....
9 00AM	Lv Chicago.......	Ar	12 30AM	.....
12 10PM	Ar Kansas City....	Lv	7 15PM	.....

OMAHA—ST. LOUIS (Rapid Air Transport)

3 45PM	Lv Omaha........	Ar	7 40PM
4 55PM	Ar St. Joseph.....	Lv	6 30PM
5 25PM	Ar Kansas City....	Lv	6 00PM

ROUND TRIP
SUMMER EXCURSIONS
(Effective Until October 16)
KANSAS CITY-DENVER
Leaving either terminal Friday, Saturday or Sunday
RETURN ANY DAY
within 30 days from date of departure
$29.50 Round Trip Rate
Excursions from other points at Low Rates

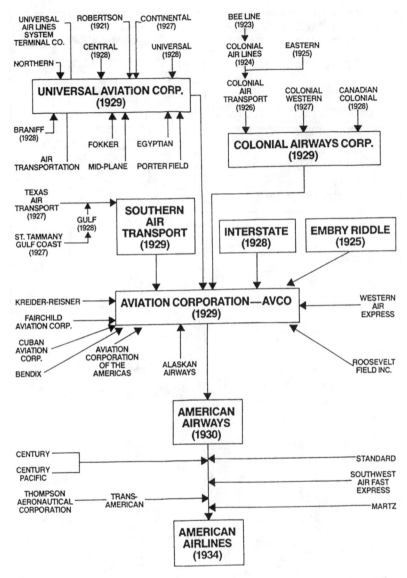

7.3   The complexity of American aviation is revealed in the early corporate genealogy of American Airlines. Within a few years a community might have had an array of companies flying into its airport.

of this scholarly work, the forces of competition which resulted from deregulation have buffeted Delta, thus becoming a major void in the recorded story. Of note is a later, more popular, heavily illustrated account of Delta that takes the carrier into the era of deregulation: *Delta: An Airline and Its Aircraft* by R. E. G. Davies (Miami, Fl: Paladwr Press, 1990). This book also features excellent historical sketches of the numerous companies that Delta either directly or indirectly acquired. Other important book-length examinations of major carriers include *The Airway to Everywhere: A History of All American Aviation, 1937–1953* by W. David Lewis and William F. Trimble (Pittsburgh, PA: University of Pittsburgh Press, 1988); *Eagle: The Story of American Airlines* (New York: St. Martin's Press, 1985) and *From the Captain to the Colonel: An Informal History of Eastern Airlines* (New York: Dial, 1980) both by Robert J. Serling.

Unfortunately, only a few in-depth histories of small "local service" companies exist. Two of the best are by I. E. Quastler: *Swift Aire Lines, 1969–1979: The History of an American Commuter Airline* (San Diego, CA: Commuter Airlines Press, 1979), and *Air Midwest: The First Twenty Years* (San Diego, CA: Airline Press of California, 1985). Also of worth are *50 Years of Aloha: The Story of Aloha Airlines* by Bill Wood (Honolulu, HI: Aloha Airlines, 1996); *Adventures of a Yellowbird: The Biography of an Airline* [Northeast Airlines] by Robert E. Mudge (Boston: Branden Press, 1969) and *The Alaska Airlines Story* by Archie Satterfield (Anchorage, AK: Alaska Northwest, 1981).

Only a few depositories hold airline corporate materials. Firms that continue to fly are likely to retain the historical papers of both the present company and predecessor firms. Examples include Delta Air Lines whose papers are found in the company's general offices at Hartsfield International Airport in Atlanta, Georgia; Trans World Airlines whose archives are situated in company headquarters in Kansas City, Missouri, but whose Public Affairs Department files, however, are in the TWA general offices in St. Louis, Missouri (both will likely change locations because of TWA's acquisition in April 2001 by American Airlines); and United Air Lines whose records remain in its general offices in Chicago, Illinois. Other noncorporate locations may hold useful materials on individual carriers. For instance, records of Braniff Airlines, a firm that closed in the 1990s after more than a half century of operations, are part of the History of Aviation Collection located in the Eugene McDermott Library at the University of Texas at Dallas in Richardson, Texas 75083.

As with other major transportation corporations, additional sources reveal aspects of company history. Trunk airlines and some of the smaller ones, issued annual reports to stockholders and regulators; these documents can aid in placing service to a particular community into a bigger context. Some carriers, usually the largest, have produced in-house magazines. In the case of Delta Airlines, the public relations department in 1941 introduced the *Delta Dispatcher*, a monthly mimeographed newssheet that quickly evolved into the quarterly *Delta Digest*. By 1945 this publication appeared on a monthly schedule. One of the several companies that Delta acquired, Chicago & Southern Airlines, also had an employee magazine, *Sky Steps*, which appeared between 1943 and 1952. Finally, minutes of the board of directors; court records, especially in cases of bankruptcies and liquidation such as those that befell Eastern and TWA, and even on-board advertising items hold historic value.

The popularity of transportation history is reflected in the aviation field. As do steam railroad, electric interurban, canal and other societies, aviation has its own major historical group, the American Aviation Historical Society (www.aahs-online.org). Founded in 1956 this educational organization produces two publications, a scholarly quarterly, the *AAHS Journal* (prior to 1980 the *American Aviation Historical Society Journal*). The Society, too, maintains an extensive collection of books, documents and other research resources at its headquarters on 2333 Otis Street in Santa Ana, CA 92704.

If learning about individuals who were associated with the airline enterprise is an objective, a good starting point for corporate leaders is the *Encyclopedia of American Business History and Biography: The Airline Industry,* edited by William Leary *(Encyclopedia of American History and Biography)* (New York: Facts on File, 1992). As with most transport industry records generated in the twentieth century, records of labor groups, especially unions, contain a wealth of information if they can be located. Prominent among these are materials associated with the Airline Pilots Association (ALPA), housed at the Walter P. Reuther Library at Wayne State University in Detroit, Michigan 48202. Similarly, the Reuther Library holds papers of the Association of Flight Attendants (AFA). Additional information on this largely female labor group is found in the files of the AFA, an affiliate of the AFL-CIO, in Washington, D.C. Interviews with active and retired aviation workers can also yield information. As with other forms of contemporary transport, groups of retirees and veterans meet on a regular basis, whether personnel associated with Braniff in Dallas, Texas, Capital in Washington, DC, Eastern in Miami, Florida, or United in San Francisco, California. Since much of the growth in the airline industry has occurred during the past fifty years, finding knowledgeable individuals may be relatively easy.

Although it is important to learn about the nature of local commercial carriers and individuals who served them, a vital dimension of "nearby" aviation history involves airports. Just as for decades steam railroads enlarged, replaced or even relocated their trackside depots, a similar phenomenon took place with airports. These changes occurred for obvious reasons. Some airports lacked room for runway and terminal expansion, especially as urban areas grew and residents fussed about aircraft noise and road congestion. A related consideration involved jets superseding piston-powered aircraft. This replacement technology made its debut in the late 1950s and within a decade had become widespread. Jet aircraft, particularly jumbo ones, required larger runways and contained a much greater passenger seating capacity. In the recent past cities in Texas, including Austin, Dallas, Fort Worth and Houston, have relocated their airports due to the pressing need to enlarge their operations, although some of the facilities replaced may remain active for private and commuter, express and freight aviation. Then, too, these are places where the initial choice for an airport proved to be a poor one. Take the case of Cleveland, Ohio. Its first airport was located in Woodland Hills Park on the east side of the city. An early replacement was also in that vicinity, largely because it adjoined the Martin airplane manufacturing plant and testing facility. Because both locations were in the infamous "snow belt" and subject to frequent wintertime snow squalls, Cleveland leaders, led by City Manager William Hopkins, in 1927 established what became today's Cleveland Hopkins International Airport in a vast, open area on the city's southwestern side, free of the worst snows and better situated for expansion.

If an airport site for a community has changed from a primitive grassy landing strip to a state-of-the-art, high-use facility, a variety of sources may be tapped to learn about earlier locations. Obvious possibilities are local individuals with ties to aviation. Newspapers and newspaper "morgues," if available, are likely sources of detailed information. A variety of maps also might be employed, whether plat maps, Sanborn fire-insurance maps or U.S.G.S. (United States Geological Survey) topographical maps. Many of the latter date from the 1930s and 1940s when new or replacement airports were constructed. They are also excellent sources for locating sites of the series of electric-powered navigational beacons that the federal government installed in the 1930s for airplane guidance. Furthermore, planning authorities generated useful documents, often with detailed charts and maps.

Over the last half century a common phenomenon has involved construction of hundreds of airports in smaller communities. With federal and state financial assistance coupled to local bond sales, the "county airport," designed mostly for business and pleasure aircraft, emerged in all sections of the country. Frequently county governments have created airport commissions to build and oversee these facilities. Whenever public bodies enter the transportation picture, a host of records result. Moreover, interviews with participants, who spearheaded airport development, remain a likely possibility, and these individuals can explain the strategies, politics and other parts of the story.

At times a visit to a functioning airport may prove revealing. The municipal airport in Lincoln, Nebraska, for instance, has three terminal buildings that date from three distinct periods of its history. In other locations these terminal structures have been recycled. The art deco style terminal in Akron, Ohio, which served the Rubber City from the early 1930s to the mid-1960s, became in the 1990s a popular local restaurant after being placed on the National Register of Historic Places and painstakingly restored. Copies of the completed forms and support materials for National Register placement are found at both the Department of the Interior in Washington, D.C., and the state preservation office, in this case at the Ohio Historical Society in Columbus.

A variety of other materials that researchers can use to discover aspects of a community's aviation past may be found elsewhere. The National Air and Space Museum Library of the Smithsonian Institution in Washington, D.C. 20560-0321 is one such place. Its photographic holdings are some of the best in the nation. As with other forms of transportation, local and state historical societies may own materials, including newspaper clippings, photographs, public timetables, airport records and assorted documents.

Gaining information about specific pieces of aircraft resembles the process of gleaning knowledge about pieces of railroad rolling stock. Just as the Library of the National Air and Space Museum holds a wealth of images of private, commercial and military aircraft, it also possesses a vast array of resource materials, including manufacturers' catalogs, along with such standard secondary works as the encyclopedic and annually published *Jane's All the World's Aircraft* (title varies). Other libraries, particularly large public and academic ones, own many of the same reference books.

A mostly ephemeral aspect of commercial aircraft, yet one particularly significant to the 1930s, involves lighter-than-air transport. Historically, this specifically meant balloons, blimps and dirigibles. The best contact for this specialized aviation equipment is the Akron, Ohio-based Lighter-Than-Air Society (www.ltas.org) that maintains its research holdings at The University of Akron Archives, Polsky Building,

7.4   In 1928 the Rand McNally Company created a small, national map of the
emerging network of commercial air carriers. If Spartanburg, South Carolina,
is the object of an inquiry, the sole service provider is identified as Pitcairn Aviation. As the key correctly notes, Pitcairn flew mail and not passengers. Since
commercial aviation was in flux, the maker sensibly warned that the map was
"Subject to frequent changes."

803 AIRPORT TERMINAL, AKRON, OHIO

7.5   Even though the picture postcard craze had subsided by the era of World War I, cards continued to be produced in sizable quantities, including ones of airports. This mid-1930s view of the art-deco terminal in Akron, Ohio, attests to the importance of this transport form. A modern city required a modern airport facility if it was to continue to prosper.

Akron, OH 44325-1708. As with other groups of transport enthusiasts, the Lighter-Than-Air Society has members who are scattered throughout the country and willingly share their expertise.

If the focus of a nearby history project involves military aircraft, resources are considerable. Indeed, they are far greater than those on commercial aircraft. Basic secondary works that might be consulted include two by Gordon Swanborough and Peter Bowers, *United States Military aircraft Since 1908* (London: Putnam, 1971), and *United States Navy Aircraft since 1911* (Annapolis, MD: Naval Institute Press, 1976). A popular Internet website for U.S. military aircraft has been created and maintained by Joseph Baugher, P.O. Box 3033, Naperville, IL 60566-7033. It is called "Joe Baugher's Encyclopedia of American Military Aircraft (www.csd.uwo.ca/~pettypi/elevon/baugher_us).

Commercial aviation remains vital to Americans. The industry is ever changing, with construction of new and refurbishing of old facilities continuous. The nearby history story has hardly ended.

Chapter 8

USING LOCAL
TRANSPORTATION HISTORY

Once the researcher has learned about that trace, canal lock or railroad depot, the question arises about what to do with this information. Fortunately, ample opportunities exist to share findings about a nearby transportation history undertaking. Since transport topics are popular with the public, discoveries find receptive local audiences. Talks to historical, educational, service, social, cultural and senior organizations can be personally satisfying experiences. Moreover, such presentations can create venues for obtaining valuable feedback. The most likely question that should be asked is: "What memories do you, as long-time residents have of your transport past?" It was this thinking that in the late 1980s prompted the National Council on the Aging (409 Third St., S.W., Suite 200, Washington, DC 20024), as part of its "Discovery Through the Humanities" program, to commission a book of primary documents, *We Got There on the Train: Railroads in the Lives of the American People,* for a series of nationwide discussion sessions with interested older citizens.

When community residents realize that there is an individual within their midst with knowledge of the general history of local transportation or a particular aspect of it, that expertise may be tapped. This information might hold considerable practical value. Examples abound. In the mid-1950s contractors building the Indiana Toll Road near Goodrum encountered an embankment that was approximately 180 feet wide at the base and two miles long that they believed to be an oddly shaped sand dune. Actually, the aborted Chicago-New York Air Line Electric Railroad had built it about 1905 to cross the wide valley of Coffee Creek, expecting that its passenger trains would operate at 100 miles per hour over a more than 750-mile proposed route between Chicago and New York. If the precise nature of this tightly compacted earthen work, which contained a buried lattice of massive bridge timbers, had been known, the routing would have been different, due to the difficulty of removal. After this expensive experience, turnpike personnel consulted an amateur railroad historian to learn if there were other hidden surprises in northwestern Indiana. A similar episode took place in Dallas, Texas. When in the 1960s a construction crew unearthed under the sticky asphalt pavement remnants of a concrete conduit for a cable car line along Elm Street, costs quickly exceeded budgeted estimates. What shocked public officials was that their city *never* had a cable car operation. Only students of local transit history knew about an ill-fated scheme of the early 1890s that had failed to turn a wheel. And on April 13, 1992, a pile driver operator, working in the Chicago River in Chicago, Illinois, ruptured a wall that allowed water to pour into the abandoned passageways of the Chicago Tunnel Company, causing a monumental disaster. The resulting inrush of water spread throughout about fifty miles of tunnels, flooding subbasements and disrupting utility service throughout the Loop. Local transit enthusiasts volunteered information about the electric-powered freight tunnel firm, which opened in 1899 but suspended operations sixty years later, including detailed drawings and movie film of its passageways.

The informational value of knowing nearby transportation history can be utilized for additional purposes. Take widespread environmental concerns about toxic wastes. Although some forms of transport were not major polluters, others caused long-term damage. For decades railroads were great perpetrators. Workers in paint shops, repair facilities, roundhouses and the like dumped toxic chemicals into adjoining streams or allowed them to penetrate the soil and enter the ground water. Maps, photographs, oral histories and other sources allow students of nearby transportation history to provide information about locations of frequently "lost" toxic sites. If a developer plans to build houses on or near a defunct tie-treating plant, a red flag should be raised. What is under the brush and weeds may hold an expensive even lethal surprise.

A happier scenario involves the expanding transportation leisure business. There is inevitably interest about the history of a particular segment of a river, canal or railroad that might convey tourists on a steamboat, canal packet or steam-powered train. If a pleasure pike is planned for an out-of-service branch-line, insights gained from historical research of the sort outlined in this book could readily contribute to the sound development of such an enterprise, not to mention personal and public enjoyment.

Knowledge of a nearby transportation topic might be shared with area students involved in a project for the popular National History

Day competition. Thousands of budding historians at the middle and high school levels annually work on exhibits and presentations on the same general topic for local, state and national contests. Although "transportation" per se may not be the current field of inquiry, aspects of this specialization may fit subject needs, whether the year's topic is changes in technology or the national response to war.

Usually transportation topics lend themselves to visual presentations. It is far easier to capture in a photograph the essence of an electric trolley than it is the nature of municipal government. Since images abound, results of nearby transportation research may be turned into heavily illustrated exhibits, ones that might be displayed in such public places as a library, museum, post office or visitors' center. For those communities in which a particular form of transportation dominated, for example a railroad shop town, such largely pictorial presentations, with appropriate caption materials and perhaps accompanied by maps or other drawings, can tell a substantial part of a locality's past. A written or oral guide to the display may also be an appropriate way to convey information and interpretations.

There may be opportunities to go beyond static visual displays. High-quality video cameras and equipment allow even amateur film makers to prepare an impressive program on a transportation topic. The proliferation of nonprofit community-access television may be the appropriate outlet for such a transportation video. After all, the History Channel, a for-profit cable network, experienced strong viewer ratings for its *Trains Unlimited* series and plans to commission additional episodes. There even may be requests by local commercial stations or national networks for a video with historic images and insights. On October 10, 1995, the criminal derailing of Amtrak's *Sunset Limited* in Arizona, which killed a passenger car attendant and injured more than 100, prompted speculation that it was inspired by a similar act of sabotage that occurred on the eve of World War II when *The City of San Francisco* wrecked on Southern Pacific rails in Nevada, killing twenty-four and injuring 115. Photographs, film footage and commentary of this earlier tragedy were in great demand.

The never-ceasing revolution in technology has resulted in rapid expansion of the Internet. It might make sense to develop a web site for the particular nearby transportation project, thus offering a way to disseminate information and to get "feedback." Assistance for creating the web site might come from a historical society, community college or other interested party.

A piece of original research that is properly crafted should have a good chance of appearing in print. See Chapter 7 of *Unlocking City Hall:*

Exploring the History of Local Government and Politics by Michael W. Homel (Malabar, FL: Krieger, 2001), for excellent commentary on how an amateur historian should conduct research and present findings. Also *Researching, Writing, and Publishing Local History* by Thomas E. Felt (Nashville, TN: American Association for State and Local History, 1976), and *Nearby History: Exploring the Past Around You* by David E. Kyvig and Myron A. Marty (Walnut Creek, CA: AltaMira Press, 2000, second edition) offer insights on writing and publishing nearby history. Although a detailed discussion of a steamboat landing or a caboose would not be appropriate for a state, regional or national history journal that is intended for scholars, it would likely be suitable for a community history magazine or newsletter or a publication oriented toward a specific group of enthusiasts. During the research process contact with such knowledgeable individuals as archivists, librarians or professors can identify such outlets. Materials gathered on a local transport subject can also potentially strengthen a broader local history writing and publishing project. It is common for community centennial, sesquicentennial and bicentennial books and pamphlets to contain a section on transportation, and usually one that is richly illustrated. Similarly, newspapers, often for their weekend editions, seek well-researched, well-written and interesting historical narratives. Weekly newspapers, too, often eagerly await such contributions. "I'll print virtually anything about the county's transportation [past]," remarked the editor of a semiweekly Iowa newspaper. "These are stories my readers want and I know they often clip and send them to the old-timers who live out-of-town." Also, regional, state or city magazines such as *Sunset Magazine, Yankee, The Iowan, Sandlapper: The Magazine of South Carolina,* and *Cleveland Magazine,* which are oriented toward a general, albeit specialized readership, might be an outlet.

Possibilities exist for "self-publication," and they should be considered. During the past decade or so scores of books and pamphlets on nearby transportation topic have appeared, which have been written and produced by the author. The range has been extensive, including works on a railroad tunnel in Illinois and an abandoned canal in Ohio. With advent of computer "desktop" publishing, costs have been significantly reduced from earlier forms of printing and overall quality has improved. Yet before any self-published study appears, others should read the manuscript for content and style. Sales can be promoted in a variety of ways. Advertisements in enthusiasts' publications would be wise and local newspapers, too, can help stimulate distribution.

Even if no exhibit or publication results from research on a nearby transportation project, notes, visuals, oral history tapes and other items

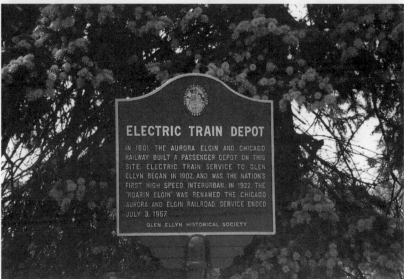

8.1–2   The results of a local transportation history project might result in the text for historical markers. (David Kyvig photographs)

should be preserved. Ask the local or state historical society if it would like either the originals or copies of the assembled findings. Such an institution, too, would surely appreciate copies of anything that has been written. Collectively, these materials will become "building blocks" for other researchers, including professional historians, who are inspired to launch inquiries into in the field of transportation history. Every result of careful research that is preserved and made accessible will help those who travel further.

Appendix I

SINGLE ROAD RAILROAD HISTORICAL SOCIETIES

Akron, Canton & Youngstown
Historical Society
P.O. Box 196
Sharon Center, OH 44274

Amtrak Historical Society
1579 N. Milwaukee Ave., Suite 350
Chicago, IL 60622

Ann Arbor Railroad Technical &
Historical Association
Box 51
Chesaning, MI 48616

Anthracite Railroads Historical
Society
(Central of New Jersey; Lackawanna;
Lehigh & Hudson River; Lehigh
Valley and Reading)
P.O. Box 519
Lansdale, PA 19446

Atlantic Coast Line and Seaboard Air
Line Railroads Historical Society
P.O. Box 325
Valrico, FL 33595

Baltimore & Ohio Historical Society
Box 13578
Baltimore, MD 21203

Bay Line Historical Society
(Atlanta & St. Andrews Bay)
517 East Market St.
Taylorville, IL 62568

Boston & Maine Railroad Historical
Society
P.O. Box 469
Derry, NH 03038

Bridge Line Historical Society
(Delaware & Hudson)
P.O. Box 7242
Capitol Station
Albany, NY 12224

British Columbia Railway Historical
& Technical Society
25852 McBean Parkway, Suite 187
Valencia, CA 91355

Burlington Northern: Friends of the
Burlington Northern Railroad
P.O. Box 271
West Bend, WI 53095

Burlington Route Historical Society
(Chicago, Burlington & Quincy;
Colorado & Southern; Fort Worth &
Denver)
P.O. Box 456
La Grange, IL 60525

Central of Georgia Railway
Historical Society
2 Turnbull Dr.
Rome, GA 30161

Central Vermont Railway Historical
Society
1070 Belmont St.
Manchester, NH 03104

Chesapeake & Ohio Historical
Society
P.O. Box 79
Clifton Forge, VA 24422

Chessie System Historical Society
163 Straith St.
Staunton, VA 24401

Chicago & Eastern Illinois Railroad
Historical Society
P.O. Box 606
Crestwood, IL 60445

Chicago & Illinois Midland Chapter
of the National Railway Historical
Society
P.O. Box 274
Sherman, IL 62684

Chicago & North Western Historical
Society
(Chicago & North Western; Chicago
Great Western; Des Moines & Central
Iowa; Fort Dodge, Des Moines &
Southern; Lichfield & Madison;
Minneapolis & St. Louis)
P.O. Box 1270
Sheboygan, WI 53082

CN Lines
(Canadian National; Grand Trunk;
Grand Trunk Western; Central
Vermont; Duluth, Winnipeg &
Pacific)

101 Elm Park Rd
Winnipeg, MB, Canada R2M 0W3

Conrail Historical Society
P.O. Box 38
Walnutport, PA 18088

Conrail Technical Society
P.O. Box 7140
Garden City, NY 11530

Cotton Belt Rail Historical Society
(St. Louis Southwestern)
Box 2044
Pine Bluff, AR 71613

Denver, South Park & Pacific
Historical Society
2725 Willow Glen Rd
Hilliard, OH 43026

East Tennessee & Western North
Carolina Historical Society
8 Hickory Hills
DeSoto, MO 63020

Erie Lackawanna Historical Society
1 La Malfia Rd
Randolph, NJ 07869

Feather River Rail Society
(Western Pacific)
Box 608
Portola, CA 96122

Fonda, Johnstown & Gloversville
Railroad Company Historical Society
115 Upland Rd
Syracuse, NY 13207

Friends of the East Broad Top
10428 Caryln Ridge Rd
Damascus, MD 20872

Frisco Railroad Museum
(St. Louis-San Francisco)
543 E. Commercial St.
Springfield, MO 65803

Grand Trunk Western Historical
Society
P.O. Box 622
Keego Harbor, MI 48320

Great Northern Railway Historical
Society
1781 Griffith
Berkley, MI 48072

Green Bay & Western Preservation
Group
702 West Green St.
Watertown, WI 53098

Gulf, Mobile & Ohio Historical
Society
Box 2457
Joliet, IL 60434

Illinois Central Historical Society
14818 Clifton Park
Midlothian, IL 60445

Illinois Traction Society
(Illinois Terminal)
5903 Vollmer Lane
Godfrey, IL 62035

Kansas City Southern Historical
Society
P.O. Box 5332
Shreveport, LA 71135

Katy Railroad Historical Society
(Missouri-Kansas-Texas)
P.O. Box 1784
Sedalia, MO 65302

Lehigh Valley Railroad Historical
Society
P.O. Box RR
Manchester, NY 14504

Louisville & Nashville Historical
Society
(Louisville & Nashville; Chicago &
Eastern Illinois; Family Lines;
Monon; Nashville, Chattanooga & St.
Louis; Seaboard System; Tennessee
Central)
Box 17122
Louisville, KY 40217

Maryland & Pennsylvania Railroad
Preservation Society
P.O. Box 5122
York, PA 17405

The Milwaukee Road Historical
Association
(Chicago, Milwaukee, St. Paul &
Pacific)
P.O. Box 307
Antioch, IL 60002

Missabe Railroad Historical Society
(Duluth, Missabe & Iron Range)
719 Northland Ave.
Stillwater, MN 55082

Missouri & Arkansas Railroad
Research Group
(Missouri & Arkansas; Missouri &
North Arkansas)
P.O. Box 1094
Harrison, AR 72601

Missouri Pacific Historical Society
P.O. Box 1876
Alvarado, TX 76009

Monon Railroad Historical-Technical
Society
P.O. Box 5303
Lafayette, IN 47903

New Haven Railroad Historical &
Technical Association
P.O. Box 122
Wallingford, CT 06492

New Jersey Midland Railroad
Historical Society
P.O. Box 6125
Parsippany, NJ 07054

New York Central Historical Society
Box 8114
Cleveland, OH 44181

New York Connecting Railroad
Society
8406 Montpelier Dr.
Laurel, MD 20708

New York, Susquehanna & Western
Technical & Historical Society
P.O. Box 121
Rochelle Park, NJ 07662

Nickel Plate Road Historical &
Technical Society
P.O. Box 381
New Haven, IN 46774

Norfolk & Western Historical Society
P.O. Box 201
Forest, VA 24551

Northern Pacific Railway Historical
Society
13044 87th Place NE
Kirkland, WA 98034

Northwestern Pacific Railroad
Historical Society
P.O. Box 667
Santa Rosa, CA 95402

Ontario & Western Railway
Historical Society
(New York, Ontario & Western)
P.O. Box 713
Middletown, NY 10940

Pennsylvania Railroad Technical &
Historical Society
Box 389
Upper Darby, PA 19082

Pennsylvania-Reading Seashore
Lines Historical Society
P.O. Box 1214
Bellmawr, NJ 08099

Pere Marquette Historical Society
P.O. Box 442
Grand Haven, MI 49417

Pittsburgh, Shawmut & Northern
Railroad Historical Society
Box 222
Angelica, NY 14709

Reading Company Technical &
Historical Society
P.O. Box 15143
Reading, PA 19612

Rio Grande Southern Historical and
Technical Society
P.O. Box 3358
La Mesa, CA 91944

Rock Island Technical Society
(Chicago, Rock Island & Pacific)
11519 N. Wayne Ave.
Kansas City, MO 64155

Rutland Railroad Historical Society
P.O. Box 6262
Rutland, VT 05701

The Santa Fe Railway Historical &
Modeling Society
(Atchison, Topeka & Santa Fe)
1704 Valley Ridge
Norman, OK 73072

Soo Line Historical & Technical
Society
2253 N. 70th St.
Wauwatosa, WI 53213

Southern Pacific Historical &
Technical Society
P.O. Box 93697
Pasadena, CA 91109

Southern Railway Historical
Association
Box 33
Spencer, NC 28159

Southern Railway Historical Society
(Southern; Central of Georgia)
P.O. Box 204094
Augusta, GA 30917

Spokane, Portland & Seattle Railway
Historical Society
6207 N. Concord
Portland, OR 97217

Terminal Railroad Association of St.
Louis Historical & Technical Society
P.O. Box 1688
St. Louis, MO 63188

Toledo, Peoria & Western Railroad
Historical Society
11618 Glenview Dr.
Orland Park, IL 60462

Ulster & Delaware Railroad
Historical Society
P.O. Box 404
Margaretville, NY 12455

Union Pacific Historical Society
P.O. Box 4006
Cheyenne, WY 82003

Wabash Railroad Historical Society
813 Ayers St.
Bolingbrook, IL 60440

Western Maryland Railway
Historical Society
Box 395
Union Bridge, MD 21791

Western Pacific Historical Society
Box 608
Portola, CA 96122

Appendix II

TRANSIT MUSEUMS

Baltimore Trolley Museum
1901 Falls Road
P.O. Box 4881
Baltimore, MD 21211

Brooklyn Trolley Museum
141 Beard Street
Brooklyn, NY 11231

Cable Car Museum
1201 Mason Street
San Francisco, CA 94108

Canadian Railway Museum
120 rue St.-Pierre
St-Constant, Quebec J5A 2G9

California Trolley and Railroad
Corporation
1600 Senter Road
San Jose, CA 95112

Charlotte Trolley Museum
2104 South Blvd.
Charlotte, NC 28203

Connecticut Trolley Museum
58 North Road
P.O. Box 360
East Windsor, CT 06088

East Troy Electric Railroad
P.O. Box 556
Waukesha, WI 53187

Edmonton Radial Railway Society
P.O. Box 45040
Lansdowne PO
Edmonton, Alberta T6H 5Y1

Fort Collins Municipal Railway
P.O. Box 635
Fort Collins, CO 80522

Fort Smith Trolley Museum
Fort Smith Streetcar Restoration
Association
2121 Wolfe Lane
Fort Smith, AR 72901

Fox River Trolley Museum
Box 315
South Elgin, IL 60177

Halton County Radial Railway
P.O. Box 578
Milton, Ontario L9T 5A2

Illinois Railroad Museum-Electric
Car Department
P.O. Box 427
Union, IL 60180

Market Street Railway
870 Market Street, Suite 984
San Francisco, CA 94102

Museum of Bus Transportation
426 South Third Street
Lemoyne, PA 17043

National Capital Trolley Museum
1313 Bonifant Road
Silver Spring, MD 20905

New York Transit Museum
130 Livingston Street, 9th Floor
Box E
Brooklyn, NY 11201

Oregon Electric Railway Historical
Society
P.O. Box 308
Lake Oswego, OR 97034

Pennsylvania Trolley Museum
1 Museum Road
Washington, PA 15301

Rockhill Trolley Museum
P.O. Box 203
Rockhill Furnace, PA 17249

Seashore Trolley Museum
P.O. Box A

195 Log Cabin Road
Kennebunkport, ME 04046

Shelburne Falls Trolley Museum
14 Depot Street
Shelbourne Falls, MA 01370

The Shore Line Trolley Museum
17 River Street
East Haven, CT 06512

Transit Museum Society
949 West 41st Avenue
Vancouver, BC V5Z 2N5

Tucson's Old Pueblo Trolley
Museum
P.O. Box 1373
Tucson, AZ 85702

Western Railway Museum
5848 Highway 12
Suisun City, CA 94585

INDEX